Sebastian Lohsse/Reiner Schulze/Dirk Staudenmayer (eds.)

Liability for Artificial Intelligence and the Internet of Things

Münster Colloquia on EU Law and the Digital Economy IV

HART PUBLISHING

Nomos

The Deutsche Nationalbibliothek lists this publication in the Deutsche Nationalbibliografie; detailed bibliographic data are available on the Internet at http://dnb.d-nb.de

ISBN:	HB (Nomos)	978-3-8487-5293-5
	ePDF (Nomos)	978-3-8452-9479-7

British Library Cataloguing-in-Publication Data
A catalogue record for this book is available from the British Library.

ISBN:	HB (Hart)	978-3-8487-5293-5

Library of Congress Cataloging-in-Publication Data
Lohsse, Sebastian / Schulze, Reiner / Staudenmayer, Dirk
Liability for Artificial Intelligence and the Internet of Things
Münster Colloquia on EU Law and the Digital Economy IV
Sebastian Lohsse / Reiner Schulze / Dirk Staudenmayer (eds.)
235 p.
Includes bibliographic references.

ISBN:	978-3-8487-5293-5	(hardcover Hart)

1st Edition 2019

Preface

As digitalisation has become a fundamental trend changing our economy into a digital economy, EU legislation is increasingly faced with the task to provide for a legal framework, a European Digital Single Market allowing to reap economic growth from digitalisation. While attention so far has mainly been paid to contract law, challenges obviously extend beyond this area of law. This becomes particularly clear with a view to Artificial Intelligence (AI). Being a key driver in building a digital economy, AI not only is an important factor for reaping economic growth but also brings about risks that have to be dealt with.

In accordance with the aim of the "Münster Colloquia on EU Law and the Digital Economy" to discuss how EU law should react to the challenges and needs of the digital economy, the 4th Münster Colloquium, held on 12–13 April 2018, focused on possible EU law responses to such risks arising from the use of AI. With "Liability for Robotics and in the Internet of Things" the Colloquium not only addressed questions relating to the reasonable allocation of these risks but also shed light on possible forms of liability taking into account traditional concepts of liability as well as possible new approaches.

This volume collects the contributions to this fourth Münster Colloquium. The editors kindly thank Karen Schulenberg for her invaluable support in organizing the Colloquium and in preparing this volume.

October 2018

Sebastian Lohsse
Reiner Schulze
Dirk Staudenmayer

Contents

Introduction

Introduction

Liability for Artificial Intelligence

Sebastian Lohsse / Reiner Schulze / Dirk Staudenmayer[*]

I. Artificial Intelligence and Liability Challenges

Artificial intelligence (AI) is a technology of ground-breaking importance. It is an 'enabling' technology which is likely to have an economic impact comparable to the effect of for instance the introduction of electricity into the economy. From the vast amount of sectors where AI will play this role agriculture could serve as example. Whereas long ago farmers used mechanical pumps driven by human or animal muscle power in order to water their fields, when electricity was introduced, such pumps were connected to a grid – the electricity network – and became electrical pumps. Now the same process is taking place with the introduction of AI. Once again, pumps are connected to a grid – the cloud – now getting access to AI and thus being turned into 'smart' pumps. Via the Internet of Things (IoT) these 'smart' pumps are connected with sensors distributed in the field which allow the pumps to decide for example which plants to water when, how much water to use and when to buy the water, i.e. to choose the time when water supply is offered at the cheapest price. The same transition can be done with practically every product: every product can become a 'smart' product[1].

AI therefore is a key driver of the transition of our economy into a digital economy and an important factor for reaping economic growth stemming from digitalisation. Promoting digitalisation and this transition is part of the connected Digital Single Market, one of the big ten priorities of the European Commission. Preparing a framework which creates the nec-

---

* Sebastian Lohsse and Reiner Schulze are Professors of Law, Centre for European Private Law, University of Münster. Dirk Staudenmayer is Head of Unit Contract Law, DG Justice and Consumers, European Commission and Honorary Professor at the University of Münster. The present contribution expresses only the personal opinion of the authors and does not bind in any way the European Commission.

1 Kevin Kelly, 'How AI can bring on a second Industrial Revolution', Ted Talk, recorded live at TED Summit June 2016 <https://www.ted.com/talks/kevin_kelly_how_ai_can_bring_on_a_second_industrial_revolution> accessed 8 August 2018.

essary technical, legal and other conditions for a successful digitalisation and transition to the digital economy would allow new business models to flourish while creating the users' trust necessary for them to embrace the advantages of the digital economy.

With regard to the tasks which the transition to the digital economy assigns to the legislation of the European Union, the attention has over the past years focused on contract law (for example the supply of digital content and the online trade of goods) and data protection. As far as AI as a part of this process of digitalisation is concerned, however, the challenges clearly extend beyond these areas of law. In particular, AI gives reason to focus also on potential risks arising from its use. Thus, the legal perspective is expanded to include a field of law which belongs to the 'classic' core fields of private law alongside contract law: non-contractual liability or 'tort law' as it is called in the Common law and several European sets of rules, e.g. the Principles of European Tort Law.

The main risks to be dealt with are related to the autonomous nature of AI powered systems and the complexity of the IoT. Autonomous systems have self-learning capacities which allow them to undertake or omit certain actions which are not necessarily predictable in advance and may therefore create undesirable results leading to injury or damage. This is coupled with the fast growing complexity of the IoT where in a multi-layered system with many actors it may be difficult, if not impossible to establish the cause for a certain damage which occurred. Thus, the acceptance of AI and the IoT and the chance of reaping the economic advantages which are promised by this new technology will very much depend on legal certainty as to the allocation of liability arising from damage associated to the use of AI and the IoT.

The Commission considered such legal certainty essential for the roll-out of IoT already in its Digital Single Market Strategy of 2015.[2] The actual discussion of liability for autonomous systems and in the IoT was initiated by the Data Economy Communication of January 2017[3] and the ac-

2 European Commission, 'A Digital Single Market Strategy for Europe' (Communication) COM (2015) 192 final, 14.

3 European Commission, 'Building a European Data Economy' (Communication) COM (2017) 9 final of 10.1.2017, 13ff.

companying Commission Staff Working document.[4] Soon afterwards the European Parliament adopted a Resolution on Civil Law Rules on Robotics which attracted a lot of political and media attention because it contained far-reaching requests to the Commission. Among others the Parliament asked the Commission in the area of liability to submit, on the basis of Article 114 TFEU, a proposal for a legislative instrument on legal questions related to the development and use of robotics and AI foreseeable in the next ten to fifteen years.[5] The mid-term review of the Digital Single Market Strategy in May 2017 announced that the Commission will consider the possible need to adapt the current legal framework to take account of new technological developments including robotics and AI, especially from the angle of civil law liability[6]. The European Council conclusions of October 2017 then invited the Commission to put forward a European approach to AI.[7] Bearing in mind their political weight these conclusions are of particular importance.[8]

A first step in the consideration whether and how to adapt the current legal framework was taken with the European Commission Communication on 'Artificial Intelligence for Europe'[9] and the accompanying Commission Staff Working Document on 'Liability for Emerging Digital Technologies'.[10] Broadly speaking, the AI Communication pursues the purpose to promote innovation and to facilitate the uptake of this new technology in order to position Europe better in the global race towards developing and mastering AI and to reap the economic advantages of the roll-out of this technology. The scope of the Communication is obviously much broader than just liability. It deals with industrial and research policy,

---

4 European Commission, Commission Staff Working document on the free flow of data and emerging issues of the European data economy, SWD (2017) 2 final of 10.1.2017, 40ff.

5 European Parliament, Resolution of 16 February 2017 with recommendations to the Commission on Civil Law Rules on Robotics (2015/2103(INL)), paras 49ff.

6 European Commission, 'A Connected Digital Single Market for All' COM (2017) 228 final of 10.5.2017, 11.

7 European Council meeting of 19 October 2017 – Conclusions, EUCO 14/17, 7.

8 On the political importance of European Council conclusions cf H Reichenbach/T Emmerling/D Staudenmayer/S Schmidt, *Integration: Wanderung über europäische Gipfel*, (1st edn, Nomos 1999) 117.

9 European Commission, 'Artificial Intelligence for Europe' (Communication) COM (2018) 237 final of 25.4.2018.

10 European Commission, 'Liability for emerging digital technologies' (Staff Working document) SWD (2018) 137 final of 25.4.2018.

mentions possible socio-economic impacts and aims at ensuring an appropriate legal and ethical framework. Considerations about civil law liability are a part of this framework.

One of the aims of this legal framework is to create legal certainty for businesses and users. For businesses producing and using smart goods and services it is key to ensure investment stability. Such businesses need to know what kind of liability risks they are running as well as whether and to what extent they need to insure themselves to cover such risks. It is also important to create users' trust. If damage happens – and in the light of recent accidents not even the strongest supporters of AI are arguing any more that AI will make accidents disappear –, effective redress schemes need to be available to ensure fair and fast compensation. This trust element is so important because it will contribute to societal acceptance. Without such acceptance, users will not embrace AI and the new technology will not therefore be able to produce the undoubtedly available economic and societal advantages which it promises to deliver.

How then should potential liability risks be dealt with? As often explained in the introductions to law on non-contractual liability,[11] the industrial revolution gave rise to a new development in this field. Whereas traditionally liability had in principle but for very few exceptions always been based on fault ('subjective liability') the 19th century's developments led to an increase of cases of 'strict liability' or 'objective liability', i.e. liability independent of fault.[12] A typical 19th century example is the steam train chugging along the tracks and endangering fields and forests with its sparks and thus leading to the introduction of statutory provisions on objective liability. The 20th century has not only experienced an expansion of the types and numbers of dangerous equipment and machines but also an expansion of the corresponding legislative responses – from cars to aeroplanes to nuclear power stations. Moreover, the legal responses to these developments have become more complex and, in part, more subtle e.g. through the different combinations of individual liability, mandatory

11 See, for example, H Kötz and G Wagner, *Deliktsrecht* (13th edn, Vahlen 2017), para 29ff, 494ff; B McMahon, 'The Reaction of Tortious Liability to Industrial Revolution: A comparison: I' [1968] 3 Irish Jurist (N.S.) 18.

12 For details see the different volumes of the series *Comparative studies in the development of the law of torts in Europe* (eds J Bell and D Ibbetson), in particular Volume 5: W Ernst (ed), *The Development of Traffic Liability* (Cambridge 2010).

insurance, limitations of liability, recourse possibilities and supplementary compensation through public-law-funds.

With the digital revolution the development of non-contractual liability has possibly reached such a new stage once again. Arguably, the complexity of issues involved calls for more than a mere introduction of another type of strict liability. In particular, it is far from sure whether and to what extent strict liability is an appropriate means of dealing with the risks of AI and the IoT, ensuring legal certainty, and guaranteeing the reaping of the economic advantages of AI at all. Accordingly, it will be necessary to consider not only whether and in how far legal approaches and instruments which have emerged since the industrial revolution can be adapted so as to deal with the challenges arising from digitalisation. Rather, one also has to ask whether completely new answers have to be found in order to deal with the specific risks of the digital age.

II. Appropriate Regulatory Level

Apart from the aspects just mentioned, the situation to be dealt with is much more complex than its 19th century predecessors due to the different regulatory levels that have been established over the last decades. Before concentrating on issues of substantive law one therefore has to decide on which of these regulatory levels an appropriate framework should ideally be created. Should one act at national level, i.e. adapt existing national law or create an independent national law? Or would it be more appropriate to have a harmonised or unified law in the European legal framework? Or does a model or binding international law respond better to the global dimension of the digital world?

From a policy perspective, seeking solutions at the regional level, i.e. from the European legislator, seems to be the most efficient way. In many respects, isolated national answers would not satisfy the cross-border – or better borderless – character of data flows and transactions in the digital world and the associated risks. The share of smart products in cross-border trade flow is likely to increase significantly. Just to take a banal example: Amazon's AI powered ('Alexa') loudspeaker Echo Dot was the best-sell-ing of all products on Amazon.com during the last Christmas season[13]. Having different national laws regulating smart products would create barriers to cross-border transactions. Global responses through international conventions would thus seem the best approach. However, such responses seem to be unrealistic bearing in mind the present global race for leadership in AI in which the big players China and the US are enjoying a pole position. With its 'Next Generation Artificial Intelligence Development Plan'[14], China wants to become global leader in AI by 2030. In the US, where industry makes considerable investments, the role of government as a regulator is seen as minimal[15]. Given these different political perceptions and economic interests such worldwide agreements are rather unlikely. For the time being, a European response is thus called for, and Europe's chance is to develop AI in a way which ensures societal acceptance[16], while at the same time making the most out of the growth potential of AI for the Digital Single Market.

III. Actors to be held responsible

With a view to the concrete rules to be adapted or established the most fundamental question to be discussed is which actors in the value chain should be responsible for which risks when putting AI powered products on the market or using them, thereby creating the risk of damage. Two approaches spring to mind for the attribution at European level of risks to private actors in the use of AI and in the IoT. On the one hand, there is the question of the responsibility of the producer.[17] On the other hand, it is to

13 <https://www.businesswire.com/news/home/20171226005146/en/Amazon-Celebrates-Biggest-Holiday-Million%C2%A0People-Trialed-Prime> accessed 10 July 2018.

14 <https://flia.org/notice-state-council-issuing-new-generation-artificial-intelligence-development-plan> accessed 10 July 2018.

15 European Political Strategy Center, 'The Age of Artificial Intelligence' (Strategic Note) 3, <https://ec.europa.eu/epsc/sites/epsc/files/epsc_strategicnote_ai.pdf> accessed 10 July 2018.

16 cf ibidem, 5.

17 At the Colloquium on which the present volume is based, this question was central to the discussions within the section on 'Traditional Liability Requirements and New Sources of Damages'; see the contributions by G Wagner, 'Robot Liability', J-S Borghetti, 'How can Artificial Intelligence be Defective?' and C Amato, 'Product Liability and Product Security: Present and Future', in this volume.

be considered whether and in which manner it is appropriate to introduce specific liability for the operator or user of an autonomous system.[18] Both approaches could also be considered together as part of an overall regulatory landscape. As these approaches are dealt with in more detail in the contributions to this volume, we confine ourselves to a short introduction.

As to the former approach, one could build on the earlier pioneering European legislation in liability law, namely the Product Liability Directive (PLD)[19], which was passed in 1985 and has since been revised, discussed, and interpreted by the courts. This is one of the approaches which has already been picked up by the Commisson. Already before the adoption of the AI Communication, the Commission had launched the Expert Group on Liability and New Technologies[20] with its two branches, one looking at the interpretation and possible revision of the PLD and the other one at liability for new technologies from a holistic point of view. The aim of the Product Liability branch is to help the Commission to interpret the provisions of the PLD and assess the extent to which its provisions are adequate to solve questions of liability in relation to traditional products but also new technologies. It will assist the Commission in drawing up guidance on the application of the PLD, among others with a particular view to emerging technologies like AI, IoT and robotics. Questions to be faced with respect to this approach mainly relate to the scope and the means by which the Directive gives rise to liability for autonomous systems and/or whether legislative measures to clarify or amend the Directive are necessary. Just to give an example of one of these issues: Would a software programmer be liable if a mistake in the code resulted in damage caused by the IoT-hardware or does Art 2 of the Product Liability Direc-

18 This question was discussed at the Colloquium on which the present volume is based within the section on 'New Approaches: Basis for Liability and Addressees'; see the contributions by B A Koch, 'Product Liability 2.0: Mere Update or New Version?', E Karner, 'Liability for Robotics: Current Rules, Challenges, and the Need for Innovative Concepts', G Spindler, 'User Liability and Strict Liability in the Internet of Things and for Robots', G Borges, 'New Liability Concepts: the Potential of Insurance and Compensation Funds' and G Comandé, 'Multilayered (Accountable) Liability for Artificial Intelligence', in this volume.

19 Council Directive 85/374/EEC of 25 July 1985 on the approximation of the laws, regulations and administrative provisions of the Member States concerning liability for defective products (Product Liability Directive) [1985] OJ L 210, 29–33.

20 cf <http://ec.europa.eu/newsroom/just/item-detail.cfm?item_id=615947> accessed 10 July 2018.

tive prevent such liability because only 'moveables' are to be regarded as products for the purposes of the Directive?[21] Generally speaking the question arises to what extent the Directive's notion of products stemming from the time before the digital revolution can cover new types of 'products' like 'software' or 'data'. As far as such adaptations based on the existing provisions cannot be regarded as sufficient, it will have to be considered whether, and by which means, the legislator should further develop product liability for the 'digital age'.[22]

However, as just mentioned, it is by no means clear whether or in how far the producer's liability is indeed an appropriate means of dealing with the risks arising from AI and the IoT. As the scope of the Expert Group with its two branches shows, the Commission wants to analyse all relevant aspects in a comprehensive manner. The New Technologies formation thus has a broader scope. It shall assess whether and to what extent existing EU and national liability schemes are apt to deal with the new technologies such as AI, IoT and robotics. It shall identify the shortcomings and assess whether the overall liability regime is adequate to facilitate the uptake of these new technologies by fostering investment stability and users' trust. In case the existing overall liability regime is deemed not to be adequate, the New Technologies formation shall provide recommendations on how it should be designed. The regulatory framework to be considered for analysis should include national tort law as well as any possible specific national liability regimes, the rationale or contents of which may be relevant. Questions of liability should be analysed holistically

---

21 On this question, see, for example, D Fairgrieve et al, 'Product Liability Directive' in P Machnikowski (ed), *European Product Liability. An Analysis of the State of the Art in the Era of New Technologies* (Intersentia 2016) 17 (46 ff); B A Koch, 'Produkthaftung für Daten' in F Schurr and M Umlauft (eds), *Festschrift für Bernhard Eccher* (Verlag Österreich 2017) 551–570; as well as the contributions by B A Koch, 'Product Liability 2.0: Mere Update or New Version?', 104–106, G Spindler, 'User Liability and Strict Liability in the Internet of Things and for Robots', 128–129, and G Wagner, 'Robot Liability', 41–42, in this volume.

22 On this issue, see, for example R de Bruin, 'Autonomous Intelligent Cars on the European Intersection of Liability and Privacy' [2016] 7 EJRR 485–501; S Horner and M Kaulartz, 'Haftung 4.0. Rechtliche Herausforderungen im Kontext der Industrie 4.0' [2016] InTeR 22–29; H Zech, 'Gefährdungshaftung und neue Technologien' [2013] JZ 21–29; as well as the contributions by C Amato, 'Product Liability and Product Security: Present and Future', 'B A Koch, 'Product Liability 2.0: Mere Update or New Version?' and H Zech, 'Liability for Autonomous Systems: Tackling Specific Risks of Modern IT', in this volume.

looking at various actors (e.g. liability of owners/operators, insurers) and legal relationships (e.g. questions of redress in the technology value chain). The New Technologies formation shall also assist the Commission in developing EU-wide principles which can serve as guidelines for possible adaptations of applicable laws at EU and national level.

As far as liability beyond the scope of the PLD and thus liability of persons other than the producers is concerned, a starting point for the discussion obviously is the aforementioned development since the industrial revolution of strict, objective liability of operators and users of dangerous objects and equipment. This question would steer European legislation into unchartered territory because the development of strict liability so far has primarily been within the national context (and was extended by international agreements rather than through European law).[23] Accordingly, it remains to be seen whether the European legislator's level of reluctance in the field of non-contractual liability can indeed be maintained, or whether the central importance of digitalisation for the internal market rather requires the introduction of strict liability rules at European level.

The finding that product liability alone is unable to deal with the challenges and thus has to be supplemented by a 'strict liability' of the user or the operator of the AI in autonomous systems[24] is supported by the fact that numerous risks are dependent on the type and the extent of the use of AI, but can hardly be traced back to a defect. In principle, in this context, the same rules apply to the 'vehicle without a driver' as to vehicles with a driver[25] for which the strict liability of the user or the operator – in addition to product liability – is generally regarded as necessary. Besides, the development of the risk potential of AI is not only regularly dependent on the interference with numerous different digital products (including services such as the various information services for 'self-driving cars' re-

23 On this development, see, for example, from a comparative legal perspective G Brüggemeier, 'European Union', *International Encyclopedia for Tort Law* (2nd edn, Kluwer Law International 2018) in particular 241–242.

24 On this issue, see also the contributions by G Spindler, 'User Liability and Strict Liability in the Internet of Things and for Robots' and G Wagner, 'Liability for Autonomous Systems: Tackling Specific Risks of Modern IT', 45–47, in this volume.

25 For German and Austrian law see E Karner, 'Liability for Robotics: Current Rules, Challenges, and the Need for Innovative Concepts', 121, in this volume.

garding the nature of the road, the traffic situation, the weather etc.).[26] Rather, this risk potential varies also depending on the constant change which the respective 'autonomous system' and its AI themselves are subject to through learning processes with the help of external artificial intelligence. The result of this change of 'self-learning' AI may even not be predictable for its operator and insofar justify the characterisation of 'autonomous systems' as 'black box'[27]. Such lack of predictability might be seen as an argument to deny the operator's responsibility and thus his liability. Such argument, however, seems to be highly doubtful. Instead, it has to be considered that the operator has created the increased risk potential by continuously operating the 'autonomous system' and thereby obtaining benefits.

Obviously, dealing with these issues of strict liability would by no means be a trivial task. It is not simply a case of introducing a new category of risk into the catalogue of provisions on 'strict liability'. Rather, one has to take into account that there are different types of risk and to consider which party should ultimately bear the economic costs. Especially the latter question is of key importance if one keeps in mind the objective to facilitate the roll-out of the new technology and to harvest its economic and societal advantages. Concretely speaking, this translates into the need not to disincentivise producers to produce and put smart products on the market and users to purchase and use them.

The type of risk can be relevant in different ways. One would need to decide if all risks should be covered or whether a distinction should be made. Such distinctions could be done according to the likelihood of materialisation of the risk in form of a damage or in terms of what the damage relates to, i.e. death, bodily harm, health, damage to property, financial loss. Linked to this is the question whether only natural persons should be compensated or also legal persons.

---

26 See also the contribution by G Spindler, 'User Liability and Strict Liability in the Internet of Things and for Robots', in this volume, 126–128.

27 For more details see the contributions by G Spindler, 'User Liability and Strict Liability in the Internet of Things and for Robots', 139, and H Zech, 'Liability for Autonomous Systems: Tackling Specific Risks of Modern IT', 190–119, in this volume.

IV. Overall Concept of Liability

Apart from all this, the development of new concepts relates to the determination of the substantial frame of reference. Would one conceptually start from the use of 'artificial intelligence' or the use of 'autonomous systems'? How would these concepts be defined and which parts of these concepts would actually be sufficiently relevant (and determinable) in order to be covered by a provision on liability?

The latter leads to a number of further questions which would be crucial for the contours of any possible future liability framework in this field, independently of the premise on which it is based. In particular, it would have to be considered whether a general provision for liability of operators or users of AI in the IoT would be appropriate or whether sector specific provisions would be preferable.[28] For both approaches there are models to be found in the Member States' liability law and in the scientific projects for European liability law.

A general rule for objective liability offers i.a. the advantage of a higher flexibility regarding its application in the case of new risks arising in the course of technological development and would insofar also serve a uniform application of law. However, it would certainly be associated with all disadvantages entailed by general clauses and undefined legal concepts with regard to predictability and legal certainty. In particular, it may prove especially difficult to describe the particularities or the necessary degree of a special, extraordinary risk in a sufficiently precise way (in order to prevent, for example, that every use of AI in a smartphone could be covered by strict liability).

Sector specific regimes could partly follow models which liability law has already developed for certain areas long before the introduction of AI (for example the liability for vehicles in road traffic or the liability provisions for medical products). They would insofar at least partly be based on experiences of the hitherto existing legislation and could better ensure the legal coherence in the areas concerned. Admittedly, the price that would inevitably have to be paid for this approach is the liability law always 'lagging behind' the technological development due to the time period needed

---

28 See also the contributions by J-S Borghetti, 'How can Artificial Intelligence be Defective?', 72, E Karner, 'Liability for Robotics: Current Rules, Challenges, and the Need for Innovative Concepts', 122–123, and G Spindler, 'User Liability and Strict Liability in the Internet of Things and for Robots', 134–136, in this volume.

for the evaluation of risks, the discussions of legal policy and the legislative procedure.

Furthermore, the conditions of any liability claim for AI related damages would need to be examined in depth. Should there be a possibility to avoid liability on the basis that the potentially liable person, e.g. the producer or operator, has undertaken certain efforts or done everything possible in this sphere, e.g. respected all safety standards or downloaded all updates, to avoid the damage. If such a defence is possible, what would be the benchmark? This is particularly relevant for self-learning autonomous systems which may develop undesirable behaviour which is not or cannot be foreseen at the time of putting them on the market. At the same time this is one of several points where the link with the applicable safety legislation creating safety standards is particularly relevant.

Other modalities are also linked to this 'black box' character of self-learning algorithms. It raises the questions whether any kind of 'defect', wrongful behaviour or omission of action or any other relevant facts would need to be a necessary condition for a successful damages claim or whether the sheer damage occurred would be sufficient to establish liability. Very closely linked to this would be the question who would bear the burden of proof for which relevant facts. Another modality would be important for the insurability of damages. It would be relevant to decide whether liability claims would have a threshold, which would ensure that only claims of a certain significance could be raised, and a cap which would exclude damage beyond a specific amount.

Furthermore, setting such a set of provisions on liability will not be sufficient. It will rather have to be incorporated into the (in part not yet existing) context of European and national liability law as well as to take into account economic needs like allowing the insurance of such new risks. For example, 'strict liability' for mobile 'autonomous systems', be these self-driving cars or other systems such as devices used in a 'smart home', in medical care or in other fields, will probably not survive without adequate voluntary or mandatory insurance and therefore without including insurance in the economic and legal system of liability.[29] In addition, careful consideration will have to be given to the relationship between such 'strict

29 See also the contributions by G Borges, 'New Liability Concepts: the Potential of Insurance and Compensation Funds', B A Koch, 'Product Liability 2.0: Mere Update or New Version?', 100, 112, and G Spindler, 'User Liability and Strict Liability in the Internet of Things and for Robots', 134, 141, in this volume.

liability' of the operator or user to the (contractual and non-contractual) responsibility of producers and suppliers of digital content – which is a particular challenge in light of the concurrence between the numerous and greatly varying 'deliveries' of data for the operation of such equipment and systems.

V. Outlook

Overcoming all these challenges will no doubt require cooperation between jurists, economists and IT specialists. Where the jurists' tasks de lege ferenda in this team effort are concerned, an element of legal creativity will probably be necessary. The economic developments are still in progress and in any case may only be predicted, whereas the legal answers will have to cover the recent as well as the unknown future developments. However, as the discussions at the conference have shown, a careful readjustment of traditional concepts of liability will probably be sufficient and completely new concepts seem not be called for. Well established concepts such as the general concept of fault liability, the notion of strict liability in certain sectors, and concepts such as product liability, vicarious liability, compulsory third party insurance or compensation funds seem well apt to deal with the new challenges and do not have to be questioned as such. Yet at the same time probably none of these traditional concepts in itself will be sufficient to deal with the new challenges. Rather, a multi-layered sector-specific approach based on a combination of carefully readjusted traditional concepts of liability seems to be called for. Thus, the main task appears to lie in the arrangement and balancing of relevant sectors, appropriate layers, and their readjustment. All that remains a difficult task. This volume's contributions will hopefully be regarded as helpful in this respect, not least with a view to possible regulatory responses. A next step has already been announced in the AI Communication. The Commission will publish by mid-2019 a report on the broader implications for, potential gaps in and orientations for the liability and safety framework for AI, IoT and robotics.[30]

30 cf European Commission (n 9) 17.

Traditional Liability Requirements and New Sources of Damages

Robot Liability

Gerhard Wagner[*]

I. The Concepts of Robots, Autonomous Systems and IoT-Devices

Since the invention of the steam engine, technological progress has served as a driver of innovation for liability systems.[1] The arrival of the railroad and of the motor-powered automobile led to the introduction of strict liability regimes in many European jurisdictions.[2] Today, society faces a similar challenge that may run even deeper than those that came before. The development of robots and other technical agents operating with the help of artificial intelligence will transform many, if not all product markets. It will also blur the distinction between goods and services and call the existing allocation of responsibility between manufacturers, suppliers of components, owners, keepers and operators of such devices into question. In this paper, the concepts of a 'robot' and of 'autonomous systems' will be used interchangeably. The characteristic shared by both entities is that their 'behaviour' is determined by computer code that allows some room for 'decision-making' by the machine itself, in the particular accident situation. In other words, the behaviour of the machine is not entirely under the control of human actors. The concept of 'Internet of Things'-devices (IoT-devices) partly overlaps with the ones of robots and autonomous systems, but this overlap is not necessary. Many interconnected products are already marketed, and they are mostly governed by computer-code that is

---

* Professor of Civil Law, Commerical Law and Economic Analysis of Law, Humboldt-University of Berlin.

1 As to the U.S., the *locus classicus* is Morton J. Horwitz, *The Transformation of American Law, 1780–1860* (Oxford UP 1977) 67–108; for a more nuanced view Gary T. Schwartz, 'Tort Law and the Economy in Nineteenth-Century America: A Reinterpretation' 90 Yale L.J. 1717, 1734–1756 (1981).

2 As to Germany, Olaf von Gadow, *Die Zähmung des Automobils durch die Gefährdungshaftung* (Duncker & Humblot 2002); Werner Schubert, 'Das Gesetz über den Verkehr mit Kraftfahrzeugen vom 3.5.1909' (2000) 117 Zeitschrift der Savigny-Stiftung für Rechtsgeschichte, Germanistische Abteilung 238.

deterministic in the sense that it does not allow for autonomous decisions of the machine or even machine learning.

II. The European Parliament Resolution of February 2017

The European Parliament Resolution of 16 February 2017 on Civil Law Rules on Robotics identified civil liability for damages caused by robots as 'a crucial issue'.[3] The Parliament suggests that this issue be dealt with at Union level for reasons of efficiency, transparency and consistency in the implementation of legal certainty for the benefit of citizens, consumers and businesses. The European Commission is asked to submit a proposal for a legislative instrument addressing the liability for harm caused by robot activity or interaction between humans and robots.

In substance, the European Parliament suggests a choice between two different approaches which it labels as the'risk management' and 'strict liability' approaches.[4] In the eyes of the Parliament, a strict liability rule requires proof of three elements only, namely damage, a harmful functioning of the robot, and a causal link between the two.[5] Whether 'harmful functioning' of a robot is equivalent to its malfunctioning, i.e. requires a deviation from the behavioural design of its manufacturer, remains an open question. The risk management approach, envisaged to serve as an alternative to strict liability, should not, it is said, focus on the person who acted negligently but rather on the individual who was able to minimise risks and deal with negative impacts.[6] But once this person is found, what will the requirements for a finding of liability be? It seems that the risk management approach is in urgent need of a principle of attribution and further elaboration upon the principle that has been chosen.

Beyond these two approaches the Parliament also envisages, as a long-term perspective, the creation of a special legal status for robots, i.e. their recognition as electronic persons.[7] Such an electronic person would be liable for any damage caused by the autonomous behaviour of the robot.

3 European Parliament, Resolution of 16 February 2017 with recommendations to the Commission on Civil Law Rules on Robotics, P8_TA-PROV(2017)0051, para 49.
4 Parliament (n 3) P8_TA-PROV(2017)0051, para 53.
5 Parliament (n 3) P8_TA-PROV(2017)0051, para 54.
6 Parliament (n 3) P8_TA-PROV(2017)0051, para 55.
7 Parliament (n 3) P8_TA-PROV(2017)0051, para 59 lit. f).

This is, of course, the most innovative, interesting and stimulating idea within the Parliament's resolution.

Finally, the Parliament touches upon insurance issues and considers that there might be a need for mandatory liability insurance, as is already in place for cars.[8] Such a mandatory insurance mechanism could be supplemented by a fund that would pick up losses not covered by liability insurance. Again, similar solutions already exist in the area of motor traffic.

III. The Commission Communication on 'Building a European Data Economy'

A week before the Parliament Resolution outlined above was adopted, the Commission published its Communication on a European Data Economy.[9] It discusses liability issues with a view to IoT-devices as they are believed to be of 'central importance to the emergence of a data economy'.[10] The existing framework of Directive 85/374/EEC on product liability[11] is found to involve uncertainties in its application to robots, regarding, for example, the classification of autonomous systems as products or rather as services.[12] The Commission also distinguishes between risk-generating and risk-management approaches, depending on whether liability is attached to the party who created the risk or to the party who is in the best position to minimise risk or avoid its realisation altogether.[13] In addition, the issue of insurance is raised, which could be either voluntary or mandatory.

---

8 Parliament (n 3) P8_TA-PROV(2017)0051, para 57f.

9 Communication of the Commission to the European Parliament, the Council, the European Economic and Social Committee and the Committee of the Regions 'Building a European Data Economy', 10.1.2017 COM(2017) 9 final.

10 Commission (n 9) COM(2017) 9 final, 14.

11 Council Directive 85/374/EEC of 25 July 1985 on the approximation of the laws, regulations, and administrative provisions of the Member States concerning liability for defective products, OJ L 210/29.

12 Commission (n 9) COM(2017) 9 final, 14.

13 Commission (n 9) COM(2017) 9 final, 15.

IV. Normative Foundations

Before delving into the substantive issues, it seems helpful to identify the normative foundations on which a liability regime for new technologies may be built. It is often said that the objective of the liability system is to compensate victims. While this is certainly true, the compensation goal cannot inform lawmakers and courts as to which party is the optimal risk bearer. Furthermore, it is submitted that the EU should not only, and not even primarily, aim to shift the costs of injuries to one particular party or another. The EU Member States operate complex systems of social and private insurance for personal injuries,[14] and with respect to property damage, private insurance is widely available.[15] Thus, compensation of victims may be achieved in many ways, not only through non-contractual liability.

On the other hand, shielding businesses from liability for the harm that they cause, for instance, with a view to fostering innovation, also seems problematic. This is not to say that innovation is unimportant or that incentives to innovate should not be generated. It is doubtful, however, whether the liability system is the preferred tool to create such incentives. To shield certain parties from responsibility for the harm that they actually caused amounts to a subsidisation of dangerous activities, leading to an oversupply of such activities.[16] Furthermore, immunity from liability undermines incentives to take precautions against harm. For both reasons, shielding parties from liability may impose a net cost on society, at the expense of victims. New technologies that promise substantial benefits will be able to 'pay their way' into the world and do not need a subsidy in the form of (partial) immunity from liability.

As a consequence, lawmakers thinking about a framework of liability for autonomous systems should do so with a view to maximise the net surplus for society by minimising the costs associated with personal injury and property damage. This objective requires to keep an eye on the different components that together represent the costs that accidents impose on

14 Ulrich Magnus (ed), *The Impact of Social Security Law on Tort Law* (Springer 2003).

15 Gerhard Wagner (ed), *Tort Law and Liability Insurance* (Springer 2005).

16 For a general exposition of the relationship between the liability system, the price system, and production levels cf Steven Shavell, *Foundations of Economic Analysis of Law* (Harvard UP 2004) 208–212.

society. One important component is the cost that accidents impose on victims, another is the cost that potential injurers incur for taking care, i.e. for taking precautions that prevent accidents from occurring.[17] Insofar as individuals suffer losses that they cannot bear easily, accidents impose additional harm on them in the form of the costs of risk-bearing.[18] The premiums paid to insurance companies, insofar as they exceed expected harm, reflect these additional losses. Finally, the administrative costs of operating a liability system must not be ignored. Liability rules should not be based on elements that are difficult and therefore costly to establish in legal proceedings before a court or in settlement negotiations with responsible parties or their insurers.[19]

In a situation that is as complex as the one described, finding the right solution is no trivial task. In order to minimise the losses suffered by victims, together with the costs of precautions incurred by potential injurers, it is essential to target incentives towards those actors who are best-situated to take precautions against harm, i.e. to develop and deploy safety measures that cost less than alternative safety measures available from other actors and less than the costs of harm that they help to avoid. There is another reason why it is important to hold actors who engage in dangerous activities accountable. Only if the cost of harm caused by dangerous activities is attributed to the actor engaging in such activities, cost internalisation is achieved so that the price of the activity in question reflects its full costs. Where all or part of the risk remains externalised, as it continues to fall on third parties, the cost of the activity is too low and the extent to which individuals will engage in such activity will be excessive. Lawmakers should aim for a system that not only minimises the costs of accidents but also maximises the difference between the gains derived from activities and their full costs, including the costs of accidents.

17 These two factors were together placed under the rubric of 'primary accident costs' in the classic work by Guido Calabresi, *The Costs of Accidents* (Yale UP 1970) 26–27, 68–94.

18 Calabresi (n 17) 27–28, 39–67: so-called 'secondary accident costs'.

19 Calabresi (n 17) 28: 'tertiary accident costs'.

V. The Range of Responsible Parties

In the following analysis, the various actors involved in the creation and the operation of autonomous systems and IoT-devices will be grouped together into two distinct camps, namely the camp of the manufacturers and the group of the users. The manufacturer group includes all actors, usually businesses, who contribute to the development, design and production of autonomous systems, including software developers and programmers. The other group comprises everyone who interacts with an autonomous system or IoT-device after it was put into circulation, i.e. owners, keepers and operators of such devices. The composition of these two groups of manufacturers and users is not purely phenomenological. It also pays tribute to the fact that, within each group, it seems fairly easy to allocate the costs of liability to any one member or to share it between several members. The obvious tool for re-allocation of the costs of liability within one of the groups is a contractual agreement. Already today, standard supply agreements among the members of the manufacturer group, i.e. end-producers and component suppliers of different layers routinely include clauses that provide for the allocation of the costs of product recalls and other costs caused by defective components.[20]

The same can happen within the group of users, i.e. between owners and operators, be they employees or independent contractors. Take the example of motor cars. Here, the keeper of a car is required to take out liability insurance under the applicable European directives.[21] If the car is rent-

---

20 Omri Ben Shahar & James J. White, 'Boilerplate and Economic Power in Auto Manufacturing Contracts' (2006) 104 Mich. L. Rev. 953, 959–960; G Wagner, in: *Münchener Kommentar zum BGB* vol 6 (7th edn, C. H. Beck 2017) § 823 para 789.

21 Art 3 Directive 2009/103/EC of 16.9.2009 relating to insurance against civil liability in respect of the use of motor vehicles, and the enforcement of the obligation to insure against such liability, OJ L 263/11; cf also Council Directive 72/166/EEC of 24.4.1972 on the approximation of the laws of the Member States relating to insurance against civil liability in respect of the use of motor vehicles, and to the enforcement of the obligation to insure against such liability, OJ L 103/1; Second Council Directive 84/5/EEC of 30.12.1983 on the approximation of the laws of the Member States relating to insurance against civil liability in respect of the use of motor vehicles, OJ L 8/17; Third Council Directive 90/232/EEC of 14.5.1990, OJ L 129/33; Council Directive 2000/26/EC of 16.5.1990, OJ L 181/65; Directive 2005/14/EC of 11.5.2005, OJ L 149/14; Directive 2009/103/EC of 16.9.2009, OJ L 263/11.

ed out to somebody else, the costs of such insurance are shifted to the lessee-driver, as a component of the price he or she has to pay for the lease. The same happens where a business operates an IoT- machine in its production process. Here, the prices for products manufactured by an IoT-machine will include a component reflecting the expected costs of harm caused by the IoT-machine. Again, costs are shifted within the group of entities that operate or benefit from the use of the IoT-device. In all of these cases, as long as responsibility is attributed to one member of the group, the re-allocation of accident costs within the group may be left to the parties and freedom of contract.

VI. The Legal Background

1. National Tort Law as the Default System

Within the European Union, the law of non-contractual liability, i.e. the law of torts or delict, is a domain of the legal systems of the Member States. Each Member State operates its own liability system, and the differences among these systems are manifold. While it is not possible at this point to engage in a comparative analysis of Member States' laws, it may be said with confidence that they share common principles.[22] These principles formed the building blocks of efforts by comparative law scholars to identify the 'common core' of European tort law. Prominent examples are Book VI of the Draft Common Frame of Reference[23] as well as the 'Principles of European Tort Law', compiled by the European Group on Tort Law.[24] Without going into any detail, it is safe to say that a general rule of liability for fault is part of the legal systems of all the Member States,[25] and it also remains central to the principles restating the common

---

22 For a thorough analysis cf Christian von Bar, *The Common European Law of Torts* vol 1 (C.H. Beck 1998), vol 2 (C. H. Beck 2000).

23 Christian von Bar and Eric Clive (eds), *Principles, Definitions and Model Rules of European Private Law, Draft Common Frame of Reference (DCFR)* vol 4 (Sellier 2009); cf also Christian von Bar, Eric Clive & Hans Schulte-Nölke (eds), *Principles, Definitions and Model Rules of European Private Law, Draft Common Frame of Reference (DCFR) – Outline Edition* (Sellier 2009) 395–412.

24 European Group on Tort Law (ed), *Principles of European Tort Law* (Springer 2005).

25 von Bar (n 22) vol 1, para 11–12.

core of European Private Law.[26] Thus, where an actor fails to take due care and this negligence causes harm to another, or where a wrongdoer causes such harm intentionally, this actor is liable to compensate the victim. The principle of fault-based liability covers harm done to a set of fundamental interests of the person, i.e. life, health, bodily integrity, freedom of movement, and private property; in some legal systems the list of protected interests also includes purely economic interests and human dignity.

The general principles of liability for fault also apply to the parties associated with the manufacture and use of robots and IoT-devices. Therefore, the conclusion presented in the Commission's evaluation of Directive 85/374/EEC, that no less than 18 Member States are lacking rules on extra-contractual liability of service-providers,[27] must be taken with a large grain of salt. While it is certainly true that many European legal systems lack rules on extra-contractual liability protecting consumers from harm caused '*specifically* by defects of either intangibles (software) or services',[28] the conclusion drawn from this statement, that there are large gaps in the respective liability systems, would still be misguided. As a matter of course, the general rules of non-contractual liability also apply to providers of services, regardless whether the customer is a business or a consumer. Here, as in other areas, fault-based liability serves as the workhorse of the liability system in protecting victims of any status or calling against harm caused by any entity or activity. What remains true is that many European legal systems have no *special* rules in place that are specifically gauged towards service providers and premise liability on 'defective' performance of services, rather than fault. The difference between the requirement of 'defective performance of a service' on the one hand, and negligence in the carrying out of a service, is slight indeed, if it exists at all. In conclusion, it must be noted that everyone involved in the manufacture and use of autonomous systems and IoT-devices remains subject to the general rule of fault-based liability, as supplied by the legal systems of the Member States.

---

26 European Group on Tort Law (n 24) Art 1.101 (1) and (2) (a); von Bar and Clive (n 23) Art VI. – 1:101 (1).

27 Commission, Evaluation of Council Directive 85/374/EEC of 25 July 1985 on the approximation of the laws, regulations and administrative provisions of the Member States concerning liability for defective products, SWD(2018) 157 final, 51.

28 Commission (n 27) SWD(2018) 157 final, 5, emphasis added.

2. The Products Liability Directive

European Union law is not entirely devoid of statutes governing extra-contractual liability. Directive 85/374/EEC on product liability is the exception.[29] It supplies a comprehensive framework for damages claims based on harm caused by products, which Art 2 of the Directive defines as 'movables'. A damages claim based on the Directive does not require a finding of fault on the part of the manufacturer. The recitals of the Directive emphasise that liability under its rules is strict, not fault-based.[30] However, for a finding of liability it is not sufficient that a product caused harm to another. Rather, it is required that the product was defective, and that the defect was the cause of the harm complained of. The concept of defect is defined in Art 6 of the Directive with a view to the reasonable expectations regarding product safety, measured at the time when the product was put into circulation (Art 6 (1) (c) Directive). What this means in application to particular cases is not entirely clear.[31] In international comparative scholarship, it is well-settled that product liability regimes of the kind inaugurated by the Directive are co-extensive with fault-based liability, at least in the important areas of design defects and liability for failure to warn.[32] And even in the case of a manufacturing defect, the Directive does not impose a pure form of strict liability, as it is known, for example, from the French doctrine of 'responsabilité de fait de choses',[33] but rather a watered-down version of negligence liability, with the concept

29 supra (n 11).

30 Directive 85/374/EEC, recitals 2, 3: 'liability without fault'.

31 Simon Whittaker, *Liability for Products* (Oxford UP 2005) 481–494; Wagner (n 20) 731–733.

32 Gert Brüggemeier, *Tort Law of the European Union* (Wolters Kluwer 2015) para 306, 314; David G. Owen, *Products Liability Law* (3rd edn, West 2015) 315–334; Simon D. Whittaker, 'The EEC Directive on Product Liability' (1985) 5 Yearbook of European Law 234, 242–243; Hein Kötz, 'Ist die Produkthaftung eine vom Verschulden unabhängige Haftung?' in Bernhard Pfister (ed) *Festschrift für Werner Lorenz* (J.C.B. Mohr 1991) 109; Peter Schlechtriem, 'Dogma und Sachfrage – Überlegungen zum Fehlerbegriff des Produkthaftungsgesetzes' Manfred Löwisch (ed), *Festschrift für Fritz Rittner* (C.H. Beck 1991) 545; Wagner (n 20) Einleitung ProdHaftG para 18.

33 Francois Terré, Philippe Simler and Yves Lequette, *Droit civil – Les obligations* (11th edn, Dalloz 2013) para 767, 794; Wagner, 'Custodian's Liability' in Klaus J. Hopt, Reinhard Zimmermann & Andreas Stier (eds), *The Max Planck Encyclopedia of European Private Law*, vol I (Oxford UP 2012) 441–443.

of product defect containing much of the elements necessary for a finding of negligence.

Where a defective product has caused harm to another, recovery under the Directive is not without limits. Art 9 allows recovery for damage caused by death or personal injury, as well as damage to property, provided that the property item adversely affected is not the product itself, that it was intended for private use and that is was actually used mainly for private purposes. Even then, a threshold of EUR 500 applies. Some Member States have transposed this threshold as a deductible applicable to all claims for compensation of property damage, while others allow the victim to sue for full compensation, provided only that the threshold has been overcome.[34] Where an infringement of one of the protected interests listed in Art 9 is lacking, liability does not apply. This leaves purely economic interests as well as harm to human dignity outside of the protective perimeter of the Directive.

3. *The Proposed Directive on the Liability of Service Providers*

Attempts to supplement the Products Liability Directive by another legal instrument covering the liability of service providers have failed so far. The Commission proposal for a directive on the liability of service providers of 1990, which was designed to supplement the Products Liability Directive never matured into a binding legal instrument.[35] From the perspective of European law, the isolation of the Products Liability Directive may seem regrettable. However, it would be wrong to conclude that service providers are exempt from extra-contractual liability. As has been pointed out above (*supra*, 1), the legal systems of the Member States invariably provide for fault-based liability of actors of all callings, including service providers. The Commission proposal for a directive on the liability of service providers was not predicated on the concept of a 'defective service' but embraced the same principle of fault that also governs in the systems of the Members States. Under Art 1 of the Proposal, the service

34 Commission (n 27), SWD(2018) 157 final, 25.

35 Commission, Proposal for a Council Directive on the liability of suppliers of services, COM(90) 482 final, OJ 1991, C 12/8 ff; cf Emmanuela Truli, *Probleme und Entwicklungen der Dienstleistungshaftung im griechischen, deutschen und Gemeinschaftsrecht* (Duncker & Humblot 2001) 29–39.

provider would have been liable for harm to protected interests 'caused by a fault committed by him in the performance of the service'. Even without careful analysis of the legal systems of the Member States, it is safe to say that service providers face liability for damage caused through their fault under these systems anyway.

4. Conclusion

In summary, the current situation is characterised by a fragmentation of European law and a comprehensive scope of national law. The responsibility of the business that puts a product into the chain of commerce, together with the responsibility of upstream suppliers, is covered by the uniform regime of the Products Liability Directive. Where businesses do not distribute 'products' but rather licence rights or provide a service, the Products Liability Directive does not apply and consequently, no uniform European system of liability is applicable. Furthermore, the responsibility of those actors who own, keep or operate a certain product remains subject to national liability regimes. As far as manufacturers are concerned, approaches towards law reform must therefore start with a re-consideration, and possibly also a supplementation, of the Products Liability Directive. In contrast, with regard to the 'group' of owners, keepers and operators, a European liability framework is missing entirely.

VII. Shifts in Control Induced by Technology

1. The Shift from User Control to Manufacturer Control

While it is difficult and not without serious risk of error to predict the safety characteristics of robots and IoT-devices, it seems reasonable to assume that the advent of such technology will shift control over these machines and appliances away from users and towards manufacturers. Legacy products rely on mechanical technology that is designed and produced by manufacturers, but that needs to be operated by users. While the manufacturer determines the general design of the product, including its safety features, and provides the interfaces between the product and its user – buttons, steering wheels, pedals and the like – it is the user who exercises control in real-world situations and determines the 'behaviour' of the mechanical device. The most obvious example is that of cars. Conventional cars are operated by individual users who determine their direction of movement and their speed. It is also within their power and their responsibility to avoid impact with other cars, property or persons. It is for the driver to hit the brakes and slow the car down, to stop it or to change its direction in order to avoid an accident. The manufacturer is far removed from the accident scene and is unable to influence the behaviour of the vehicle in the relevant situation. Of course, the car manufacturer determines the safety features of the cars he or she produces and may be held liable under the Products Liability Directive where these features are found wanting. However, cars that fail to satisfy the requisite standards of product safety are a rare exception. By far the most traffic accidents are caused by human failure of the driver,[36] with speeding and mistakes in turning representing the most important causes of accidents.[37]

In contrast to conventional cars, autonomous vehicles will be steered and controlled not by a human driver but by an algorithm developed and installed into the car by its manufacturer. Fully autonomous cars that satisfy Level 5 of the classification system for automated vehicles do not require any human intervention when in operation. On the contrary, the intervention of the passenger into the process of driving is prohibited or rather prevented through technical safeguards. As a consequence, the 'behaviour' of the autonomous car is not in the hands of the human driver but in those of the manufacturer. With regard to other autonomous systems and IoT-devices, matters will be similar. The whereabouts and movements of an automated lawnmower are determined by the software operating within the device. The user of the lawnmower can hardly do anything except switching it on and off at a particular location.

---

36 Europe: TRACE, Project No. FP6-2004-IST-4-027763, 16; USA: 94%; NHTSA, National Highway Traffic Safety Administration, Federal Automated Vehicles Policy (2016) at 5, <http://www.nhtsa.gov/AV> accessed 8 August 2018. Germany: 88,1%; Statistisches Bundesamt, Fachserie 8 Reihe 7, Verkehr, Verkehrsunfälle 2016 (Statistisches Bundesamt 2017) at <https://www.destatis.de/DE/Publikationen/Thematisch/TransportVerkehr/Verkehrsunfaelle/VerkehrsunfaelleJ2080700167004.pdf?__blob=publicationFile> accessed 8 August 2018, 49.

37 SafetyNet, Alcohol (2009) 3, at <https://ec.europa.eu/transport/road_safety/specialist/knowledge/alcohol_en> accessed 8 August 2018; SafetyNet, Speeding (2009) 3, at <https://ec.europa.eu/transport/road_safety/sites/roadsafety/files/specialist/knowledge/pdf/speeding.pdf> accessed 8 August 2018; Statistisches Bundesamt, ibid.

The shape of current liability systems is adapted to the division of power and control between manufacturers and users. In short, the main focus of liability rules and the legal practice developed under them is on the users of technical appliances, not on the manufacturers. Again, motor cars provide the best example. The systems of motor traffic liability existing in the Member States differ greatly from one another, but they have in common that they target the users of cars – keepers and/or drivers – rather than manufacturers.[38] Of course, car manufacturers may be held liable under the Products Liability Directive as well as under national law, but the enforcement of such claims is the rare exception.[39] By far the greater share of the total cost of traffic accidents is internalised by the users, or rather by their liability insurers.

Continuing the example of motor traffic, autonomous cars of the future will transform the user from a driver into a passenger, i.e. into a person who travels inside the car, but has no control whatsoever over it. Even without legal analysis it seems obvious that this shift of control will upset established modes of cost attribution through the liability system. From a functional perspective, the focus of the extra-contractual liability must track the shift in the focus of control. As a first approximation, the liability of manufacturers will increase in size and relevance, and the responsibility of users will diminish proportionally.[40] The following analysis accounts for this shift in control by zooming in on manufacturers first (*infra*, VIII.), and by discussing the liability of users in second rank (*infra*, IX.).

2. *Dispersion of Control: Unbundling*

The future is inherently uncertain, and it is impossible to predict with sufficient probability the design and operating mode of technological systems that are yet to be developed and marketed. There is a serious possibility that autonomous systems and IoT-devices may follow an open-system approach that allows users to intermingle with the software that operates the

38 Cees van Dam, *European Tort Law* (2nd edn, Oxford UP 2013) 408–420.

39 For Germany: Statistisches Bundesamt (n 36) 49: less than 1% of traffic accidents are caused by mechanical failure and poor maintenance.

40 Mark A Geistfeld, 'A Roadmap for Autonomous Vehicles: State Tort Liability, Automobile Insurance, and Federal Safety Regulation' (2017) 105 Cal. L. Rev. 1611, 1691.

device. It is conceivable that hard- and software will not be marketed in a bundle, as envisaged for autonomous cars, but separately – so that it is for the user to decide what software product to combine with which kind of hardware product. Further, one can imagine that users will be authorised and enabled to modify the software running a robot or IoT-device, e.g. by adding new features, by choosing between different modes, or by combining the original software with products made by other software companies. If such unbundling takes place, it no longer makes sense to place the manufacturer of the original product on the center stage. The task of attribution of responsibilities may become rather complicated, as it must be somehow shared or divided between original equipment manufacturers, suppliers of additional components, and users. Whatever principle is adopted in this area, it will almost certainly make it more difficult for the victim to identify the responsible party and to furnish proof that the requirements of liability are in fact satisfied vis-à-vis that party.

It seems that this is the situation that the European Parliament had in mind when it articulated the idea to take the autonomous system or robot itself and accord it the status of a legal entity, or 'ePerson'.[41] Doing so would relieve the victim of the burden to identify the responsible party and would spare courts the task to allocate liability between a multitude of defendants. However, as we shall see, the proposal to create ePersons is not without problems that need careful analysis (*infra*, X.). Once this has been done, they must be balanced against the costs of such a move in the form of diminished incentives to take care and adjust activity levels.

VIII. Liability of Manufacturers

1. The Manufacturer as Best Cost Avoider

Manufacturers of robots and IoT-devices will be able to exercise much more control over the performance and behaviour of their creatures than manufacturers of mechanical products. To the extent that manufacturers do or can exercise control, liability must follow. This is particularly obvious in the case of a closed software system that prevents third parties, including the user, from tampering with the algorithm that runs the device.

41 supra, I (n 6).

Here, it is only the manufacturer who is in a position to determine and improve the safety features of the device; nobody else can. Phrased in economic terms, the manufacturer is clearly the cheapest cost avoider.[42] Legal doctrine aligns well with this insight, as it is well accepted that the duty to take care is contingent on the actual availability of precautions and their economic reasonableness.[43] Precautions are economically reasonable if they generate gains in the form of reduced accident costs, which exceed their cost. In the case of a machine or device that comes as an integrated and closed system of hard- and software, the manufacturer is not only the cheapest cost avoider but the only party in a position to take precautions at all. This suggests that the focus of the liability system must be on the manufacturer.

2. *The Scope of the Products Liability Directive*

The movement of manufacturers of robots and IoT-devices onto the central stage of the liability system raises a number of important issues for the Products Liability Directive. An initial question concerns its scope and applicability. Art 2 of the Directive limits its application to 'movables'. This term is understood to refer to corporeal objects or things.[44] Where a corporeal object, such as a car, a machine or a household appliance, is operated by software, it is generally accepted that the bundle of hard- and software together represents the product or 'movable' within the meaning of the Directive.[45] Thus, even if only the software was defective, the Directive applies and the manufacturer may be held liable.

A problem arises if software is distributed as a separate product that is acquired through the internet in the form of a download. In this case, there is no 'movable', i.e. no corporeal asset that the manufacturer placed into the stream of commerce. Computer code is intangible and does not qualify as a 'thing'. Therefore, the Directive may not be applicable to defective software that was distributed separately from the hardware for which it

42 Calabresi (n 17) 136–150; but see also Shavell (n 16) 189–190.

43 van Dam (n 38) 235–246; von Bar, *The Common European Law of Torts* vol 2 (C.H. Beck, 2000) 251–254; Wagner (n 20) § 823 para 421–429.

44 Brüggemeier (n 32) para 293.

45 Wagner (n 20) 714–715.

was designed and also without a corporeal storage device, such as a USB-stick that itself qualifies as a corporeal asset.

It is not entirely clear that the Directive does not apply to computer code. One option is to operate with an expanded notion of 'movable' that includes anything that is neither real estate nor a service,[46] regardless whether the object was tangible or intangible. The other options are an expanded, 'digitalised' interpretation of the concept of 'movable'[47] or the application of Art 2 of the Directive by analogy in order to capture 'quasi-things'. Both options are problematic, as Art 2 is rather elaborate as to the meaning of 'movable', listing a number of examples that all refer to corporeal objects. And the last sentence of Art 2 reads: '"Product" includes electricity'. Against this backdrop, it is not easy to argue that the framers had a broad notion of 'movable' in mind, one that was not limited to corporeal objects. Otherwise, it would not have been necessary to explicitly include electricity. It may also be argued, however, that electricity is mentioned merely as an example of a non-corporeal object that is to be treated like a corporeal asset, and that software is another, and even better example. On this view, the Products Liability Directive, already in its current form, does apply to software 'products'. This expansive view, that applies Art 2 of the Directive in a functional way, excluding only real estate and services, is preferable. The Directive should not be limited in scope to 'old-school' products, and its application should be independent of the mode in which computer programs are stored, copied and distributed.

3. *The Requirement of a Defect*

The Products Liability Directive does not impose pure strict liability on manufacturers of movables but makes liability contingent on the finding of a product defect. The concept of a defect is defined in Art 6 of the Directive with a view towards the safety standard, which a reasonable person was entitled to expect at the time when the product was put into circulation. The problem with this definition is that product users rarely form

---

46 Services are clearly outside of the scope of the Directive; ECJ, 21.12-2010, Case 495/10 (Centre hospitalier universitaire de Besancon v. Dutrueux), para 39; cf also ECJ, 10.5.2001, Case 203/99 (Veedfald v. Arhus Amtskommune) para 17; Brüggemeier (n 32) para 298.

47 Wagner (n 20) 717–718.

specific expectations regarding product safety, and even where they do, these expectations are not determinative, as they are subject to the requirement of reasonableness, encapsulated in the 'entitled to expect' language. As consumer expectations are often lacking or illusive, and not determinative anyway, courts and commentators of products liability law in the USA and Europe therefore favour the so-called risk/utility-test.[48] Notably, it was also embraced by the German Federal Court of Justice (Bundesgerichtshof – BGH).[49]

A finding of defectiveness is relatively straightforward in the area of so-called manufacturing defects. It is characteristic of a manufacturing defect that the product that was put into circulation does not fit the description of the manufacturer because something went wrong in the production process. Examples involving digital products include the incomplete installation of software in an autonomous car or IoT-device, as well as accidents caused by software bugs that were inadvertently included in the computer code. Even though a quality level of 'zero defect' is unattainable, manufacturers of legacy products have worked hard and successfully in recent decades to minimise the occurrence of manufacturing defects. Whether they will be as successful with digital appliances that run on software remains to be seen. It is often said that it is impossible to write perfect computer code, free of any defects. However, to avoid liability for defective products an item need not be perfect but only risk minimising. A bugged computer program in an IoT-device, for instance, does not trigger liability if the system shuts down orderly and safely when the software crashes.

Design defects are by far more serious than manufacturing defects. A product has a defective design if its layout, chosen by the manufacturer during the research and development process, is found wanting. Under the risk/utility-test, the layout of a product is defective if the court is able to identify an alternative design that would have helped to avoid the accident in question, provided that the accident costs avoided by the added safety feature of the alternative design would have exceeded the added costs of the alternative design. Applying the risk/utility-test to autonomous systems and IoT-devices requires an inquiry into software programming. The court or other decision-maker will need to identify shortcomings of the

48 Owen (n 32) 482–503; Whittaker (n 31) 487–488; Terré, Simler and Lequette (n 32) para 989; Wagner (n 20) 731–733; cf also Brüggemeier (n 32) para 306.

49 BGH, 16.6.2009, VI ZR 107/08, BGHZ 181, 253 para 18.

software that could have been avoided by an alternative program that would have performed as well as the one that was used – but would have avoided the accident in question. This issue, of whether the software is defective by design, will require the involvement of a technical expert. This alone is not problematic as, also in cases involving mechanical products, the involvement of technical experts into the fact-finding process is standard practice.

However, autonomous systems probably will pose special problems when it comes to design defects. A first inclination may suggest to compare the performance of an autonomous system to the one of a legacy product, operated by a human being. As to autonomous cars, this solution would amount to a 'human driver test'. Whenever the autonomous system caused an accident, which a reasonable human driver would have been able to avoid, the algorithm would be found defective in design. Intuitive as the human operator test may seem, its application to autonomous systems is misguided.[50] Autonomous systems are expected to decrease the number and severity of accidents dramatically, but accidents will continue to occur. The critical point is that the pool of accidents that an autonomous system still causes will not be the same as the pool of accidents a reasonable driver is unable to avoid. For instance, an autonomous car operating in orderly mode will never speed, and it cannot be drunk. However, it might fail to observe and account for a freak event that any human would have recognised and adapted his or her behaviour to. To subject autonomous systems to a human operator test would miss the mark as it would hold the system to a standard that it cannot live up to.

By definition, an autonomous system cannot and shall not be controlled by humans, neither by its manufacturer nor by its user. In particular, the software engineer who programs the algorithm running the system does not use a finite set of commands of an 'if ... then' nature.[51] Rather, the algorithm is trained on sets of data, and then evolves through self-learning. The learning process unfolds not within one particular car or device, but rather with respect to the whole fleet of cars or devices designed by the same manufacturer. What is required, therefore, is a system-oriented concept of design defect.[52] The crucial question must be whether the system in question, e.g. the fleet of cars operated by the same algorithm, causes an

50 Geistfeld (n 40) 1644–1647; Wagner (n 20) 733–734.
51 Geistfeld (n 40) 1644–1645.
52 Geistfeld (n 40) 1645–1647; Wagner (n 20) 737–740.

unreasonable number of accidents overall. Whether the individual accident in question would have been avoided by a reasonable human driver or by another algorithm, these questions should be irrelevant.

To develop a system-oriented concept of defect is easier said than done. It is difficult to see how an alternative design could be identified other than by comparing the algorithm in question to the ones used by other manufacturers. However, under such an 'optimal algorithm test' the algorithm that caused the accident will always be found defective, whenever there is an algorithm in the market that would have avoided that particular accident. And even applied to the full class of accidents caused by any one fleet of autonomous cars operated by the same algorithm, this method would lead to finding all the algorithms in the market defective – except for the safest of them all.[53] Assuming that one and the same algorithm is operating in a whole fleet of cars or other products marketed by a particular manufacturer, only the manufacturer with the best algorithm would be spared, while all the other manufacturers would be saddled with the full costs of accidents caused by their products. This outcome would be problematic as it would overburden the manufacturers of sub-optimal algorithms and, in doing so, stifle competition in the respective product market.

At this point of the technological development, it is not easy to predict how serious the problems just described will turn out to be. Possibly, courts will be in a position to identify design defects without comparing the performance of the algorithm involved in the accident with other algorithms operating in similar products. This may be true for programming bugs and other shortcomings of the algorithm that may be easy to identify and isolate.

4. *Burden of Proof – Strict Liability as a Response?*

The study that underlies the European Commission's evaluation of the Products Liability Directive suggests that the burden of proof poses a serious obstacle for victims seeking compensation from the manufacturer.[54] Pursuant to Art 4 of the Directive, the burden of proving defect, damage,

53 Wagner (n 20) 737–740.

54 Commission (n 27) SWD(2018) 157 final 25–26.

and the causal link between the two, is upon the injured person. Some observers expect that the burden of proof will weigh even more heavily upon the person injured by a digital product than the one injured by a legacy product.[55]

At this stage, where very few autonomous products are operating in the market, it is difficult to know whether these concerns are justified. On one hand, it is to be expected that the digital revolution will make products even more complex than they previously were.[56] In particular, it may become increasingly difficult to analyse and evaluate self-learning algorithms and complex operating systems more generally. On the other hand, digitalisation also offers unprecedented opportunities to monitor the operation of an autonomous system or IoT-device and to store this information for the benefit of victims. Robots and IoT-devices that were involved in an accident will offer victims, courts and regulators the same comprehensive sets of data that are now available in the case of an airplane crash. This will greatly diminish the evidentiary burden on victims and courts. After a recent reform, the German Road Traffic Act (Straßenverkehrsgesetz – StVG) already includes a right for victims of motor accidents to access the 'black box' of a car equipped with autonomous driving functions (Section 63a (3) StVG). This is meant to enable the victim to identify the true cause of the accident, i.e. whether the automated system or the human driver was responsible.

With access rights like the one just described already in place or readily conceivable, it cannot be said that the remaining difficulties with proving product defect will pose a serious obstacle against recovery. Therefore, lawmakers are well-advised to remain cautious, to hold their fire, and to resist the urge to legislate, i.e. to sharpen the liability system. It is one of the virtues of legal systems in general, and of the development of private law in particular, that the system is able to evolve on a case-by-case basis. In the rather slow process of case-by-case adjudication, society can engage in an iterative process of learning and adjusting that promises better results than aiming for bold goals and easy solutions through early legislation.

---

55 Jeffrey K Gurney, 'Sue My Car Not Me: Products Liability and Accidents Involving Autonomous Vehicles' (2013) University of Illinois Journal of Law & Technology, 247, 265–266; Lennart S Lutz, Tito Tang & Markus Lienkamp, 'Die rechtliche Situation von teleoperierten und autonomen Fahrzeugen' (2013) Neue Zeitschrift für Verkehrsrecht 57, 61.

56 Wagner (n 20) 747.

If it should turn out that, indeed, victims face excessive difficulties to establish product defectiveness with regard to autonomous systems or IoT-devices, two remedies come to mind. One would be to reverse the burden of proof with regard to the requirement of defect, i.e. to turn Art 4 Products Liability Directive around and to hold the manufacturer liable unless he or she is able to prove that the product was not defective. Moving even further, it would be conceivable to abandon the concept of defect altogether and to switch to a system of pure strict liability for autonomous systems and IoT-devices. Under such a system, the manufacturer would be responsible to make good any injury caused by the autonomous system, unless the harm was caused through the fault of the victim, the fault of a third party or force majeure. The switch from quasi-fault-based liability for defective products towards strict liability for autonomous systems may seem revolutionary, but, in reality, it would not be so. To the extent that the manufacturer shapes the algorithm that, in turn, determines the 'behaviour' of the technical system or device, strict liability may be appropriate. Other than with legacy products, the user cannot do anything to prevent accidents from occurring and thus need not be incentivised through the liability system. Incentives to take care of users and third parties as victims would be held in check by the defence of contributory fault, as provided for in Art 8 (2) Products Liability Directive.

5. Unbundled Products

The situation just described, where the manufacturer of the autonomous system fully controls its 'behaviour' in the real world, would change rather dramatically, however, if digitalised products such as autonomous cars and IoT-devices would not be marketed as a bundle of hard- and software that remains closed to user interference. Where the user had acquired hard- and software separately, and from different suppliers, it may be very difficult, in the event of harm, to figure out whether the hardware component or the software component or the mismatch of the two was the cause of the accident. The same problem arises where the user acquired hard- and software together, from a single manufacturer, but was in a position to add software to the programs already installed by the original equipment manufacturer or to tamper with the operation of the pre-installed software. Here, again, it will be very difficult to figure out whether a particular accident was caused by the original software or by add-ons or alterations executed by the user. In both cases, it remains innocent, from the perspective of the liability system, that the user was able to add software that remained outside of the program that operates the system, like entertainment software in an autonomous car. As long as it is assured that the software that governs the safety features of the car or other device remains isolated from user interference, it qualifies as a closed system for purposes of product liability law.

The upshot of the distinction between open and closed systems is that manufacturer liability is of paramount importance with regard to closed systems of hard- and software bundles. This is much less so where hard- and software are manufactured by different suppliers and marketed separately, or where the user is in a position to modify or supplement the safety features of the original software. In the latter case, it does not make sense to channel liability exclusively towards the hardware manufacturer, or towards the software manufacturer. Rather, it is important for the liability system to provide incentives to take care for everyone who is in a position to impact the safety characteristics of the autonomous system or IoT-device.

Thus, much will depend on the characteristics of autonomous systems and IoT-devices and the development of markets for these products. With regard to bundles of hard- and software that remain closed to the user, liability of the manufacturer who placed the bundle on the market is of utmost importance. For unbundled products, the proper solution is much more obscure. In theory, there is a simple remedy, namely a combination of liability for manufacturers of hard- and software and fault-based liability of users and third parties. Of course, this is exactly what the law provides for today, as the Products Liability Directive not only applies to end-manufacturers but also to component suppliers of any layer (Art 3 (1) Directive), while users and third parties are liable for fault under national tort law. In practice, however, the current state of the law may pose serious obstacles towards recovery, as the victim needs to prove who of the various actors involved in the accident does bear responsibility. While Art 1 and Art 3 (1) Directive hold end-producers responsible for the safety of the entire product, this does not apply to product bundles, in which the components are marketed separately. Thus, the victim would have to investigate whether the accident was caused by defective hardware, defective software marketed by the supplier of the original software, software manufactured by a third party and added to the device by the user, or by other modifications made by the user subsequent to acquisition of the device.

This burden may deter many victims from bringing suit and may seriously undermine the success even of meritorious actions. Under Art 4 Products Liability Directive, it is the risk of the victim that the court may fail to identify the true cause of the accident. The same applies under the fault-based liability systems of the several Member States.

Again, there is no easy way out of this conundrum. Reversing the burden of proof offers no remedy. It makes no sense, from a deterrence perspective, to reverse the burden of proof against manufacturers of hardware, for example, when, in all likelihood, the accident was caused by defective software. The same applies with a view to the other parties involved. Where users are authorised to access the safety-related software of the system, the manufacturers of the original components may no longer be held responsible for the performance of the aggregate product. For unbundled products, there simply is no single responsible party that controls the safety feature of all components. Thus, liability must be apportioned between all the actors who contributed to the safety features of the device that caused the accident, at the time of the accident.

It seems that the only solution that would alleviate the burden on the victim of identifying the responsible party when the accident was caused through the interaction of unbundled products is to hold the system itself liable, i.e. to create some form of 'robot liability'. This solution will be examined in more detail below (*infra*, X.).

IX. Liability of Users

There is no European liability regime for users of autonomous systems or IoT-devices, or in fact any kind of product. This does not mean, that users go scot-free. Rather, they are subject to national tort law. In all of the Member States, fault-based liability is the first and central pillar of the liability system. Liability for fault applies to all members of society, including the users of products of any kind, and notably autonomous systems and IoT-devices (*supra*, VI. 1.). Thus, the user of such an appliance is answerable in damages, where he or she misused or abused it and harmed others. For example, if the user of an autonomous car overrides the software's firewall in order to steer the vehicle off the streets or in order to use it like a weapon against another person, his or her liability is out of the question. Further, as has just been explained (*supra*, VIII. 5.), the user is responsible for any software installed subsequent to the purchase of the original system, and for any modifications made to the original software. It has also been noted that it may be difficult for the victim to prove that it was the user – rather than the end- or component manufacturers – who is responsible for the defect that caused the harm complained of.

Some legal systems have gone beyond fault-based liability and subjected users to strict liability for harm caused in the operation of an installation, appliance or machine. The most widespread of these categories is strict liability of keepers of motor cars.[57] The most notable exception to this principle – the United Kingdom that holds on to fault-based liability even in the area of motor traffic – is about to leave the EU. On the other end of the spectrum, France has moved far beyond subjecting motorists to strict liability, in providing a liability system for traffic accidents that is even farther removed from fault and rather settles on mere involvement (implication) in a traffic accident.[58] Outside the special area of motor traffic, France subjects any keeper of a 'thing' to strict liability for any harm, regardless whether the 'thing' was defective or not.[59]

The French solution of strict liability for keepers of any 'thing' did not win over the drafters of the Common Frame of Reference or the European Group on Tort Law. Art VI.–3:202ff Draft Common Frame of Reference provide several categories of strict liability, namely for immovables that are unsafe (Art VI.–3:202 DCFR), animals (Art VI.–3:203), defective products (Art VI.–3:204), motor vehicles (Art VI.–3:205) and dangerous substances and emissions (Art VI.–3:206), but not for simple 'things'.[60] Under Art 5:101 Principles of European Tort Law strict liability is confined to abnormally dangerous activities, while national lawmakers retain the option to extend strict liability to activities that are dangerous, though not abnormally so.[61] The advent of autonomous systems and IoT-devices may force European lawmakers to reconsider the issue. If markets developed towards unbundling, and original equipment manufacturers lost

---

57 supra (n 38).

58 Geneviève Helleringer & Anne Guédan-Lécuyer, 'Development of Traffic Liability in France' in: Wolfgang Ernst (ed), *The Development of Traffic Liability, Comparative Studies in the Development of the Law of Torts in Europe* (John Bell & David Ibbetson, eds), vol 5 (Cambridge UP 2010) 50, 67–69; van Dam (n 38) 408–411; Terré, Simler & Lequette (n 32) 984–1012.

59 supra (n 33).

60 von Bar & Clive (n 23) 3544, 3558; von Bar, Clive & Schulte-Nölke (n 23) 401–405.

61 European Group on Tort Law (n 24) 5–6, 104.

control over the safety features of the products they put into circulation, responsibilities become blurred. It will thus become increasingly difficult for the victim to single out the actor who bears responsibility for the accident in question. To the extent that the victim fails to pinpoint responsibility, the damages claim fails and incentives to take care are lost. Such outcomes could be avoided if users were held strictly liable for any harm caused in the course of the operation of an autonomous system. The question as to who bears responsibility for a particular accident would then be shifted towards the user and his or her insurers who, in turn, would seek recourse against hardware- and software manufacturers.

It seems that, at this point in time, it is too early for such a sweeping solution. Up to the present day, unbundling has not taken place, and the evidentiary burden for the victims of digital products is no greater than the burden for victims of any other product. As long as the situation remains as is, there is no need to discuss the introduction of broad strict liability of users of digital appliances.

On the other hand, the national legal systems are well-advised to keep systems of strict user liability in place, where they are already established. This advice is particularly important for road traffic liability, which provides the backbone of the tort system in many jurisdictions. In Germany and other countries, liability is channeled towards the keeper of the car, who in turn is required, under European law, to cover the risk through liability insurance.[62] The result is a two-step system of strict liability for motor accidents that offers victims a 'one-shop-stop'-solution to compensation. The question of who bears responsibility for the accident, be it the driver who drove too fast, the owner keeper who failed to afford proper maintenance of the car, the shop owner whose repairs were deficient or the manufacturer who failed to meet the required standard of safety, is not a concern of the victim. Whoever the culpable party may be, the insurance company that insured the keeper against liability will indemnify the victim. The attribution of liability and the enforcement of legal claims are shifted to recourse actions by the motor insurer against the responsible party. These are managed by the insurance carriers, who are professional and well-informed parties willing and able to enforce such claims. It would be foolish to abolish or restrict these well-oiled systems of compensation for traffic accidents that exist in the Member States. Also, in a

62 van Dam (n 38) 408–420; as to the duty to take out liability insurance supra (n 21).

world with autonomous cars, traffic victims should be able to obtain compensation from the keeper of the car, or rather, the liability insurer of the car, and not be forced to identify the party within the group of manufacturers, service providers, keepers and users who bears responsibility for the accident in question.

In the same vein, proposals to restrict the rights of recourse of motor insurers against manufacturers of autonomous cars should also be resisted.[63] If rights of recourse against these manufacturers were removed or restricted, the costs of their failure to take precautions against harm would be externalised to motor insurers and, ultimately, the keepers of cars, who would have to pay higher insurance premiums. This consequence does not raise distributive concerns as the keepers must front the costs of compensation anyway, be it in the form of higher premiums for their insurance policies, be it in the form of a higher purchase price for the car, reflecting a component of liability insurance running with the sale. The real concern is behavioural: To isolate auto manufacturers from rights of recourse would effectively remove any financial incentive for them to take care and to avoid accidents from occurring. These incentives are needed, however, to entice manufacturers to invest in the safety of the autonomous driving machines they are about to market.[64] Contrary to popular thought, these incentives are no less needed in case of a new technology, but even more so. It is unavoidable that manufacturers know less about the safety requirements of new technologies than they know about the features and risks of long-established technological appliances. Thus, at the early stages of a technology, it is particularly important to provide incentives to take care as manufacturers still have a lot to learn. Abolishing the rights of recourse of insurance carriers against manufacturers would essentially remove the financial incentive to do so and provide a subsidy to manufacturers of new technologies.

63 Wagner (n 20) 760–764.

64 Horst Eidenmüller, 'The Rise of Robots and the Law of Humans' (2017) Zeitschrift für Europäisches Privatrecht 765, 771–772; Gerald Spindler, 'Roboter, Automation, künstliche Intelligenz, selbst-steuernde Kfz – Braucht das Recht neue Haftungskategorien?' (2015) CR 766, 771–772; Wagner (n 20) 762.

X. Liability of the IoT-Device, the Robot Itself

1. A Legal, not a Philosophical Question

The fanciest topic in the area discussed in this paper is, of course, the liability of the robot itself. The fact that robots are anthropomorphic may lead to the idea that they should be treated as persons, so-called 'ePersons' for that matter. In a more serious way, scholars of sociology and philosophy of law have pointed to the fact that, with the advances in technology that are now visible on the horizon, the gap between humans and machines becomes increasingly blurred.[65] If the distinctive feature of being human is to be able to 'think' and to autonomously set goals for oneself, then it might be conceivable that artefacts acquire these same capabilities. And if they do, it seems, they must lose their status as 'objects' and be recognised as persons, i.e. subjects, by the legal system.

The suggestion to promote autonomous software agents to legal subjects raises a number of issues that cannot and need not be discussed in the present context. One obvious question that troubles academics and the public alike, is whether it is at all realistic that machines will get to the level of 'artificial intelligence' or whether they will remain confined to execute the computer program they were trained on. This question is obviously of a technological nature, and, as such, not for lawyers to discuss and decide. The legal question rather, is whether autonomous software agents should be accorded entity status, on the assumption that and at the point in time when they have acquired the requisite capabilities.

Another interesting question is of anthropological nature: What does it take to be human? This goes to the level of cognitive capabilities an entity must possess in order to be qualified as 'intelligent'. The next step then is to determine whether intelligence is enough for acceptance into the group of humans or whether it takes more. If it does take more, what else is required? Autonomous goal-setting, moral agency, the capacity for empathy

---

65 Pathbreaking Gunther Teubner, 'Rights of Non-humans? Electronic Agents and Animals as New Actors in Politics and Law' (2006) 33 Journal of Law and Society 497–521; idem, 'Digitale Rechtssubjekte? Zum privatrechtlichen Status autonomer Softwareagenten' (2018) 218 Archiv für die civilistische Praxis 155–205; cf also F Patrick Hubbard, '"Do Androids Dream?": Personhood and Intelligent Artifacts' (2011) 83 Temple Law Review 405, 418–433; Erich Schweighofer, Thomas Menzel & Günther Kreuzbauer (eds), *Auf dem Weg zur ePerson: aktuelle Fragestellungen der Rechtsinformatik* (Verlag Österreich 2001).

and for emotions more generally? Again, these questions are not of a legal nature. Legal systems take it for granted that humans are persons, i.e. legal subjects, not objects, without discussing what it takes to qualify as a human. More precisely, legal systems refer to 'speciecism', i.e. they classify living organisms as humans and accord them the status of persons if they belong to the species of *homo sapiens*.[66] Whether a particular human being is really able to think for him- or herself, whether it has a moral sense, whether it sets its goals autonomously, and develops emotional ties towards others, is irrelevant.

This strategy of defining legal subjectivity not with a view towards certain intellectual and emotional capabilities, but simply on the basis of belonging to the human race, suggests that the expansion of entity status to non-human actors is not a question of capabilities. It is rather a decision for the legal system to make. The legal system is a creation of and operated by humans. The same people who (virtually) agreed on a constitution and who inaugurated a legislature to make laws can and will decide on whether to accord entity status to autonomous software agents. Even the closest similarities between machines possessing artificial intelligence and humans will not predetermine the answer to this question.

The 'anthropocentric' approach to the question of entity status for robots, outlined above, is confirmed by the concept of the juridical person as it exists in modern legal systems, including the Member States of the EU. Juridical persons are formed of groups of humans who together pursue a certain purpose, usually to run a business for profit.[67] On the basis of statutory instruments or other legal norms, corporations and certain kinds

66 The term 'speciecism', originally coined by Richard D. Ryder, is popular in the animal rights community; cf, eg, Paul Waldau, 'Speciecism: Ethics, Law, and Policy' in Marc Beckoff & Jane Goodall (ed), *Encylopedia of Animal Rights and Animal Welfare* (2nd edn, Greenwood Press 2009) 529–534; Peter Singer, *Animal Liberation* 1975; idem, 'Ethics Beyond Species and Beyond Instincts' in Cass R. Sunstein & Martha C. Nussbaum (eds), *Animal Rights* (Oxford UP 2004) 78, 79; Richard Dawkins, 'Gaps in the Mind' in Paola Cavalieri & Peter Singer (eds), *The Great Ape Project* (St. Martin's Griffin 1993) 81–87. Without subscribing to the propositions of the animal rights movement, the point that existing legal systems are anthropocentric, in that they endow only humans with rights, is uncontroversial.

67 John Armour, Henry Hansmann, Reinier Kraakman & Mariana Pargendler, 'What is Corporate Law?' in Reinier Kraakman, John Armour, Paul Davies, Luca Enriques, Henry Hansmann, Gerard Hertig, Klaus Hopt, Hideiki Kanda, Mariana Pargendler, Georg Ringe & Edward Rock (eds), *The Anatomy of Corporate Law:*

of partnership enjoy 'entity status', i.e. they qualify as a distinct legal person, even though they are not human. The classification of groups of people operating a business as a 'legal person' obviously rests on decisions made and institutions supplied by the legal system itself. It is not 'in the nature of things' that corporations are legal entities, but it is a matter of legislative fiat.

Advocates of ePersons often point to the example of corporations in order to argue that entity status is not strictly confined to humans. As we have seen, this argument is correct, but it cuts both ways. There is nothing in the concept of a legal entity or in philosophy that stands in the way of recognition of autonomous software agents as legal persons. On the other hand, there is nothing in the concept of the legal person or in anthropology or philosophy that requires the legal system to accord entity status to autonomous software agents. These may be as human-like as they get, the decision whether they qualify as persons still needs to be made by humans, and they can decide not to take this step.

Even if humans decided to accord entity status to autonomous software agents, they need not do so wholesale. As for corporations, legal systems take a nuanced approach, treating them like persons in the commercial area, but withholding other privileges, such as the right to vote. Whether corporations are within the protective perimeter of fundamental rights like free speech or freedom of religion is a much-discussed issue on both sides of the Atlantic.[68] In the present context, it is neither possible nor necessary to delve into the discussion on fundamental rights. Entity status is no black-and-white decision but allows for graduation; the accordance of legal status in one context need not lead to an award of the same status in another. Within the context of non-contractual liability, the crucial question that needs to be answered is whether robots should be recognised as wrongdoers or otherwise liable parties, i.e. whether they should be accorded entity status for purposes of ascribing liability. Again, this question

---

A Comparative and Functional Approach (3rd edn, Oxford UP 2017) 1–15; for an historical perspective Andreas M. Fleckner, *Antike Kapitalvereinigungen* (Böhlau 2010) 239–496.

68 Citizens United v. Federal Election Commission, 558 U.S. 310 (2010); Burwell v. Hobby Lobby, 573 U.S. __ (2014); Thomas Ackermann, 'Unternehmen als Grundrechtssubjekte' in Susanne Baer, Oliver Lepsius, Christoph Schönberger, Christian Waldhoff, Christian Walter (eds), *Jahrbuch des öffentlichen Rechts der Gegenwart*, vol 65 (Mohr Siebeck 2017) 113.

must not be approached in a fundamentalist or essentialist way, asking whether robots are sufficiently similar to other persons who may become 'liability subjects', i.e. entities that may be held liable under the applicable legal rules, in the same way that humans, corporations, and perhaps partnerships may be held liable. According entity status to non-humans is not a question for anthropology but one for the liability system to answer. The question is: Does it make sense, for the liability system, to recognise autonomous software agents as legal entities who may be held liable in damages?

2. *Externalisation of Risk through Recognition of ePersons as 'Liability Subjects'*

As a first approximation, the answer to the question posed above, whether robots should qualify as entities capable of attracting liability, must be 'no', i.e. autonomous software agents cannot be recognised as 'liability subjects'. The obvious explanation is that robots have no assets for paying off damages claims. If they were nonetheless accepted as legal entities, victims would receive nothing. Entity status would result in a complete externalisation of accident risk, and incentives to take care would be lost.

In this context, it is important to note that recognising robots as ePersons would protect all the actors 'behind' the robot from liability. The creation of a distinctive legal entity, such as a corporation, works as a shield against liability for the actors who created the entity, in the example of corporations the shareholders.[69] The purpose of this shield is to stimulate risk bearing; shareholders cannot lose more than the money they invested into the corporation.[70] Applying the principle of limited liability to ePersons, manufacturers and users of robots would be exempt from liability as they qualify as quasi-shareholders of the robot. Its manufacturers, programmers, and users would no longer be liable as the 'behaviour' of the robot would no longer be ascribed to them – but instead to the robot itself.

69 Frank H. Easterbrook & Daniel R. Fischel, *The Economic Structure of Corporate Law* (Harvard UP 1991) 40–62; Stephen M. Bainbridge & M. Todd Henderson, *Limited Liability* (Elgar 2016) 44–85; John Armour, Henry Hansmann, Reinier Kraakman & Mariana Pargendler (n 67) 5–6.

70 Frank H. Easterbrook & Daniel R. Fischel (n 69) 40; Stephen M. Bainbridge & M. Todd Henderson (n 69) 2.

This could be tolerated, in the sense of a price worth paying, if the newly created legal entity itself were capable of responding to the threat of liability. This is emphatically not true for robots. It seems that, under the proposition of ePerson liability, no one responsive to the financial incentives of the liability system would in fact be exposed to it.

For purposes of deterrence, such an outcome is intolerable. The quasi-shareholders of the robot would have no financial incentive to manufacture the robot and operate it in a way that reduces the risk of harm. No incentives to take precautions would exist. Furthermore, the price charged for the robot would not reflect the true social cost of its creation and operation, as the harm caused to third parties would remain with the victims. Thus, entity status externalises the risks created by the robot itself, but also the risk created by those who put the robot into circulation and others who decided to put the robot to a certain use or otherwise release it into society.

3. *Incentives for Robots?*

In the case of limited shareholder liability, at least the corporation is not immune from liability. As an organisation that ties together individuals through a nexus of contracts, it may respond to the incentives generated by the liability system.[71] It is essential to understand that matters are different when it comes to ePersons. The reason is that robots – however 'intelligent' they may become – will never be able to respond to the incentives generated by the liability system. Sure enough, an autonomous software system can be programmed to 'learn' from past experience in the sense that the algorithm improves with every accident it becomes involved in. However, the capacity of the algorithm for improvement is based on its programming, i.e. on the decisions of software programmers. Whether or not the autonomous system will be held liable for the consequences of an accident it has caused, is irrelevant to the learning curve, or lack thereof, of the algorithm. Obviously, software can be programmed to improve itself even without the concept of an ePerson. Thus, autonomous software agents are immune to the financial incentives generated by a credible threat of being hold liable for harm caused. The fact that potential ePer-

71 Frank H. Easterbrook & Daniel R. Fischel (n 69) 40–41.

sons are unreceptive to financial incentives to avoid harm, raises serious concerns with a view to deterrence, even if minimum asset requirements or insurance mandates apply.

4. Risk Internalisation through Asset Requirements and Insurance Mandates

It is true that the problem of risk externalisation, together with the frustration of incentives to take care, may be addressed by the legal system, and this is what serious advocates of ePersons actually propose. The remedies are similar to the ones employed in corporate law. The robot could be required to be endowed with minimum assets in order to qualify as a legal entity. Such a minimum asset requirement would force other parties to provide the funds necessary to satisfy potential damages claims. These funds would then be transferred to the robot and held in its own name. From this pool of assets, damages claims would be paid off.

An alternative means to minimum asset requirements that serves the same end is mandatory liability insurance. The law could simply stipulate an insurance mandate, as a precondition for incorporation of a robot as an ePerson. Again, the burden for providing the mandatory liability insurance would fall on the natural and legal persons who put the robot into circulation or operate it. They would have to supply the insurance contract and pay the premiums, as the robot would have no assets to pay them from. Looked at solely through the eyes of the liability system, mandatory liability insurance seems preferable over minimum asset requirements. Other than for the largest of enterprises, who can easily self-insure, market insurance is usually more efficient than self-insurance through the setting aside of assets. Tellingly, liability insurance for business enterprises is very common even though there is no legal requirement for it. The main advantage of insurance over other forms of hedging risk is that there is no saving period until a sufficient pool of assets has been compiled, and that the assets remain liquid as they need not be set aside as savings for the benefit of victims. This suggests that mandatory insurance may be the better solution also for ePersons.

Within the scope of the insurance cover or asset cushion, the crucial issue is as to who will be liable to contribute. The robot cannot pay for insurance, so somebody else needs to do that. The usual suspects are already familiar: the manufacturers of the robots and their users. If the manufacturers have to front the costs of insurance, they will pass these costs on to the buyers/keepers of the robot. In one form or another, they would end up with the users. The same outcome obtains if the users contribute directly to the asset cushion or become liable for the insurance premiums. In the end, therefore, the producers and users of the robot have to pay for the harm caused by the robot. The ePerson is only a conduit to channel the costs of cover to the manufacturers and users.

Whatever tool would be chosen by the legal system, both, minimum asset requirements and mandatory insurance are well-suited to avoid risk externalisation. At least up to the amount of the insurance ceiling or the value of the minimum assets, victim compensation is assured. Beyond this amount, however, risk externalisation would persist.[72] Again, the essential point about entity status for robots is that this move helps to shield other parties from liability, namely manufacturers and users. Within the corporate context, the protective function of limited liability is acceptable for voluntary creditors who can easily protect themselves against risk externalisation, but it is much more problematic for involuntary creditors like tort victims who lack any means to do so.[73]

It may well be argued that manufacturers and users should be protected from excessive liability so that caps on liability are in order. There is also no doubt that limited liability of the quasi-shareholders, such as the manufacturers of robots, is functionally equivalent to a cap on the direct liability of these same manufacturers. Here, as in corporate law, the creation of a legal entity helps to limit the exposure of the individuals who created the entity and thus may stimulate them to take on more risk at lower cost.[74] However, it must be remembered that any 'liability subsidy' accorded to certain activities stimulates an excessive amount of such activities (*supra*, IV.). If autonomous systems really generate the great savings in accident costs that they are promised to, then no liability subsidy is needed.

As a general matter, it is submitted that the issue of limited liability should be addressed and discussed head-on rather than hidden in the issue of recognition of autonomous systems as ePersons. Whether caps are use-

---

72 Frank H Easterbrook & Daniel R Fischel (n 69) 49–50.

73 Frank H Easterbrook & Daniel R Fischel (n 69) 50–54; Wagner, 'Deliktshaftung und Insolvenzrecht' in Eberhard Schilken, Gerhard Kreft, Gerhard Wagner & Diedrich Eckardt (eds), *Festschrift für Walter Gerhardt* (RWS 2004) 1043, 1048–1051.

74 Stephen M. Bainbridge & M. Todd Henderson (n 69) 2, 47–48, 69.

ful and, if so, what their appropriate level shall be, must be discussed separately from and independently of the ePerson issue. Art 16 (1) Products Liability Directive provides such a cap with regard to the liability of the manufacturers; their exposure is limited to 70 million ECU. Pending reform of the Directive, this cap also applies to manufacturers of robots and IoT-devices, however intelligent they may be. On the other hand, the liability of users, insofar as it is fault-based, is typically unlimited.

5. The Benefit of Robots as Liability Subjects

As has been pointed out, it is conceivable to develop tools that aim to preserve, or restore, the incentives generated by the liability system. In particular, ePerson liability could be supplemented by rights of recourse that the robot, or rather its liability insurer, would have against the manufacturer of the robot, and perhaps also its user. If such rights of recourse are generously granted, manufacturers and users may be exposed to the exact same incentives that they would face if the robot would not have been promoted to a liability subject. However, under this assumption, the question arises as to the purpose of the whole enterprise. If ePersons do not effectively shield the parties that created and operated them from liability, then why the effort?

The best answer to this question seems to be that the creation of a new entity may solve the evidentiary problems victims may face in markets for unbundled digital products. As has been explained above (*supra*, VIII. 5.), persons injured by a robot may face serious difficulties in identifying the party who is responsible for the misbehaviour of the device. Where robots are no longer marketed as a closed bundle of hard- and software, the mere malfunctioning of the robot is no evidence that the hardware product put into circulation by the manufacturer or the software downloaded from another manufacturer was defective. Likewise, the responsibility of the user may be difficult to establish. In a market of unbundled products, the promotion of the robot to a liability subject may serve as a tool for 'bundling' responsibility. The burden to identify the party who was in fact responsible for the malfunction or other defect would then be shifted away from victims and onto the liability insurers of the robot. Liability insurers, in turn, are professional players who may be better able to investigate the facts, evaluate the evidence and pose a credible threat to hold hardware manufacturers, software programmers or users accountable. The first question liability insurers would consider is, however, whether the investigation of the facts for the purpose of identifying the responsible party is worth the cost.

Whether the evidentiary problems to be expected from markets with unbundled products are worth the cost of creating a new legal entity is doubtful. Moreover, digital technologies offer unique opportunities to record evidentiary data and to provide access to them at zero cost. It may well be that the information stored in the 'black boxes' that will be installed in robots and IoT-devices will allow victims to identify the responsible party easily and accurately. Until it has been proven that these hopes will not materialise, legislation to create ePersons as liability subjects is not recommended.

XI. Conclusions

As the preceding analysis has revealed, the advent of robots and IoT-devices poses some challenges to the liability system. From a European perspective, it is noteworthy that the legal rules governing the liability of manufacturers are harmonised by the Products Liability Directive while the liability of users is subject to the legal systems of the Member States. Unfortunately, there is some uncertainty as to the responsibility of software programmers under the Directive, as it may be argued, incorrectly, that computer code does not qualify as a 'movable' within the meaning of Art 2 of the Directive. This uncertainty will remain inconsequential as long as autonomous systems are marketed as a bundle of hard- and software, as such bundles surely qualify as products. Once the bundle is unpacked and software is distributed separately, the situation changes. In this case, the need arises to add a clarification to the Products Liability Directive that software qualifies as a movable.

The difference between bundled and unbundled products turns out to be of crucial importance in other respects as well. In the former case, when hard- and software are marketed together and in a package that remains closed to the user, the manufacturer is the pivotal actor. Here, it is only the manufacturer who determines the safety features and the behaviour of the robot or IoT-device. In other words, the manufacturer clearly is the cheapest cost avoider, in fact, he or she is the only person in a position to take precautions at all. In the interest of meaningful incentives of the manufacturer to employ available safety measures and to balance their costs and benefits, manufacturer liability is essential. In the case of closed systems marketed as a bundle, the incentives of users are secondary, as the user cannot influence the behaviour of the robot. The temptation of users to tamper with the system, to override firewalls or otherwise abuse the robot, is effectively held in check by fault-based liability that exists in the legal systems of all the Member States.

Matters are much more complex when it comes to unbundled products. Here, it may be difficult for the victim to identify the responsible party, be it the hardware manufacturer, the software provider, or the user. Reversing the burden to prove a defect under Art 4 Products Liability Directive, makes no sense as long as the question of who the responsible party is remains unsettled. Robot liability, i.e. the promotion of autonomous systems and IoT-devices to legal entities or liability subjects, would offer a solution. The downside of entity status for robots is that a technical appliance, artificially intelligent as it may be, is never responsive to the financial incentives generated by the liability system. For this reason, and also for the purpose of avoiding the externalisation of risk, it is essential that the parties who created and operated the robot, i.e. hardware manufacturers, software programmers and users, are made accountable for the cost of harm. This end can be achieved by requiring ePersons to take out liability insurance in an amount that reflects the amount of harm that they might potentially cause, and to force manufacturers and/or users to front the premiums for such insurance cover. Whether the advantage in terms of victim compensation is worth the price of shielding the truly responsible parties, namely manufacturers and users, from liability remains to be seen. As long as autonomous systems and IoT-devices do not arrive in large numbers, there is no need for legislative action.

How can Artificial Intelligence be Defective?

*Jean-Sébastien Borghetti**

While it is not always clear how the Internet of things (IoT) and artificial intelligence (AI) should be defined precisely, it is a fact that the new technologies associated with algorithms and the Internet attract an increasing amount of attention from lawyers, and rightly so. The issues that are raised are very diverse, but liability is definitely one of them. Who can be held liable for damage associated with the IoT or AI, and under what conditions? This is a central, and very complex question. This short contribution obviously will not attempt to give a complete and final answer to it, but will rather focus on the element that can or should trigger liability associated with the IoT or AI.

The element that triggers liability, and which French lawyers suggestively call *fait générateur* (literally: the generating fact, but the expression is often translated into English as the 'event giving rise to liability'), depends on the liability regime that is being applied. It is often a human conduct, as is the case when liability is based on fault, but it can also be a certain type of event or a given characteristic in a thing, as is the case when liability is based on a product's defect. A preliminary question is therefore: what are the liability regimes which may or should apply in case of harm caused by, or in connection with the use of, the IoT or AI?

Depending on the circumstances and on the legal systems, different regimes may be applicable. A general distinction can be made, however, between sector-specific regimes and non-sector-specific regimes. The former are relevant every time that the IoT or AI is used in a field of activity covered by such a specific regime. For example, in many countries, if an autonomous car or vehicle is involved in a traffic accident, a specific (strict) liability regime designed to cover such accidents will apply[1]. Sector-specific regimes will not be considered at this stage, since they come

---

* Professor of Private Law, University Panthéon-Assas (Paris II).

1 See infra II.

in all shapes and sizes, and there is no uniformity in the events, facts or conducts that give rise to liability under them.

Non-sector-specific regimes are quite different in that respect. Each country has of course its own rules, but there are two types of regimes that can be found in most (Western) legal systems and whose application can at least be contemplated in case of damage caused by or in connection with the use of, the IoT or AI: product liability and liability for fault.

Most Western legal systems have special product liability regimes. The developments which took place in the USA as of the 1930s, and especially in the 1960s and 1970s, were a source of inspiration for the 1985 European Directive on product liability[2]. This text, in turn, served as a model for legislation in many countries outside the EU. The result is that there are many common features between the special product liability regimes applicable all over the world. For the sake of simplicity, however, the focus here will be on the common European regime based on the 1985 Directive.

Whether this regime is applicable to the IoT or AI has been the subject of some debate. There is actually no doubt that it applies to robots or any device in which a software program or algorithm is embedded. The question is whether it should also apply to 'stand-alone algorithms'. It seems quite clear that the Directive's drafters did not contemplate this issue, and the few official declarations there have been on the subject are contradictory[3]. If one considers the implicit rationale of the Directive, however, and the need to meet the challenges raised by the mass distribution of standardised products, then it can be accepted that the Directive and the liability it establishes should apply to stand-alone algorithms, at least when they have not been designed to meet the specific needs of a particular customer, but are made available to the general public, like physical products can be[4].

2 Council Directive 85/374/EEC of 25 July 1985 on the approximation of the laws, regulations and administrative provisions of the Member States concerning liability for defective products [1985] OJ L210/29.

3 See Jean-Sébastien Borghetti, *La responsabilité du fait des produits. Étude de droit comparé* (LGDJ 2004) para 495.

4 See Cédric Coulon, 'Du robot en droit de la responsabilité civile : à propos des dommages causés par les choses intelligentes' (2016) Responsabilité civile et assurances, étude 6, para 12; Gerhard Wagner, 'Produkthaftung für autonome Systeme' (2017) AcP 217, 707, 717–718.

The application of liability for fault in case of damage caused by, or in connection with, the IoT or AI is not self-evident. Of course, if it is proven that a person was negligent or at fault when designing an algorithm, he can be made liable for any damage caused by his fault or negligence. The real question is whether a software program or algorithm can itself be at fault. That a non-human could be negligent or commit a fault seems at first sight preposterous, and yet the suggestion cannot be discarded outright. After all, if there is really any such thing as AI, it is conceivable that this intelligence could err and be at fault[5]. Besides, should robots be granted some sort of legal personality or be considered as agents, as some suggest[6], then this might create an incentive to recognise a concept of 'robot's fault'. This fault could then become the basis for the robot's personal liability, or for the liability of the robot's principal, if the robot is considered as an agent.

Assuming, be it only for the sake of discussion, that there could be such a thing as a robot's fault, how should this fault be characterised? The assessment of fault is normally based on a comparison between the defendant's behaviour and the behaviour which a model person, such as the *bonus paterfamilias*, the reasonable (wo)man or the (wo)man on the Clapham omnibus, would have adopted in similar circumstances, and one could think of recognising the figure of the reasonable robot, or of the autonomous Clapham omnibus. It is doubtful, however, if the test of the reasonable robot could be anything else than a restatement of the requirement that the robot should not be defective. A negligent robot is just a defective one. The conclusion therefore seems to be that, whether product liability or liability for fault applies, and leaving aside the issue of who should answer for damage attributable to the IoT or AI, the basis for liability will be defectiveness.

---

5 Discussing the extent of the robots' autonomy, see eg Andrea Bertolini, 'Robots as Products: The Case for a Realistic Analysis of Robotic Applications and Liability Rules' (2013) Law, Innovation and Technology, 5:2, 214–247, DOI: 10.5235/17579961.5.2.214; Bartosz Brozek and Marek Jakubiec, 'On the legal responsibility of autonomous machines' (2017) Artif Intell Law 25:293; Jaap Hage, Theoretical foundations for the responsibility of autonomous agents, (2017) Artif Intell Law 25:255.

6 This option is considered in Mady Delvaux (rapp.), Report with recommendations to the Commission on Civil Law Rules on Robotics (2015/2103(INL)), January 2017. For a clear rejection of this option, see eg Horst Heidenmüller, 'The Rose of Robots and the Law of Humans' (2017) ZEuP 765, 775.

Defect thus appears as a central and unavoidable concept when one contemplates the application of traditional non-sector-specific liability regimes to damage caused by, or in connection with, the IoT or AI. It is also a complex and protean one, as all those who have even a slight interest for product liability know.

A preliminary distinction should be made between defects in a software program or algorithm, on the one hand, and 'physical' defects in the objects that are governed or animated by the algorithm, one the other hand (for example a non-functioning brake or sensor in an autonomous vehicle). The latter are just ordinary defects, even if they were caused by the operation of the IoT or AI, and the ordinary rules of product liability should therefore apply to them.

More problematic is the application of these rules, and especially of the concept of defect, to software programs or algorithms. Some further distinctions need to be made. As a matter of fact, certain types of defect that can be associated with software programs or algorithms, and more generally with AI, are quite easy to handle conceptually, if not to demonstrate: an erroneous code line in a program, or an abnormal vulnerability of the program to viruses or to hackers, for example. In such cases, it is quite clear that the program is not as it should and could have been, and there is therefore no difficulty in regarding it as defective (provided the shortfall is significant enough). It is also conceivable that the information or warnings that accompany the software or algorithm were not sufficient, in which case a warning defect could be recognised.

In many cases, however, there will be neither an obvious design defect nor a warning defect. There will only be a possibility or a suspicion that the algorithm was defectively designed. The practical question will therefore be: what is the test to assess the defective design of an algorithm? This is a central issue, whose significance for potential plaintiffs cannot be underrated. The problem, as shall be seen, is that demonstrating an algorithm's defective design is bound to be a very difficult, if not impossible, task for plaintiffs (I). It should therefore be considered whether liability for the IoT or AI could be based on another notion than defect (II).

I. How can the defectiveness of an algorithm be assessed?

The mere fact that a product, including an algorithm, caused harm or damage does not make it defective. Under the 1985 Directive, a product is defective 'when it does not provide the safety which a person is entitled to expect' (article 6). Another and simpler way to put it is to say that a product is defective only if it is unreasonably or abnormally dangerous. Whichever way you phrase it, the standard for defectiveness is quite vague. However, the central issue is not so much the standard itself as the test or tests that can be used to establish defectiveness, in particular when it is the product's design that is allegedly defective.

Looking at what courts do in several countries suggests that a product's defect, and especially a design defect, is normally established in one of the following ways[7]:

- proof that the product malfunctioned;
- proof of the violation of safety standards;
- balancing the product's risks and benefits;
- comparing the product with other products.

None of these methods, however, seems well suited for algorithms.

The proof that the product malfunctioned is a common way of establishing defectiveness, with the malfunctioning creating a presumption that the product was defective. Malfunctioning, when the product was apparently used in reasonably foreseeable circumstances, is actually an illustration of *res ipsa loquitur*. It is only in certain cases, though, that the product's malfunctioning is obvious. Some of these cases might involve the IoT or products with AI (for example a connected toaster that explodes, or an autonomous car that drives off the road even though there was no obstacle and the road was as good as it could be). But the chances are that there will be no obvious malfunctioning in most cases where damage occurs in association with the use of the IoT or AI. If an algorithm designed to make medical diagnoses delivers a wrong diagnosis, for example, this might be the result of a defective design, but there is no obvious malfunctioning that could be the basis for a presumption that the algorithm was defective. A plaintiff would therefore have to turn to another way of establishing the algorithm's defect.

The violation of safety standards is another, and theoretically quite simple way of establishing defectiveness. Safety standards are all the more important as they powerfully contribute to making products safer and to avoiding damage – probably much more than liability and the incentive it

7 Borghetti (n 3) para 277ff.

presumably creates for producers. Safety standards are not always up to date, however, and, especially in a fast-moving field such as the IoT or AI, it might take some time before plaintiffs can rely on adequate standards to try and establish defectiveness.

Risk-benefit analysis is yet another method to assess defectiveness. One way of carrying it out is to compare the product's risks with the benefits associated with its use. This method is deceptively simple, however, since, most often, the benefits and the risks associated with one product are of totally different natures, and comparing them is just like adding apples and oranges. 'Absolute' or 'internal' risk-benefit analysis is thus adapted only to very specific products, such as pharmaceuticals, whose benefits and risks are of a similar nature.

Another approach to risk-benefit analysis is to confront the respective risks and benefits of two products. This is just a specific type of comparison, though, which brings us to the fourth and most common method to assess defectiveness. As far as 'normal' products are concerned, a comparison can be made in two ways: the product under investigation can be compared to *existing* comparable products; or, it can be compared to *hypothetical* comparable products, using the famous reasonable alternative design test. In the case of algorithms, a comparison between the algorithm under investigation and other algorithms, either existing or virtual, is of course conceivable, but the way in which this comparison should be carried out is open to discussion. A comparison with what a reasonable person would have done in the same circumstances is the other option. These two types of comparison should therefore be contemplated, starting with the latter one.

1. Comparing the outcome of the algorithm with the behaviour of a reasonable human being

A comparison between the outcomes of an algorithm, on the one hand, and of reasonable human behaviour, on the other hand, may be appropriate to decide if the algorithm should be put on the market in the first place[8]. As a matter of fact, one of the points about using algorithms is that they should do things better and more safely than humans, and it therefore does

8 Wagner (n 4) 735.

not make sense to put into circulation an algorithm which creates more dangers than the human actions it is intended to replace.

Once this initial requirement has been satisfied, however, a comparison with what a reasonable human being would have done in the same circumstances is not an adequate test to decide if an algorithm was defectively designed. The first reason for that is obviously, as has just been said, that algorithms ought to be better than humans at what humans do, or used to do. Besides, algorithms should also be or become able to do things that humans are not capable of doing, in which case a comparison with a reasonable human behaviour is pointless[9].

2. Comparing the algorithm under investigation with another algorithm

Comparing an algorithm with another algorithm is probably the most obvious way to assess the former's defectiveness. How this should be made is not self-evident, however. One could think of comparing the outcome of the first algorithm in the situation under investigation with the outcome of another algorithm in the same situation, but this method is actually not a convincing one, as it is rather the overall outcomes of the two algorithms that should be compared.

a) Comparing the outcome of the algorithm in the situation under investigation with the outcome of another algorithm in the same situation

When one tries to assess the existence of a human fault or negligence, one always compares the behaviour of the defendant with the one which a model human being would have adopted in the same circumstances. Such a comparison is valid and pertinent because we assume that all human beings share the same kind of rationality and should be able to figure out what is reasonable in any kind of circumstances. The problem is that algo-

---

9 Jean-Sébastien Borghetti, 'L'accident généré par une intelligence artificielle autonome', *Le droit civil à l'ère du numérique. Actes du colloque du Master 2 Droit privé général et du Laboratoire de droit civil – Paris II – 21 avril 2017* (LexisNexis 2017) 23, para 23, available at <http://web.lexisnexis.fr/Fb/Droit_civil_a_l_ere_numerique_112017/> accessed 31 July 2018.

rithms do not function the way human beings do, and the outcomes they produce may not be the product of a human-like rationality. Besides, two algorithms designed to perform the same tasks might function along different types of rationality and may therefore face one same situation in very different ways. As Gerhard Wagner has convincingly argued, this means that one algorithm can cause an accident in a given situation where another algorithm would not, without the former being unreasonably dangerous, or even more dangerous than the latter[10]. In other words, if one wants to compare meaningfully an algorithm to another algorithm, one should take into account the overall results of the two algorithms, and not just the outcome of each one of them in a single set of circumstances.

b) Comparing the overall outcomes of the algorithm with the overall outcomes of another algorithm

Comparing the overall outcomes of two algorithms therefore seems to be the right way to decide if one of them is defective. Yet, the fact that an algorithm has overall outcomes that are not as good as those of another algorithm (i.e. that it causes a greater number of, or more serious accidents) does not necessarily mean that the former is defective. If this were the case, then, in any given field, all algorithms on the market, save the best one, would be defective. And since the outcomes of 'self-learning' algorithms are normally a function of how long they have been running, this means that the first algorithm on the market would normally be immune from liability. Such a solution would hardly be satisfying and one must therefore find a standard for defectiveness that is not as strict as 'not as good as the best algorithm on the market'[11].

A possibility would be to consider that an algorithm is defective when its overall outcomes are less than X % as good as the reference algorithm. This approach, however, raises several questions. The first one is of course how the reference algorithm should be identified. A further one is how the value of X should be set. Should the standard be 90, 80, 70, or even 50 % of the performance of the reference algorithm? Yet another question, more practical in nature but no less important, is how to obtain information on

10 Wagner (n 4) 733.
11 Wagner (n 4) 737.

the overall outcomes of algorithms. All these questions are not easily answered and cast a serious doubt on the practicability of the defectiveness test when the IoT or AI are at stake.

The 'less that X % as good' standard also creates a risk of unfair treatment among defendants[12]. Let us assume that two algorithms are respectively (X-1) and (X+1) % as good as the reference algorithm. The first one will be regarded as defective and its producer will answer for all accidents caused by it. The second one, on the other hand, will not be defective and its producer will not have to answer for the accidents it causes, even if their number or seriousness is well nigh equivalent to those of the accidents attributable to the first algorithm. This all-or-nothing approach is hardly satisfying, and yet it is a necessary consequence of the defectiveness test in the context of the IoT or AI, where defectiveness can normally be assessed only on the basis of the overall outcomes of an algorithm.

*

Assessing the defectiveness of an algorithm is easier said than done. As has just been shown, exactly what method should be used is open to discussion, and what the author thinks is the most convincing method is not easily put into application. In any event, highly technical expertise will in most cases be needed to decide if an algorithm was defectively designed. This calls for the conclusion that defectiveness is not an adequate basis for liability, if individuals or consumers who have suffered harm through the use of the IoT or AI are to be adequately protected. In most circumstances, it will be too difficult or expensive to prove the algorithm's defect. Thus, if one regards it as socially desirable that compensation should be available on the basis of liability rules when the use of the IoT or AI causes harm that cannot be regarded as normal, and if this availability should not remain purely hypothetical, then another requirement than defectiveness must be adopted, on which liability could be based.

This does not mean that the notion of defect should be discarded altogether in the context of the IoT or AI. In the absence of more precise contractual standards, it is probably the right test to adjudicate regress claims against producers or designers of algorithms by primary respondents, who will be directly liable to the victims of harm caused by those algorithms[13].

12 Wagner (n 4) 738.
13 Wagner (n 4) 760.

The question thus becomes: to what standard should these primary respondents be held?

II. What are the other possible bases for liability?

Given the closeness of fault and defect when algorithms are at stake, fault-based liability cannot be an alternative to liability based on defectiveness in the field of the IoT and AI.[14] It is only some form of strict liability, not based on defect, that can offer an effective remedy to those harmed through the use of algorithms. However, a broad strict liability regime applying to the IoT and AI generally, regardless of the field in which they are used and of the dangers they create, and not resting on defectiveness, seems neither realistic nor desirable. A sector-by-sector approach is probably more appropriate. The basis and nature of liability would then depend upon the type and the intensity of the risk that is associated with the use of the IoT or AI.

There are obviously drawbacks inherent in such a piecemeal approach, the first one being that it might take some time between the moment when the IoT or AI starts to be broadly used in a new sector and the moment when an adequate ad hoc liability regime is established. It is a general feature of the law, however, that new rules are often a response to new social issues, and that the development of the law always trails the evolution of society.

At this stage, there are at least three fields in which the IoT and AI are being increasingly used, and for which the opportunity to create a specific liability regime, not based on the algorithm's defect, should be contemplated: autonomous motor vehicles, medical robots and algorithms, and domestic robots.

1. Autonomous vehicles

Autonomous motor vehicles undoubtedly constitute the application of AI that has attracted the greatest attention from tort lawyers so far. In many countries, however, existing legal rules should be able to cope adequately

---

14 See supra p. 63.

with the accidents in which such vehicles are involved, or will be involved in the future[15].

As a matter of fact, many legal systems, especially in continental Europe, have adopted specific strict liability regimes, which apply to traffic accidents. Liability under those regimes very often rests on the mere use of a motor vehicle[16] or the mere happening of an accident[17], which means that no inquiry needs to be made into the driver's negligence or the vehicle's defect in order to assess liability, at least as far as the compensation of bystanders injured in the accident is concerned. Those systems can readily accommodate accidents involving autonomous vehicles, since it will not be necessary to decide whether a defect or malfunctioning of the vehicle's algorithm was causal in the accident[18]. This is even truer in the few legal systems, such as Quebec's, which have established pure no-fault compensation systems for traffic accidents that totally bypass civil liability.[19]

Since all those systems rest on insurance, the real issue with autonomous vehicles is to determine who should pay for the insurance that will cover the harm caused by those accidents in which such vehicles may be involved. Some have suggested that robots, including autonomous vehicles, should be granted legal personality, so that the vehicles themselves would pay for their insurance[20]. This is an unnecessary complication, however, for someone will have to build up the robot's assets in the first place, so that the latter can meet its obligations as a legal person. It is simpler to have that pre-existing person who choses to use the robot pay directly for the robot's insurance[21].

---

15 Since there are very few countries in which such vehicles are already allowed to drive on the road.

16 See § 7 of the German *Straßenverkehrsgesetz* (StVG), which provides that liability should arise from the 'operation' (*Betrieb*) of a motor vehicle, or art 2054 of the Italian civil code (*Codice civile*), which associates liability with the circulation (*circolazione*) of a vehicle.

17 See the French *loi Badinter*, on which see Jean-Sébastien Borghetti, 'Extra-Strict Liability for Traffic Accidents in France', 53 Wake Forest LR 2 (2018) 265.

18 For a discussion in French law, see Borghetti (n 9) para 6ff; in German law, see Wagner (n 4) 757.

19 See Daniel Gardner, 'Automobile Accident and Pure No-Fault Scheme: The Quebec Experience', 53 Wake Forest L. Rev. 2 (2018) 357.

20 Discussing this possibility, see eg Grégoire Loiseau and Matthieu Bourgeois, 'Du robot en droit à un droit des robots', La Semaine juridique édition générale (JCP G) 2014, doctr. 123, para 6ff.

21 Borghetti (n 9) para 41.

In the case of motor vehicles, it is therefore the person who choses to put the autonomous vehicle on the road, and who thus takes the risk of its being involved in an accident, who should pay for the vehicle's insurance. In most countries, however, there is no need to adapt existing legislation, since it is already the owner of a vehicle, who normally decides to put it on the road, who has an obligation to insure against civil liability in respect of the vehicle.

It is in countries or legal systems where traffic accidents are still handled through ordinary fault- or negligence-based liability, like in England or in most North American States, that autonomous vehicles appear as most problematic from a tort law perspective. In the absence of a driver, and unless it is proven that an autonomous vehicle involved in the accident was defective – a most difficult task, as has been seen –[22], the victims of such an accident could never be compensated. It is in those countries that the adoption of specific rules for accidents involving autonomous vehicles seems more likely[23]. And it should come as no surprise if the British Parliament recently adopted a special statute, which paves the way for a *sui generis* insurance-backed regime in which the insurer of an autonomous vehicle will be liable for any harm suffered in consequence of an accident caused by the insured vehicle[24].

2. *Medical robots and algorithms*

Some countries have some sort of strict liability applicable to medical devices, or have special compensation mechanisms for harm caused by medical accidents[25]. While the exact framework of these systems may vary,

22 See supra I.

23 Some authors argue that existing tort rules offer a comprehensive framework for accidents associated with new technologies, however; see eg Mark A Geistfeld, 'A Roadmap for Autonomous Vehicles: State Tort Liability, Automobile Insurance, and Federal Safety Regulation' (2017) 105 Cal. L. Rev. 1611; see also David C. Vladeck, 'Machines Without Principals: Liability Rules and Artificial Intelligence' (2014) 89 Wash. L. Rev. 117.

24 The Automated and Electric Vehicles Act 2018 received the Royal Assent in July 2018. It provides for a secondary liability on the owner in the event of a failure to insure.

25 See eg in French law art L. 1142-1, II, of the public health code (*code de la santé publique*).

they generally should be able to accommodate accidents involving medical robots and algorithms.

In those legal systems – a majority – in which medical liability is still negligence-based, the compensation of harm caused by medical robots will be more challenging, especially if the doctors who take the initiative of using such devices have adequately discharged all their information duties. The problem, however, has probably less to do with the IoT or AI than with the fact that establishing liability is always a complex issue when medical treatments or pharmaceuticals are at stake. One reason for that, though not the only one, is the difficulty to assess causation when the functioning of the human body is involved. The answer to the problem, if any, probably lies in a system that can handle medical or pharmaceutical accidents generally, and not just accidents involving medical robots.

3. Domestic robots

While household appliances increasingly rely on the IoT and AI, it is not obvious if a specific liability regime is needed for the compensation of the accidents that may be caused by such devices. From a historical perspective, this has been an important field of application for product liability, and the 'classic' product liability regimes are probably apt to handle most cases involving domestic robots. As a matter of fact, accidents involving household appliances are often the result of a product's malfunctioning, in which case the product's defect can be fairly easy to establish, regardless of whether the IoT or AI is involved in the matter.

*

The broad liability regimes which have been designed to handle damage caused by humans (fault-based liability) or by physical products (product liability) are ill-suited for the compensation of harm caused by, or associated with, the use of the IoT or AI. Fault is not a relevant concept when algorithms are at stake, and establishing an algorithm's defect will probably be too difficult in most cases. This should and will not result in the designers of algorithms, or the producers of devices that use them, enjoying immunity from civil liability, however. In many of the fields where the IoT or AI are used, sector-specific liability regimes or compensation mechanisms are applicable, whose implementation does not require that an abnormal behaviour or conduct be established. The fact that damaging devices are governed by self-learning algorithms usually makes no difference for these regimes. This is especially true for most strict liability or no-fault schemes that apply in the field of traffic accidents. In the end, and despite the excitation that robots in general, and autonomous vehicles in particular, have created among tort lawyers, it may be that national legal systems will be able to handle harm caused by robots without too much strain – even if, in order to do so, they cannot always rely on the hallowed regimes inherited from the Age of Enlightenment and from the first industrial revolutions.

Product Liability and Product Security: Present and Future

Cristina Amato[*]

I. Introduction

According to Art 6 para 1 Directive 1985/374/EC ('PLD'), an unsafe product is a defective product that may result into producer's liability. In the European legislator's intent, Art 6 seems to implement the following syllogism: defect is an objective notion that refers to safety, not to utility;[1] the identification and qualification of the properties of a product depend on what the public at large expects. Consequently, it is up to the courts to determine the legitimate safety expectations of the public at large. The legitimate expectations of a person concerning safety represent an objective standard, assessed on the public's expectations but not on the injured. It is, therefore, a normative standard, not a factual one.[2] The *nobile officium* of

---

* Full Professor of Comparative Law – University of Brescia (Italy).

1 Directive 1985/374/EC recital 6: 'whereas, to protect the physical well-being and property of the consumer, the defectiveness of the product should be determined by reference not to its fitness for use but to the lack of the safety which the public at large is entitled to expect'. See Hans C Taschner, 'Product Liability: Basic Problems in a Comparative Law Perspective' in Duncan Fairgrieve (ed), *Product Liability in Comparative Perspective* (Cambridge University Press 2006) 159: 'Whether a product is serviceable or not does not apply here. Serviceability is a term which is appropriate to be used for the law of sales. But the question here is not whether the product worked or not (…). The goal is to protect life and limb, and to a certain extent the property, of the product user. The corresponding notion to this requirement is safety, not utility'. See more recently the Commission Notice of 5 April 2016, the 'Blue Guide' on the implementation of EU product rules 2016 C(2016) 1958 final ('the Blue Guide'), 12: 'The fact that a product is not fit for the use expected is not enough. The Directive only applies if a product lacks safety'.

2 *A v National Blood Authority* [2001] 3 All ER 289: it was a very well-known English case concerning recovery of damages arising out of the patients' infection with Hepatitis C; the blood was considered defective under Article 6 PLD and the defendants had no escape within Article 7(e). See also Cees C van Dam, 'Dutch Case Law on the EU Directive', in Duncan Fairgrieve (ed), *Product Liability in Comparative Perspective* (Cambridge University Press 2006) 129: in a case concerning transfused blood containing the hepatitis C virus, it was held that, even though one

judges in determining the legitimacy of the public's expectations is a delicate and a hard one.

To sum up: there are only three conditions for a product liability claim, enumerated in Article 4 of the PLD: damage, defect and causation. The producer's conduct is entirely unimportant. The producer's liability is 'defect' based, not 'fault' based. Foreseeability or avoidability is irrelevant. 'Defect' is an objective notion. It refers to safety, and to nothing else. The identification and qualification of the properties of a product depend on what the public at large, not the consumers, believes. It is up to the courts to decide what the public at large believes.[3]

The safety or the degree or level of safety depends on what persons generally are entitled to expect, that is, on what their legitimate expectations are.[4] The test is not that of an absolute level of safety: the degree of safety is reduced to a question of social acceptance.

In this reasoning, safety is reduced to a discretionary, though objective, notion hold tight to social circumstances: a) the presentation of the product; b) the use to which it could reasonably be expected that the product would be put; c) the time when the product was put into circulation (art 6 para 1 PLD). The argument is that once the mass and large-scale production gets the better of the market, the crucial test for defectiveness rests on the relationship between safety and liability. Defectiveness does not neces-

---

could argue that *the actual expectations* of the public probably were that some transfused blood was infected with viruses, a recipient could legitimately expect that the blood he got would be perfectly safe. In a similar case where a patient received HIV-infected blood during heart surgery, the district court of Amsterdam reached the same conclusion. The court held that, taking into account the importance of blood products and the lack of an alternative, the general public is entitled to expect that blood products in the Netherlands have been 100% HIV-free for some time. Even if there was a small statistical chance of infection, this does not relate to the legitimate expectations of the public (Rb Amsterdam 3 February 1999, NJ 1999, 621).

3 Hans C Taschner, 'Product Liability: Basic Problems in a Comparative Law Perspective' in Duncan Fairgrieve (ed), *Product Liability in Comparative Perspective* (Cambridge University Press 2006) 161. See also: Daily Wuyts, 'The Product Liability Directive – More than Two Decades of Defective Products in Europe': 'The standard of liability is the defectiveness of the product at hand and not the negligence or fault of the producer' JETL 1 (2014) 8.

4 *A v National Blood Authority* [2001] 3 All ER at 31, where Burton J ruled that '"legitimate expectations" rather than "entitled expectations" appeared to all of us to be a [happier] formulation'.

sarily refer to safety, and safety cannot be limited to a social perception: it can provide judges with an objective criterion to determine the expectations that the public at large is entitled to demand. My argument is that, the harmonised technical standards should represent the fundamental link[5] between safety and defectiveness: judges should rely on them in order to assess the level of risk that the public is legitimately entitled to accept. The final goal, on the one hand, is to design an *idealtypus* of the product (in any market sectors) that may reduce – though not eliminate – judges' discretionary power; on the other hand, the goal is also to provide a better balance between users' protection and producer's liability.

II. At the Roots of the Problem: National Courts and the Burden of Proof of Defectiveness

European and national courts apparently do not pay the necessary attention to the relationship between product's liability and general product safety. Concerning the burden of proof, the distance from general product safety is demonstrated by the uncertainty in the national courts. In particular, the first condition to assess producer's liability (ie, defect), as enumerated in Art 4 of the PLD, deserves some considerations in regard to the burden of proof. The PLD does not define the standard of proof, it simply states that: 'The injured person shall be required to prove the damage, the defect and the causal relationship between defect and damage' (Art 4 PLD). According to European reports,[6] courts should facilitate the burden of proof on claimants. In some situations, proof of the defect poses difficulties for the consumer because of the technical complexity of certain products, the high costs of expert evidence, the parties' unequal access to information (particularly about the production process) and the fact that some products are not retrievable after they have been used (eg, defective fireworks). Therefore, there is much liberty for Member States' courts and courts' discretion in assessing the defectiveness of a product.

5 U Carnevali, 'Prevenzione e risarcimento nelle direttive comunitarie sulla sicurezza dei prodotti' (2005) 1 Responsabilità civile e previdenza 3–20.
6 COM (1999) 396 final [20]–[22] (Green Paper on liability for defective products) and COM (2000) 893 final, [13]–[15] (Report from the Commission on the Application of Directive 85/374 on Liability for Defective Products).

Although courts have to take into account other possible explanations of the damage, one cannot lose sight of the fact that the claimant has sufficiently proved the defect if he gives evidence that the product did not provide the safety he was legitimately entitled to expect. It would infringe the purpose of the PLD and the definition of 'defect' to expect the claimant to prove the exact cause or nature of the defect. Thus, in cases concerning the defectiveness of breast implants that prematurely ruptured, the Italian High Court affirmed that the products' defect is a binding evidence of the producer's liability.[7] Contrary to that, an English court refused to infer the defectiveness of the breast implants merely from the fact that they had malfunctioned and in the absence of probable proof of what exactly went wrong.[8] In one more well-known case, the English Court of Appeal ruled that the mere fact that a product deviates from the production standards does not prove the existence of a defect.[9] Moreover, usually High Courts take into account the target group (ie, children) and the legitimate safety expectations of the public on the target group.

---

7 Cass. civ. (3) No 20985 of 8 October 2007 (2008) 2 Responsabilità civile e previdenza 354ff, note U Carnevali, 'Prodotto difettoso e oneri probatori del danneggiato'.

8 *Foster v Biosil* [2000] 59 BMLR 178, where the Plaintiff alleged that the breast implants, manufactured by the defendant, were defective in that the left implant ruptured prematurely, and the right implant leaked silicone. Consequently, both implants had to be removed.

9 *Tesco Stores Ltd v Pollard* [2006] CA, Civil Division (EWCA Civ) 393: it was held that, even though a manufacturing glitch made a container of dishwasher powder less childproof than it was intended (the child ate the powder), the container was still safe enough to live up to the public's legitimate expectations and, therefore, not defective. On the facts, the Judge held that the legitimate expectations of the public only extended so far as it could expect a child-resistant cap to open with more difficulty than a regular one and ruled by this standard that the product was not defective. See also *Richardson v LRC Products Ltd* [2000] Lloyd's Rep Med 280, where it was alleged that a condom burst during a sexual intercourse and that the claimant conceived as a result. Nevertheless, the court held that the condom was not defective and rejected the claim. One interpretation of this judgment is that, even if it could be proved that the rubber was damaged before it left the factory, the condom was not defective because the public knows and accepts the risk that a small proportion of condoms will burst in the course of use, and it does not matter whether this is by way of a large rupture or a small invisible tear. Therefore, the legitimate safety expectation is not that a condom provides 100% protection from the risk of conception.

A consolidated judicial technique comprises the use of presumptions. In the case of bursting bottles, in particular, the *res ipsa loquitur* reasoning has been largely used by Member States' courts.[10] In one important Italian case,[11] a surgeon suffered damages in using forceps that provoked him with a paraesthesia of two of the right hands' fingers. The surgeon alleged the producer's liability for the defectiveness of the forceps, but the Italian High Court ruled that the injured asking for damages shall give evidence of the foundations of the affirmed right. To this purpose, it is not sufficient for the injured person to infer the defect from the very causality relationship between the use of the product (the forceps) and the personal injury suffered (the paraesthesia), thus transferring on the producer the burden of proving that the product was not defective, or the burden of proving the exemptions (listed at Art 7 PLD). Nevertheless – the Italian High Court continues – this argument does not exclude presumptions: they can be still used, provided that they are serious, specific and consistent.

Seeking help from presumptions, this approach has recently been affirmed by the European Court of Justice,[12] according to which such rules do not require the victim to produce, in all circumstances, certain and irrefutable evidence of a defect in the product and of a causal link between the defect and the damage suffered, but authorise the court, where applica-

---

10 SAP Cadiz of 16 March 2002, JUR 2002, 140327; Trib Rome of 17 March 1998, Foro It 1998, 3060; Rb Namen of 21 November 1996, JLMB 1997, 104; Antwerpen of 10 January 2000, RW 2004–2005, 794 and HR 24 of December 1993, NJ 1994, 214. In all these cases, national courts applied the *res ipsa loquitur* rule in establishing the evidence of the defect.

11 Cass. civ. (3) No 13458 of 29 May 2013 (2013) I Foro italiano 2118, overruling the previous approach of the 'Corte di Cassazione' No 20985/2007 (n 7). In Germany, most influential are the cases of the exploding sparkling water bottles, close to the tripartite American approach distinguishing manufacturing, design and warning defects: Bundesgerichtshof (Federal Court of Justice, BGH) Neue Juristische Wochenschrift (NJW) 1995, 2162. See: S Lenze, 'German Product Liability Law: Between European Directives, American Restatements and Common Sense', in Duncan Fairgrieve (ed), *Product Liability in Comparative Perspective* (Cambridge University Press 2006) 107–113. cf also in Belgium: Rb Namen of 21 November 1996, Revue de Jurisprudence de Liège, Mons et Bruxelles (JLMB) 1997, 104. In this case the producer argued that the consumer had exposed the bottle to extreme changes in temperature, making it more fragile. However, the Belgian court held that it was foreseeable to the producer that consumers might chill their soda bottles, especially during the summer.

12 European Court of Justice of 21 June 2017, Case C–621/15 *W and Others v Sanofi Pasteur MSD and Others*, paras 28–29.

ble, to conclude that such a defect has been proven to exist, on the basis of a set of evidence the seriousness, specificity and consistency of which allows it to consider, with a sufficiently high degree of probability, that such a conclusion corresponds to the reality of the situation. However, such evidentiary rules do not bring about a reversal of the burden of proof which, as provided for in Article 4 of Directive 85/374. It is for the victim to discharge, since that system places the burden on the victim to prove the various elements of his case which, where applicable, taken together will provide the court hearing the case with a basis for its conclusion as to the existence of a defect in the vaccine and a causal link between that defect and the damage suffered.

This recent approach on presumptions confirms that the standard of liability is based on defect and not on fault, provided that the injured shall be able to produce evidence of the defect, in the form of serious, specific and consistent presumptions.

III. The EU Quality Chain

1. Social State of Art v Technical Standards

In the EU, quality chain technical regulations represent the transfer of rules of art into standardised data: they should, therefore, be considered as the crucial link that provides a unique, objective standard on which judges from different national legal systems can identify defectiveness and release harmonised decisions. Apparently, the reason why product safety law is concerned with generally accepted rules of the art, or with justified safety expectations that manufacturers have to comply with, instead of threshold values, lays on the fact that nuclear powers or pharmaceutical products require specific standards related to their risks, which can be legally assessed in terms of defectiveness. On the other hand, 'product' is a very general category that includes sophisticated technological devices as well as simple tools.[13] Nevertheless, the issue at stake is the legal assessment of defect, which should be connected to the level of risk that any product implies. Standardisation of production, mass products and large

13 C Joerges, 'Product Safety, Product Safety Policy and Product Safety Law' (2010) 6 Hanse L Rev 115, 117–118.

scale production[14] (eg, cars, pharmaceutical products, electronic components, mobiles, 3D printers, etc) have changed the relationship between consumers/users and producers and, in particular, the legitimate safety the public at large is entitled to expect. In fact, any defectiveness of products may potentially affect a large number of users/consumers because of their large scale of production. This is the reason why in Europe the old liability regime, based on producer's fault, was abandoned in favour of the new regime of strict liability, as such happened in the 'seventies of last century in the United States'.[15]

The goal of these legislations was clear: to match users' protection with the enhancement of competition in a free market. Most mass products, as well as high technological products, distributed on large scale are required to comply with technical standards; while others – usually outside the large-scale market or free from technological complexity: shoes, clothes, furniture and stationery – are not. For the second category of products, it is correct to refer to legitimate consumer's expectations that can be interpreted by judges with reference to a social state of art. The most complex issue on liability concerns the first category of products, mass products distributed on a large scale and large-scale technology. Until now, pharmaceutical products and chemicals represented the most quoted examples of policy treatment of their risks, and the same can be said today of high-tech projects and Artificial Intelligence ('AI') in particular. Anyone who does not wish to leave safety decisions to market forces, but also does not wish to abide by the average level or the state of the art and sees the guaranteeing of safety as a political task will assign this task to either State authorities (as this is the case in Europe) or independent agencies (as this is the case in the United States of America). 'The alignment of corresponding decisions to technical standards specifying general safety duties is equivalent to setting a threshold value establishing the extent of permissible risks in general terms'[16].

---

14 E Al Mureden, 'La responsabilità del fabbricante nella prospettiva della standardizzazione delle regole sulla sicurezza dei prodotti' in E Al Mureden (ed), *La sicurezza dei prodotti e la responsabilità del produttore* (Giappichelli 2017) 6.

15 The reference is to the well-known Restatement (Second) of Torts (American Law Institute, 1965) § 402A and now to Restatement (Third) of Torts, Products Liablity (American Law Institute, 1998).

16 C Joerges, 'Product Safety, Product Safety Policy and Product Safety Law' (2010) 6 Hanse L Rev 118.

2. The European Layout of the New Approach and the New Legislative Framework

Since Directive 73/23/EEC[17] ('low voltage'), a cross-reference method to harmonised technical standards has been enhanced within the Union. Since then, following the *Cassis de Dijon* case[18] and the European Commission Communication of 31 January 1985, the Council of Ministers on 7 May 1985 indicated the regulatory technique that products placed on the EU market must meet if they are to benefit from free movement within the EU (the 'New Approach').[19] The New Legislative Framework ('NLF')[20]

---

17 Council Directive of 19 February 1973 on the harmonisation of the laws of Member States, relating to electrical equipment designed for use within certain voltage limits. Article 5, in particular, referred to safety provisions of harmonised standards, 'drawn up by common agreement between the bodies notified by the Member States' (para 2). Later on, the cross-reference method was pursued by the Council Directive 83/189/EEC of 28 March 1983, laying down a procedure for the provision of information in the field of technical standards and regulation.

18 European Court of Justice of 20 February 1979,– Case 120/78 *Rewe-Zentral AG v Bundesmonopolverwaltung für Branntwein*, [1979] ECR I–649.

19 Council Resolution of 7 May 1985 on a new approach to technical harmonisation and standards (85/C 136/01). The 'New Approach' is grounded on Four Principles (Annex II): (1) legislative harmonisation is limited to the adoption of the *essential safety requirements*; (2) the task of drawing up the technical specifications needed for the production and placing on the market of products conforming to the essential requirements established by the Directives, while taking into account the current stage of technology, is entrusted to organisations competent in the standardisation area; (3) *these technical specifications are not mandatory* and maintain their status of voluntary standards; (4) at the same time, national authorities are obliged to recognise that products manufactured in conformity with harmonised standards (or, provisionally, with national standards) are presumed to conform to the 'essential requirements' established by the Directive. This signifies that the producer has the choice of not manufacturing in conformity with the standards but that in this event he has an obligation to prove that his products conform to the essential requirements of the Directive.

20 The NLF (<https://ec.europa.eu/growth/single-market/goods/new-legislative-framework_en> accessed 8 August 2018) consists essentially of a package of measures aiming at setting clear rules for the accreditation of conformity assessment bodies; providing stronger and clearer rules on the requirements for the notification of conformity assessment bodies; providing a toolbox of measures for use in future legislation (including definitions of terms commonly used in product legislation, procedures to allow future sectorial legislation to become more consistent and easier to implement); and improving the market surveillance rule, through the RAPEX alert system for the rapid exchange of information among EU countries

was adopted in 2008 in order to promote the quality of conformity assessment. It represents:

'a complete system bringing together all the different elements that need to be dealt with in product safety legislation in a coherent, comprehensive legislative instrument that can be used across the board in all industrial sectors, and even beyond (environmental and health policies also have recourse to a number of these elements), whenever EU legislation is required'.[21]

The result is a complex, multilevel layout:[22] at the first stage, technical harmonisation is achieved through *general* regulatory rules concerning specific products, categories, market sectors and/or types of risks, implemented by European[23] and national standards institutions.[24]

There is a mandatory general standard of safety (Directive 92/59/EC of 29 June 1992, now superseded by Directive 2001/95/EC of 3 December 2001, on general product safety: 'GPSD') intended to ensure a high level of product safety throughout the EU for consumer products that are not covered by sector-specific EU harmonisation legislation, and mandatory

---

and the European Commission. These measures are: Regulation (EC) 765/2008 (setting out the requirements for accreditation and the market surveillance of products); Decision 768/2008 on a common framework for the marketing of products; Regulation (EC) 764/2008 laying down procedures relating to the application of certain national technical rules to products lawfully marketed in another EU country.

21 Commission Notice of 05.04.2016, The 'Blue Guide" on the implementation of EU product rules 2016 ('Blue Guide'), 11. The *Transatlantic Trade and Investment Partnership* (TTIP), aiming at harmonising Europe and the American safety standards and imposing a new and deeper reflection on this relationship: RW Parker and A Alemanno, 'A Comparative Overview of EU and US Legislative and Regulatory System: Implications for Domestic Governance & the Translatlantic Trade and Investment Partnership' (2015) 22 Colum. J. Eur. L. 61ff.

22 E Al Mureden, 'La responsabilità del fabbricante nella prospettiva della standardizzazione delle regole sulla sicurezza dei prodotti' in E Al Mureden (ed), *La sicurezza dei prodotti e la responsabilità del produttore* (Giappichelli 2017) 2ff.

23 In Europe: European Committee for Standardisation (CEN) and the European Committee for Electrotechnical Standardisation (CENELEC), European Telecommunication Standards institute (ETSI). See Annex I of Regulation (EU) No 1025/2012.

24 In Italy: Ente Nazionale di unificazione (UNI); Comitato Elettrotecnico Italiano (CEI).

specific safety standards contained into vertical directives.[25] GPSD complements the existing sector-specific (vertical) legislation, and it also provides for market surveillance provisions.[26] The wide range of products covered has to be sufficiently homogeneous for common essential requirements to be applicable, and the product area or hazards also have to be suitable for standardisation (see the First Principle of the Council Resolution 7 May 1985, fn 19).

In both horizontal and vertical legislation, the producers' duties to comply with standardised rules are still general (ie, they provide the goal of safety to be achieved and the type of risks to be avoided). The wording of the essential requirements contained in the sections of the acts or in their annexes[27] is intended to:

'facilitate the setting up of standardisation requests by the Commission to the European standardisation organisations to produce harmonised standards. They are also formulated so to enable the assessment of conformity with those requirements, even in the absence of harmonised standards or in case the manufacturer chooses not to apply them'.[28]

Consequently, in most cases, the essential requirements of different harmonisation acts need to be applied simultaneously in order to cover all relevant public interests.

Harmonised technical standards are focused on a second level of intervention.[29] They are European standards adopted by recognised standardisation organisations, upon requests made by the European Commission

---

25 See the list of specific Directives and Regulations at <https://ec.europa.eu/growth/single-market/goods/new-legislative-framework_en> accessed 30 September 2018.

26 RAPEX, Rapid Alert System set up between Member States and the Commission; to certain conditions, Rapid Alert System notifications can also be exchanged with non-EU countries.

27 As an example, see Directive 2009/48/EC on the safety of toys: art 10, § 2 runs: 'Toys, including the chemicals they contain, shall not jeopardise the safety or health of users or third parties when they are used as intended or in a foreseeable way, bearing in mind the behaviour of children'. In Annex II, particular safety requirements are then listed: Physical and Mechanical Properties, Flammability, etc. The same can be said on directives and regulations on cosmetics, machinery, medical devices, etc.: < https://ec.europa.eu/growth/single-market/goods/new-legislative-framework_en> accessed 30 September 2018.

28 The 'Blue Guide' (n 1) 37–38.

29 There are several instruments to promote safety: preventive approval regulations, performance standards, certification procedures, voluntary standards and safety

for the correct implementation of the harmonisation legislation. Such organisations have a private nature: they operate on a mutual agreement, maintaining their status of voluntary application, and their technical standards never replace the legally binding essential requirements. Regulation (EU) No 1025/2012 on European standardisation defines the role and responsibilities of the standardisation organisations, and it gives the Commission the possibility of inviting, after consultation with the Member States, the European standardisation organisations to draw up harmonised standards. It also establishes procedures to assess and to object to harmonised standards. More deeply, the Commission (assisted by a committee, consisting of representatives of national states: Art 22 of Regulation (EU) No 1025/2012) issues standardisation mandates[30] (ie, after consulting sectoral authorities at the national level), addressing the European standardisation organisations that will formally take a position on the request and finally start up the standardisation work.[31] Harmonised technical standards can also step in absence of vertical legislation, and in compliance with Directive 2001/95/EC on general safety. This is the case, in particular, for furniture, ladders/staircases. At the end of this complex process, standards are published on the European Official Journal. From publication, the standards shall mandatorily be applied by national standards institutions or by national notified bodies that are authorised to issue marks or certificates of conformity. Moreover, publication of references of harmonised standards sets the date from which the presumption of conformity (to the essential requirements) takes place.

The essential feature of this layout is to limit legislative safety harmonisation to the essential requirements that are of public interest, such as

---

symbols, warnings, safety campaigns, follow-up market controls (recalls and bans) and rules on liability. Nevertheless, positive regulation of all safety aspect is impracticable, although in principle the justification for preventive safety regulations is undisputed.

30 See the *Vademecum* on European standardization: SWD(2015) 205 final, 27 October 2015 available at <http://ec.europa.eu/growth/single-market/european-standards/vademecum/index_en.htm> accessed 8 August 2018.

31 About the content of the harmonised standards and their relationship with the essential requirements of the harmonised legislation, see more extensively the Blue Guide (n 1) 4.1.2.2., 39ff. 'A specification given in a harmonized standard is not an alternative to a relevant essential or other legal requirement but only a possible technical means to comply with it', 40.

health and safety of users, sometimes even including property, scarce resources or the environment.

Essential requirements define the results to be attained, or the hazards to be dealt with, but do not specify the technical solutions for doing so. The precise technical solution may be provided by a standard or by other technical specifications or be developed in accordance with general engineering or scientific knowledge laid down in engineering and scientific literature at the discretion of the manufacturer.[32]

It is up to a manufacturer to implement a risk analysis of its product and to identify all possible risks inherent to the product. Then, the manufacturer shall be able to assess what the essential requirements are in relation to the risks inherently raised by the product, as well as the harmonised technical standards necessary to ensure that the product complies with the essential requirements. It may happen that only part of the harmonised standard is applied, or it may be that the harmonised standard does not cover all applicable essential requirements, nor does it cover all risks of the product. In these cases, the manufacturer should be able to provide sufficient documents illustrating the way applicable essential requirements not covered by harmonised technical standards are dealt with.

The cross-reference method illustrated hereabove is preferred to vertical, specific legislation (the 'Old Approach'), at least for two reasons. First, it encourages flexibility: safety assessment procedures must be flexible, above all, because the hazards to be assessed vary tremendously in nature and intensity. Secondly, it provides sustainability of the imposed standards, that involves transparency and the participation of relevant stakeholders, including SMEs, consumers, environmental organisations and social stakeholders (see Regulation (EU) No 1025/2012, Art 5 ch II, in particular). This dialogue between public entities, private standardisation organisations and relevant stakeholders provides sufficient guarantees[33] that the standardisation requests are well understood in order to satisfy the es-

32 The 'Blue Guide' 38.

33 For a different view: C Joerges and HW Micklitz, 'Completing the New Approach Through a European Product Safety Policy, (2010) 6 Hanse L. Rev. 381; C Joerges and HW Micklitz, 'The need to Supplement the New Approach to Technical Harmonization and Standards By a Coherent European Product Safety Policy' (2010) 6 Hanse L. Rev. 349 – Special issue. The Authors consider the Union product safety policy as a barrier to trade and plead for a Standing Committee on Product Safety (that includes private parties like CEN/CENELEC) before setting the special standards. On the ineffectiveness of several EU instrument to ensure and control

sential requirements, on the one hand. On the other hand, the public interests are taken into account in the process, without completely delegating technical standards to industry representatives. What safety law is about is social protection, which no manufacturer nor single judge can determine unilaterally by laying down what 'safety' is.

IV. The Relationship between Safety and the Compliance Defence (Art 7 let (d) of the PLD)

1. Safety and Defectiveness

Safety laws and product liability laws respond to different assumptions and requests, but, nevertheless, they are part of a complex and united system. Product liability should be considered a complementary safety-instrument: a modern construction of the PLD that can adapt it to new technologies would create a link between the product liability system created by the PLD and the safety legislation. The occasion is provided by Art 7 let (d) of PLD: 'The producer shall not be liable as a result of this Directive if he proves: (d) that the defect is due to compliance of the product with mandatory regulations issued by the public authorities'. According to the Fourth Principle affirmed in the Council of Ministers resolution of 7 May 1985 (fn 19), there is a presumption of conformity:

'[N]ational authorities are obliged to recognize that products manufactured in conformity with harmonized standards (or, provisionally, with national standards) *are presumed to conform to the 'essential requirements' established by the Directive*. (This signifies that the producer has the choice of not manufacturing in conformity with the standards but that in this event he has an obligation to prove that his products conform to the essential requirements of the Directive)'.

The PLD does not take into account the relevant distinction between unsafe and defective products. Nevertheless, it should be recalled that one

---

the safety of products see: C Joerges, 'Product Safety, Product Safety Policy and Product Safety Law' (2010) 6 Hanse L. Rev. 115. RW Parker and A Alemanno, 'A Comparative Overview of EU and US Legislative and Regulatory System: Implications for Domestic Governance & the Translatlantic Trade and Investment Partnership' (2015) 22 Colum. J. Eur. L. 89ff, where the Authors argue for a more procedural approach of the EU consultation practices.

product is unsafe if it does not comply with technical standards or with the state of art, although it may not necessarily turn into a defective product. On the other hand, a defective product may cause damage or injury to users, even though it is perfectly 'safe' (ie, compliant) because of: a) misuse or b) it is an unavoidable unsafe product (eg, cars, mobiles, cigarettes, pharmaceutical products, etc). It is, therefore, crucial to establish what compliance means within the PLD and safety system, as it is the logical medium between safety and defectiveness. In particular, the question here is: does *any* compliance exclude producer's liability?

Once an injury has occurred, and there is evidence that the product has caused the injury, the two categories of products (ie, unsafe and defective) may eventually overlap. In order to assess the producer's liability, we can envisage two situations.

2. Non-Compliance with Harmonised Standards and Exclusion of the Presumption of Compliance

There may be cases where producer complied with general and special (mandatory) harmonised legislation but did not comply with harmonised technical standards (the latter being not mandatory: see para III.2. above). Applying the Fourth Principle of the Council of Ministers Resolution, courts can presume that the product is not compliant with the essential requirements of the GPSD, and, therefore, it is defective; thus, the producer has the burden to prove compliance, misuse or an unavoidable risk. In such a situation, although the GPSD had been respected, the producer cannot rely on the compliance defence. In essence, it was the producer's choice of not manufacturing in conformity with the standards; therefore, consequently, the producer has an obligation to prove that the products conform to the essential requirements of the GPSD. It is worth noting that detailed procedures as for conformity and quality management assessment prior to marketing of products came with the Council Resolution on the Global Approach (issued in 1990) and Decision 90/683/EEC (updated and replaced by Decision 93/465/EEC and, at present, by Decision No 768/2008/EC of 9 July 2008 on a common framework for the marketing of products).[34] These decisions developed consolidated conformity assess-

34 OJEU L 218/218 of 13 August 2008.

ment procedures and the rules for their selection and use in special (vertical) directives (the modules), involving both the Commission and private entities (the conformity assessment bodies). The modules are set up from simplest products presenting minimum risks, to very complex products and technologies presenting high risks. This presentation favours their selection and their final use into specific directives, leaving the legislator free to decide which standards are the most appropriate in each sector.

In the aforementioned situation, courts may assume the delicate *officium* of controlling that the plaintiff's claim not only is on line with a social acceptability test, but that harmonised technical standards have been ignored;[35] therefore, the use of presumptions of defectiveness (see para II above) prove to be serious, specific and consistent. Nevertheless, it should be underlined that judges remain free to rule that the respect of essential requirements – given the peculiarities of the case – proves to be a sufficient defence for the producer. They may use their discretionary power and consider the product as reasonably safe, having regard to all the circumstances listed in Art 6 of the PLD (ie, the presentation of the product, the use to which it could reasonably be expected that the product would be put and the time when the product was put into circulation). Harmonised standards, although voluntary, represent the objective transformation of the state of art for mass products distributed on a large scale into the level of safety that the public is entitled to expect. In this perspective, they represent the crucial link between safety and producer's liability: the objective test that reduces social expectations to a sustainable and shared notion of safety. Harmonised technical standards represent, therefore, the convergence of legitimate expectations of the public at large.

---

35 Cass. civ. (3) No 3258 of 19 February 2016 (2016) 17 Guida al diritto 2016 51 'The level of safety imposed by the law, beyond which a product shall be therefore considered as defective, does not correspond to its total harmlessness. It rather corresponds to the level of safety requirements generally expected by users with reference to the circumstances listed at Art 5 [of the Italian law implementing PDL] or with reference to other requirements to be evaluated by the ground court, *within which, in particular, we can and must include safety standards possibly imposed by the technical rules within the specialised area*'.

3. Compliance with Harmonised Standards and Presumption of Conformity

In a second situation, if the producer complied with harmonised regulations and/or with harmonised technical standards,[36] the Fourth Principle stated by the Council Resolution 7 May 1985 would then apply. Accordingly, applying the presumption of conformity/safety, the compliance defence of Art 7 let (d) is triggered, and the producer is not liable.[37] Therefore, a rare allergic reaction to a detergent or to a perfume that can objectively be considered safe – according to harmonised standards – does not make the producer liable under the Directive.[38] Nevertheless, a damage occurred, although provoked by a 'safe' product. In the situation at stake, if harmonised technical standards are considered as 'floors' (ie, minimum standards) and not 'ceilings' (ie, maximum standards), the injured party can rebut the presumption of conformity and provide the court sufficient social expectation that a product should reach nearly 100% of safety before reaching the market. Or, he/she can give evidence that the particular circumstances of the case rendered the safe product defective. On their side, provided that harmonised technical standards are deemed as floors and not ceilings, judges have a limited discretionary power in eventually considering the producer liable, valuing more the gap of safety in-between the (respected) harmonised technical standards and higher technical standards or higher social expectations, given the peculiarities of the case. Regarding unavoidable unsafe products, in particular, judges still maintain a limited discretionary power to either considering the producer liable, thus

---

36 The 'Blue Guide' ([4.1.3.], 48ff) specifies that the presumption of conformity can also be attained through other ways, such as 'technical specifications' consisting of national standards, European standards non-harmonised (that is: not published on the OJEU), manufacturer's own specifications.

37 Cass. civ. (3) No 6007 of 15 March 2007 (2007) 7–8 Responsabilita' Civile e Previdenza 1592, note M Gorgoni, 'Responsabilità per prodotto difettoso: alla ricerca della (prova della) causa del danno': an allergic reaction to a dyeing hair product considered safe according to harmonised standards excludes the producer's liability; Cass. civ. (3) No 25116 of 13 December 2010 (2012) I 2 Foro italiano 576: this was a case involving a tanning cosmetic product causing injury. The Italian High Court has ruled against the plaintiff's claim on the ground of misuse of the product.

38 Daily Wuyts, 'The Product Liability Directive – More than Two Decades of Defective Products in Europe', 5 JETL 1 (2014) 8. See the Italian High Court: Cass. civ. (3) No 6007 of 15 March 2007 (n 36).

discouraging enterprises from placing on the market dangerous products, or excluding producer's liability in cases of socially accepted goods (as it is the case for pharmaceutical products). The challenge for the future, in regard to high-tech products, consists of finding criteria to assess which risks must be eliminated at all costs, which risks should be reduced through design requirements and which risks are unavoidable. Even in this situation, it is not necessary to adopt the tripartite American distinction among design, manufacturing and warning defects, as the assessment of defectiveness is measured on a multi-level notion of safety.[39]

V. Final Remarks

In the era of AI and IoT, judges should adopt an approach aiming at coordinating safety rules and liability rules. If it is the judges' *nobile officium*[40] to qualify a product as defective or not, and to establish what the public's expectations are, then judgements should be grounded on evidence of compliance or non-compliance with harmonised technical standards, as objective connectors to the entitled expectations of the public at large. Provided that harmonised standards are considered as minimum requirements, thus leaving to the judge the delicate task to control that technical rules were correctly drafted within the cross-reference method, and that the dialogue among public entities, private standardisations organisations and the relevant stakeholders had taken place within the NLF system.

---

39 This is not the approach of the Italian legislator: in implementing the PLD, Art 117, para 3 Italian Consumer Code runs: 'A product is to be considered defective when it does not provide the same degree of safety as that normally offered by any other product of the same series'. The Italian vision of PLD goes in the direction of cutting short any argument on the degree of expected safety by adopting the manufacturing defect reasoning. See Daily Wuyts, 'The Product Liability Directive – More than Two Decades of Defective Products in Europe' (2014) 5 JETL 13: 'However, it has already been noted that this detracts from the normative character of Art 6 of the Directive. The standard of liability imposed by Art 6 cannot be reduced to a mere finding that the specific product deviates from the production line. In doing so the Italian interpretation violates the maximum harmonisation intended by Art 6 of the Directive, which clearly states that the only standard of liability is that of the legitimate safety expectations of the public'.

40 Hans C Taschner, 'Product Liability: Basic Problems in a Comparative Law Perspective' in Duncan Fairgrieve (ed), *Product Liability in Comparative Perspective* (Cambridge University Press 2006) 160.

Assuming harmonised technical standards as fundamental parameters on which the defectiveness of products can be objectively assessed, may represent an optimal solution to the question concerning the relationship between safety and defectiveness for the following reasons. a) Assessing defectiveness through harmonised technical standards may help in reducing the judges' discretion, thus, reaching a better harmonisation of judgments within Europe and a higher certainty. b) In the AI and IoT technology era, users' protection cannot be completely achieved, mainly because the applications of PLD to new technologies involve public or collective interests.[41] Thus, the state of art, as accepted by the public at large, implies a discretion of judgments that are not sustainable in the new era of high technology. Instead, the recourse to harmonised standards, as evidence of compliance, would represent a balanced way to coordinate the (still) actual provisions of PLD with safety regulations. c) The implementation of the safety legislation through the PLD would also reduce in the long run the placing on the market of unavoidable unsafe products. The judicial respect and support of the dialogue between public European institutions and private organisations (and stakeholders) would contribute to solve ethical questions, concerning the correct edge between promoting technology and making useless technological risks unavailable in the market. d) A better coordination between harmonised safety regulations and liability rules would enhance free competition in a free market. It should be recalled that the history of the connection between the free market movement of goods and harmonised safety regulations started with the CJEU case *Cassis de Dijon*.[42] This ruling is important not only because of the mutual recogni-

41 Piotr Machnikowsky, 'Introduction' in Piotr Machnikowsky (ed), *European Product Liability. An Analysis of the State of the Art in the Era of New Technologies* (Intersentia 2016) 9.

42 Case 120/78 *Rewe-Zentral AG v Bundesmonopolverwaltung für Branntwein* (n 18). The case concerned the sale (through a retailer, Rewe) in Germany of a type of *crème de cassis*, a blackcurrant liqueur produced in France. Because the German legislation required the fruit liqueur to contain at least 25% of alcohol, whereas the cassis de Dijon contained 10-20%, the *Bundesmonopolverwaltung für Branntwein* (a section of the German Federal Ministry of Finance) ruled that the product could be imported in Germany, but not marketed. According to the Plaintiff and to the CJEU this measure resulted into a substantial restriction of quantitative imports, against the meaning of Art 34 TFEU.

tion principle,[43] but also because the Court had the opportunity of clarifying the role of technical regulations and opening a debate on future harmonisation legislation that ended in the New Approach. According to the CJEU, Member States could only restrict or forbid the marketing of products from other Member States if they did not comply with 'essential requirements'. Consequently, non-essential requirements could not figure in the EU harmonised legislation. The voluntary nature of harmonised technical standards, as set out later by the EU Commission in the New Approach, forbids the creation of a barrier in importing and marketing Member States' products. However, at the same time, harmonised standards represent appropriate means for demonstrating conformity in a proportionate manner. e) Compliance with harmonised standards would guarantee a fairer apportionment of the risks inherent in modern technological production between the injured person and the producer, in compliance with recital 2 of the PLD. This is especially true in cases of misuse[44] of high technological products or professional machines that are intended for use of skilled and trained workers, but rented to unskilled and unsupervised end-users. f) As described at III.2., standardisation organisations are private entities in the industrial sector, but the mandates asking for specific technical standards come from the European Commission after consultation with sectoral national authorities. This procedure provides sufficient elements of expectations of public authorities, representing an objective, authoritative and competent expression of the 'safety which a person is entitled to expect' (Art 6 para 1 of the PLD).

43 Enhancing the free movement of goods is the purpose of Arts 34-36 TFEU, which prohibit quantitative restrictions. The CJEU, in the case Cassis de Dijon, with reference to the free movement of goods, has established the mutual recognition principle, according to which products lawfully manufactured or marketed in one Member State should in principle move freely throughout the Union where such products meet equivalent levels of protection to those imposed by the Member State of destination.

44 European Court of Justice of 5 March 2015, Joined Cases C-503/13 and C-504/13, *Boston Scientific Medizintechnik*,, OJ C138/9, EU:C:2015:148, para 37.

New Approaches:
Basis for Liability and Addressees

Product Liability 2.0 – Mere Update or New Version?

Bernhard A Koch[*]

I. Introduction

Other contributions to this volume address various problems with applying the standard concepts of tort law in general and of product liability in particular to modern-day scenarios. They thereby also provide answers to the question whether the historic elements built into the Products Liability Directive (PLD)[1] can still be used.[2] After all, technology has clearly changed over the past three decades and will continue to evolve.

This paper specifically addresses the question whether and to what extent the PLD needs to be amended, or – in terminology closer to this volume's main theme – whether Product Liability 1.0 needs an update or even a relaunch.

I would like to contribute to answering this question by starting from the fundamentals of tort law, using the example of damage caused by the use of a motorized vehicle.

---

* Bernhard A Koch is a Professor of Civil and Comparative Law at the University of Innsbruck.

1 Council Directive 85/ 374/ EEC of 25 July 1985 on the approximation of the laws, regulations and administrative provisions of the Member States concerning liability for defective products [1985] OJ L 210/ 29, as amended by Directive 1999/ 34/ EC of the European Parliament and of the Council of 10 May 1999 [1999] OJ L 141/ 20.

2 The following deliberations will be limited to the Directive as such and mostly ignore national variations of product or producers' liability.

II. Traditional Bases of Liability

Traditionally, of course, and in some legal systems still, the prime focus of the law of delict lies on the driver and her conduct when using the car.[3] The ultimate decision whether and to what extent she may be held liable depends upon the degree of impact of other potential causes of the harm, starting with the victim herself or third parties, unavoidable external causes commonly referred to as acts of God, or – in this context in particular – also flaws attributable to the State, for example with respect to road maintenance or traffic control.[4]

An alternative route to compensation was chosen by many jurisdictions already a long time ago by shifting the focus from the driver's behaviour to the control of and benefit from the object whose inherent risks materialized.[5] Strict liability was in essence also a response to the challenges of modern technology at the time and seems to have worked more or less fine ever since, particularly in light of a compulsory liability insurance regime often coupled with it.[6]

Then came an alternative approach co-existing with both more traditional paths towards compensation, now shifting the focus yet again from those using or controlling the vehicle to its producer,[7] requiring, however, at least in theory that the product was distributed with some inherent vice.[8] Liability is therefore attached to the manufacturer for putting a defective product into circulation via a system of distribution. Sometimes, the defect

---

3 cf Pierre Widmer in European Group on Tort Law, *Principles of European Tort Law* (Springer 2005) 80: Fault is 'the most traditional, most widespread and – apparently – most important criterion of imputation or foundation of responsibility'.

4 On the latter, see Ken Oliphant (ed), *Liability for Public Authorities in a Comparative Perspective* (Intersentia 2016).

5 See the contributions to Wolfgang Ernst (ed), *The Development of Traffic Liability* (2010).

6 This is probably why Wolfgang Ernst, 'General Introduction: legal change? Railway and car accidents and how the law coped with them' in Ernst (n 5) 5, argues that 'road accidents seem to be handled almost everywhere in a sort of "systemic", quasi-bureaucratic way. This is largely because the issue of liability has become entwined with insurance.' A recent comparative study on the interrelation of compulsory liability insurance and tort law is Attila Fenyves and others (eds), *Compulsory Liability Insurance from a European Perspective* (De Gruyter 2016).

7 See Simon Whittaker (ed), *The Development of Product Liability* (Cambridge University Press 2010).

8 On the notion of defect, see in this volume Jean-Sébastien Borghetti 63.

can be traced back to some parts built into the final product, which puts those who contributed the flawed components into the liability limelight as well.

While the PLD channelled liability onto the manufacturer of the defective product, it also took care of the other players already mentioned by providing for a co-existence of the liability theories already addressed.[9]

III. Product Liability in the Digital Age

How is all that still suitable for the Digital Age? I have chosen the car example for the obvious reason that we will sooner or later see truly autonomous vehicles on our roads, and these will probably be the first 'robots' that will be of enormous practical concern in tort law.[10] Here, the scenario clearly gets more complex, as more players will necessarily have to be considered.[11]

Apart from the ones already mentioned, other vehicles in traffic may either directly or indirectly communicate with the autonomous car that ultimately triggered the harm, as will traffic information systems, providing further input such as GPS and other data to the functioning of the car. The keeper may have to sign up for some backend services, either provided by the manufacturer herself or by some third party, which will not only transmit further input, but also send data from our car back.[12] A significant portion of all that interaction will be done via mobile communication systems, and their providers themselves will play a significant role in the overall functioning of future traffic as well.

---

9 See in particular Arts 7(d), 8, 13 PLD and ECJ Case C–402/ 03 *Skov Æg v Bilka Lavprisvarehus A/ S* [2006] ECR I-199, paras 47–48 with further references.

10 Needless to say, there are many other variants of products which will cause harm; see also infra VII.

11 See, eg, Fraunhofer-Institut für Arbeitswirtschaft und Organisation IAO (ed), *Hochautomatisiertes Fahren auf Autobahnen – Industriepolitische Schlussfolgerungen* <https://www.bmwi.de/Redaktion/DE/Downloads/H/hochautomatisiertes-fahren-auf-autobahnen.pdf> (accessed 24 May 2018) on technology aspects of autonomous driving.

12 This may include, for example, notifications about potential imminent failures of car components communicated back to the producer, arranging automatically for repair at one of her service outlets nearby.

In addition, updates and further digital input from those who originally contributed to the final product will go straight to the car, either via the Internet or at the occasion of a service stop at the vendor's or some repair shop, but most likely in bypassing the producer, and most certainly added after the car was originally put into circulation, which is the PLD's magic moment.[13]

But also the State may play a more important role in the overall assessment as it will probably contribute more substantially to the actual functioning of an autonomous traffic system, e.g. by providing infrastructure that will directly or indirectly communicate with the vehicles, such as smart traffic lights that send out data to the cars in the vicinity of the crossing.[14]

Despite these additional players, we should not forget that also the ones mentioned before remain crucial as well. This is even true for the driver, although her role may be reduced to that of a passenger in the future.[15] Nevertheless, she may still have some residual duties such as the ones foreseen by current legislation on automated driving.[16] Also third parties may continue to play decisive roles in the occurrence of accidents on the roads of the future, as there may still be pedestrians running into the streets out of the blue, but also hackers who purposefully interfere with software and communications.

---

13 cf Art 6, 7, 11 and 15 PLD.

14 See <https://www.eng.ufl.edu/newengineer/research-innovation/a-smart-city-where-self-driving-cars-traffic-lights-pedestrians-and-cyclists-all-talk-to-one-another/>, but see also <https://senseable.mit.edu/light-traffic/> both accessed 24 May 2018.

15 On the potential contributory negligence of the user of an autonomous car if she is harmed herself, see Martin Ebers, 'Autonomes Fahren: Produkt- und Produzentenhaftung' in Bernd Oppermann and Jutta Stender-Vorwachs (eds), *Autonomes Fahren* (CH Beck 2017) 115–116.

16 At least for a certain transitional period while the technology gradually replaces conventional vehicles. See, eg, sec 1a para 2 no 3 of the German Road Traffic Act (StVG), which requires that even in fully automated cars the driver always has to have the opportunity to resume control and deactivate the self-driving mechanism. But see the new Californian regulations which under certain circumstances allow automated vehicles onto the road without a person inside that can take over control if needed (but still requiring monitoring through a 'remote operator': 13 CCR § 227.38): <https://bit.ly/2IQqwHt> accessed 24 May 2018.

Does this increase in complexity (which in part is already the reality) require a new look at the role or even the details of product liability as harmonized in 1985?

IV. Traditional Requirements of Product Liability and Products of the Digital Age

1. Recoverable Loss

If we go through the catalogue of requirements for product liability, the first question is of course whether the victim suffered some harm that is deemed recoverable under the PLD's regime. Whether a reform of the directive will finally get rid of the 500 Euro threshold,[17] or whether certain property losses remain excluded from the directive's scope[18] are questions whose answers do not necessarily depend upon the technology we are looking at here.

However, it remains unclear whether damage to data falls within the ambit of the PLD. After all, the directive's language does not specify whether the 'items of property' damaged have to be corporeal.[19] Nevertheless, it is to be presumed that the drafters did not have digital content in mind when defining recoverable losses for purposes of the directive. It is

---

17 Art 9(b) PLD. cf ECJ Case C–52/ 00 *Commission v France* [2002] ECR I–3827, paras 26–35; Case C–154/ 00 *Commission v Greece* [2002] ECR–I 3879. See also the fourth report by the Commission on the application of the PLD, COM (2011) 547 final, 9–11.

18 Art 9(b) PLD excludes compensation for damage to property that is in general not 'ordinarily intended for private use or consumption' and (cumulatively) was not in fact used by the victim 'mainly for his own private use or consumption'. See the criticism against this choice raised eg by Gerhard Wagner in *Münchener Kommentar zum BGB* (7th edn, CH Beck 2017) § 1 PHG para 14.

19 However, the Austrian implementation of the PLD specifically added the term 'corporeal' to its transposition of Art 9(b) PLD in sec 1(1) *Produkthaftungsgesetz* (Act on Product Liability, 'eine von dem Produkt verschiedene *körperliche* Sache' – emphasis added). Neither the German language version of the PLD nor the German Act on Product Liability expressly qualify 'item of property' as necessarily 'corporeal'. However, this has to be seen in light of the German definition of an item of property ('thing') in sec 90 BGB (*Bürgerliches Gesetzbuch*), according to which all 'things' have to be corporeal, unlike its Austrian counterpart of sec 285 ABGB (*Allgemeines Bürgerliches Gesetzbuch*), which is broader.

therefore to be hoped that a future update of the PLD will provide for explicit clarity in this regard.

Another question unresolved is whether the exclusion of damage to the product itself in art 9(b) PLD also applies to harm caused by a mere component to the rest of the product, which in German is referred to as a 'Weiterfresserschaden' (harm caused by a 'spreading' defect). This is already a problem with tangible parts in the analogue world, but is equally relevant for digital components: What if the firmware of some battery-powered gadget fails to regulate its power usage properly, causing it to overheat, which harms other parts of or even destroys the entire gadget? The wording of art 9(b) PLD cited makes it clear that the manufacturer of the final product cannot be held liable for the damage thereto, but this does not rule out necessarily that the victim can recover her loss from the component producer instead. If the firmware is deemed a product in itself were it distributed separately, I see no reason why the developer of this file should not be held liable for the damage her product causes – after all, the mere fact that this component was integrated into another final product must not shield its producer from liability if she were liable for the very same defect to a direct customer.[20] As a manufacturer of tires should compensate losses caused by flaws of her products irrespective of whether these are first attached to a car and then distributed together with it or sold directly as spare parts to a car owner, a software developer should be liable for imperfect code both if it is already part of the original version pre-installed into some gadget as well as if it is distributed through some update or otherwise independently to the buyer of said gadget.

2. *Product*

When it comes to the notion of a product, it can easily be applied to autonomous vehicles, robots or the like as well – after all, these will be tangible items despite the integration of digital content.[21]

---

20 See already Helmut Koziol and others, *Österreichisches Haftpflichtrecht*, vol 3 (3rd edn, Jan Sramek Verlag 2014) B/ 96-B/ 99. cf Gerald Spindler, 'Roboter, Automation, künstliche Intelligenz, selbst-steuernde Kfz – Braucht das Recht neue Haftungskategorien?' [2015] CR 766, 773. *Contra* Gerhard Wagner, 'Produkthaftung für autonome Systeme', (2017) 217 AcP 707, 723–724.

21 Gerhard Wagner (n 20) 715.

However, it is very much open to debate whether the digital content itself is a 'product' within the meaning of the PLD.[22] This not only applies to software or drivers, but also to other data such as audio or video files and electronic maps for navigation systems. If all that is built into a tangible final product such as a vehicle, this question is not as pressing for the victim as long as the manufacturer of the latter is still solvent enough to compensate her loss, and it is for the latter to resolve the matter at the recourse action level (which may be a question of contractual liability anyhow).

But what if this digital content is sold separately and causes harm to persons or property due to some vice already inherent when put into circulation? This issue also arises, of course, if the victim acquires an update separately and overwrites previous versions of integrated data. While Art 2 PLD requires products to be 'movables', it does not further specify whether this is limited to tangible objects.[23] The explicit inclusion of 'electricity' in the same article does not help – one could argue that this was meant to add a singular exception, but also interpret this as merely one example for the fact that all intangible products are covered by the PLD as well.[24] While the Commission already in 1988 expressly confirmed that software is a product within the meaning of the directive,[25] this may not be decisive from today's perspective since at the time software was not yet sold online but invariably came with some tangible medium.

22 For US case law on whether software and other intangible personal property may be subject to strict products liability, see *Restatement (Third) of Torts: Products Liability* (1998) § 19 Comment d.

23 Jean-Sébastien Borghetti, *La responsabilité du fait des produits* (2004) para 494, argues in favour of such limitation, though conceding that this may be different with respect to software and other data (para 495).

24 The prime reason for mentioning electricity specifically, however, rather seems to be the fact that this is not a product in the sense of a one-time-delivery item, but rather a continuous supply over time, which makes it more challenging to identify the moment when it was put into circulation. cf Marshall Shapo, *Shapo on the Law of Products Liability* (7th edn, Edward Elgar 2017) 7-23–7-28, on the struggle of US legal systems with strict liability for problems with the supply of electricity.

25 On behalf of the Commission, Lord Cockfield replied to a question posed by the European Parliament that 'the Directive applies to software in the same way, moreover, that it applies to handicraft and artistic products' ([1989] OJ C114/ 42).

Nevertheless, I agree with Gerhard Wagner[26] that the PLD already now does (and should) extend to digital content.[27] However, it would be very helpful indeed if the wording of the directive could expressly clarify this – one way or another – in a future update.[28]

3. Liable Person

The key person in the product liability game is obviously the manufacturer of the finished product. In our scenario here, this would be whatever company that markets the self-driving car as such.

Those providing (hardware) components to autonomous vehicles are clearly covered by the existing approach – already now, those providing the steering wheel or other integral parts of the final car are deemed secondary producers by Art 3(1) PLD.

It is not entirely clear, however, whether those contributing digital input into the final product, ie software developers or those producing other digital content, can also be held liable under the PLD regime. If one agrees that purely digital content falls within the scope of the directive,[29] its developers are necessarily 'manufacturers of a component part' under Art 3(1) PLD.[30]

---

26 Gerhard Wagner (n 20) 717–718, and in this volume 41f. See also Gerald Spindler, 'Haftung im IT-Bereich' in Egon Lorenz (ed), *Karlsruher Forum 2010: Haftung und Versicherung im IT-Bereich* (2011) 41–43; and the in-depth analyses of Andreas Günther, *Produkthaftung für Informationsgüter* (2001) 668–677, and Jürgen Taeger, *Außervertragliche Haftung für fehlerhafte Computerprogramme* (1995) 108–169.

27 Bernhard A Koch, 'Product Liability for Information in Europe?' in Johann Knobel and others (eds), *Essays in Honour of Johann Neethling* (LexisNexis 2015); idem, 'Produkthaftung für Daten' in Francesco Schurr and Manfred Umlauft (eds), *Festschrift für Bernhard Eccher* (Verlag Österreich 2017).

28 Similarily Piotr Machnikowski, 'Conclusions' in Piotr Machnikowski (ed), *European Product Liability* (Intersentia 2016) 700–701.

29 See supra III.

30 Gerhard Wagner (n 20) 719–722. But see Horst Eidenmüller, 'The Rise of Robots and the Law of Humans' [2017] ZEuP 765, 772–773, who argues in favour of holding the producer of the final product exclusively liable vis-à-vis third parties, thereby deviating from the PLD's choice to allow claims against component manufacturers as well.

3D printing technology does not pose any further challenges in this respect: As long as there is an entity from which the final printout is bought through some method of distribution, the answer to the question who is the producer remains the same – it is the manufacturer who just happens to use different technology.[31] The same is true for those producing the printing material, but also for others providing digital input such as the STL design files or the software producing those files if one agrees with the inclusion of digital content as argued above. If it is not some third party, but the owner and user of a product herself who prints it out with her own 3D printer, the focus changes, but still the analysis is rather straight-forward: If the item turns out to be defective, this may be due to a problem with the printing material, the printer itself, or some flaw in the software and/or STL file. The only difference to the previous variation is that here the contributors of digital input now deliver directly to the printer/owner and become independent manufacturers putting their (final) products directly into circulation. Also, problems of identifying the defect might be more troublesome for the victim of a flawed product since she now faces challenges that would otherwise primarily arise at a recourse level. Still, this is not different to the more traditional case where someone, for example, buys wood and other components as well as tools independently from various producers in order to assemble a cupboard herself rather than buying a finished item from a furniture store.

4. Defect[32]

Product liability only attaches to defective products, which means that these fail to 'provide the safety which a person is entitled to expect, taking all circumstances into account' (art 6 PLD). The key question is of course what kind of and what degree of safety we are entitled to expect in the age of robotics and the IoT. After all, those using modern technology presumably do not even expect their new gadgets to operate flawlessly from the

---

31 However, as 3D printing (at least of less complex models) no longer necessarily requires specific skills or major investments, product liability may be barred if the final product was not 'for sale or any form of distribution for economic purpose', as this triggers the defence of Art 7 lit c PLD.

32 More specifically on defectiveness in the digital age Jean-Sébastien Borghetti, in this volume 63, and Gerhard Wagner (n 20) 724–750.

start any more – when buying a computer or a mobile phone, we are all aware of patch days and continuous updating of the embedded or pre-installed software.[33]

Does this impact upon the standard of 'safety' we are entitled to expect from modern-day technology? Of course. However, when it comes to AI products the tricky question arises whether these have to be treated differently.[34] After all, they are meant to develop their own decision-making process and to adapt to future problems independently. Nevertheless, I am confident that 'reasonable expectations of the public at large'[35] can also be identified here. While this peculiar nature of AI products is what contributes to defining said expectations, it does not overrule basic safety standards. If products are admitted to the market of which it is clear from the outset that they may show unexpected behaviour, this will nevertheless not be a clearance for causing harm to the public at large.[36]

Take the example of a driverless car that is programmed to accumulate data about other traffic participants itself according to certain generic pre-installed standards. If that vehicle in the course of this learning process misinterprets the conduct of a pedestrian who is about to cross the road as the movement of an inanimate object, the car will still be deemed defec-

---

33 But see Mark A Geistfeld, 'A Roadmap for Autonomous Vehicles: State Tort Liability, Automobile Insurance, and Federal Safety Regulation', (2017) 105 Cal LR 1611, 1639, who argues that the vision of traffic without accidents advertised by manufacturers of self-driving cars may fire back: 'Paradoxically, the safe performance promised by the technology could generate demanding expectations of safety that subject the manufacturer to liability in the event of crash.'.

34 See, eg, Martin Ebers (n 15) 106–108.

35 cf, eg, CJEU Joined Cases C-503/ 14 and C-504/ 14 *Boston Scientific Medizintechnik GmbH v AOK Sachsen-Anhalt – die Gesundheitskasse* ECLI:EU:C:2015:148, para 37, mirroring the wording of Art 6 PLD by stating that 'a product is defective when it does not provide the safety which a person is entitled to expect, taking all the circumstances into account, including the presentation of the product, the use to which it could reasonably be expected that it would be put and the time when the product was put into circulation'. The Court further emphasized 'that assessment must be carried out having regard to the reasonable expectations of the public at large.'.

36 cf Gerhard Wagner (n 20) 713: 'Insbesondere kann sich ein Hersteller nicht durch Hinweis auf die Unkontrollierbarkeit autonomer Systeme von seiner im Übrigen begründeten Haftung entlasten. Das Inverkehrbringen einer unkontrollierbaren Gefahrenquelle ist kein Grund für eine Haftungserleichterung …' He concludes that autonomous systems can only be admitted to the market if the producer has taken all objectively possible measures to prevent harming others.

tive if it runs over that pedestrian[37] – killing people will never be considered a necessary cost of society in the process of deploying new technology.

If negative effects of new technologies cannot be ruled out, as a minimum will the producer have to warn those exposed if the product is nevertheless greenlighted despite such potential dangers.[38]

5. *Burden of Proof*

Probably the biggest challenge with product liability in the digital age lies in proving the defect as the cause of harm.[39] The operation of modern products is no longer predominantly determined by their inherent features given to them by their manufacturers, but depends heavily on the subsequent interaction of these products with others.

In addition, the afore-mentioned problems of continuous updating, often by those already contributing to the original product, but subsequently bypassing the manufacturer by delivering updates directly to the user, makes it very hard to determine what actually caused the harm. Even if it can be allocated somewhere within the operation of the vehicle, it often remains unclear whether it was really a problem inherent within the product already at the time it was put into circulation, triggering the defence of art 7 lit (b) PLD.

A reflex response by some is to call for a reversal of the burden of proving the defect in product liability,[40] but this would effectively be noth-

---

37 This was exactly the reason why a Uber self-driving car killed a lady who crossed the street with a bicycle: see the preliminary NTSB report at <https://www.ntsb.gov/news/press-releases/pages/nr20180524.aspx> accessed 24 May 2018.

38 As Gerhard Wagner (n 20) 729, put it: 'Solange die Erwerber über die mit dem Betrieb autonomer Fahrzeuge verbundenen Schadensrisiken adäquat informiert werden, geschieht ihnen auch kein Unrecht, wenn ihnen die unvermeidbaren Restrisiken der neuen Technologie auferlegt werden.' See also Geistfeld (n 33) 1639.

39 On problems of causation, see Miquel Martín-Casals in this volume 201.

40 Eg Roeland de Bruin, 'Autonomous Intelligent Cars on the European Intersection of Liability and Privacy' [2016] EJRR 485, 495 (despite realizing that this 'could foster a "claims culture", and have a negative impact upon innovation').

ing less than reallocating the overall risk in disguise.[41] One should also keep in mind that with automated vehicles in particular, it is highly likely that these will be equipped with event logging or recording systems such as black boxes or similar devices which may put even better data about the actual cause of a collision (ultimately) into the hands of the victim than before.[42]

V. Reasons for Allocating the Loss

The final decision who should bear the risk of uncertainty is at the same time a verdict allocating the loss in light of competing interests. Let us therefore have a closer look at just two of the players envisaged here, the keeper of the self-driving car and its manufacturer.[43]

If we go through the checklist of arguments commonly raised,[44] one often cited in support of product liability is that the manufacturer is the one who is (or should be) in control of the defect. It is her who should prevent it or at least properly inform the users of the risks coming with the product. On the other hand, at the time of the accident it is the keeper who is (or should be) in control of the vehicle itself, which inter alia also includes the possibility to install software updates if made available. Then again, it is the manufacturer who should have better access to the facts helping to prove (or disprove) the defect, although the log files mentioned before might shift the balance a little. However, it is the keeper who is the one who benefits from the use of the vehicle at the time of the accident, which brings it into contact with the victim.

When it comes to the question who of the two might be the best loss spreader, the answer is not so easy, at least not if motor vehicles are the

---

41 See also Gerhard Wagner (n 20) 728–729, who speaks against absolute liability of a producer for the mere fact that her products caused harm: 'Die Produkthaftung ist keine absolute Haftung für sämtliche Schäden, die durch ein Produkt verursacht worden sind, sondern eine Haftung für die Pflichtverletzung durch Inverkehrbringen fehlerhafter Produkte. … Hundertprozentige Unfallfreiheit kann von einem autonomen Fahrzeug genauso wenig erwartet werden wie von dem Menschen, der ein herkömmliches Fahrzeug steuert.'.

42 cf Gerald Spindler (n 20) 772.

43 If the keeper is injured herself, however, the focus will be on the latter alone, of course.

44 cf Horst Eidenmüller (n 30) 772.

products at stake, in light of the elaborate motor insurance regime functioning fairly well throughout Europe.

There are other factors such as deep pocket arguments or how we can foresee incentives for manufacturers for producing flawless products,[45] but let us note as an interim result at this stage that the answer to identifying the 'best' defendant for the victim of an autonomous car is not self-evident at first sight.

VI. The Needle in the Haystack

As mentioned before, the focus on just the manufacturer and the keeper alone will necessarily be too narrow, as there are other players we need to keep an eye on, starting with those producers of digital information that continue to deliver updates and other input to the vehicle after it was put into circulation. Similarly, those providing the vehicle with further data, if only for its continuous operation, also come into play as additional producers, even though the borderline to the provision of services may be tricky to draw.[46]

Some of the players listed in the scenario outlined above clearly belong to the manufacturer's sphere, at least originally, and it seems appropriate to stick to the channelling idea of the PLD also in the future, focusing primarily on the party who puts the final product onto the market, but at the same time preserving alternative claims against providers of components and other parts.

Similarly, the keeper of the final product who is (or should be) in control of it at the time it causes harm should continue to be at the centre of our attention when it comes to attributing risks brought about by the product's ordinary use, whether or not this can be traced back to some defect already inherent in the product when it was put into circulation, as long as such a defect triggers strict liability itself, since the prime reason for sub-

45 See eg Gerald Spindler (n 20) 774.

46 cf Art 3 para 5 lit a of the draft directive on certain aspects concerning contracts for the supply of digital content in the version of the general approach by the Council, 2015/ 0287 (COD), which excludes from the directive's scope contracts on 'the provision of services where the digital form is used by the supplier only for transmitting the products of such services to the consumer'. This seems to be a very useful approach towards identifying the proper boundaries in this context as well.

mitting it to a no-fault regime is the likelihood of harm caused in its ordinary operation.[47] As some strict liability statutes provide, it makes even sense to extend the keeper's liability to the fault of the actual user of the product if the latter had control over it at the time of the accident with the consent of the former (without necessarily barring direct claims against the user herself, though).[48]

However, there are several other players remaining which are not similarly related, and amongst them, there is no obvious single prime target onto whom liability could and should be channelled.[49] The only possibly connecting element is perhaps the mere fact that these are all third parties with respect to the production or the use of the product, even though the latter may be doubtful in light of its necessary interaction with input from or contact with these third parties in order to function properly.

Considering that the primary goal of the PLD is to find 'a fair apportionment of the risks inherent in modern technological production',[50] and if this is what we still strive for, then it is not necessarily just the manufacturer onto whom liability should be channelled. While the PLD only addresses the risks of production, strict liability eg for motor vehicles instead focuses on the risks of motorized traffic, which is of course a significantly different problem. If we expand our view to those who participate in this risky traffic scenario, it might be preferable to consider a liability system linked to the latter coupled with a risk pool such as compulsory liability

---

47 On the interplay of the various reasons for introducing strict liability, see Bernhard A Koch and Helmut Koziol, 'Comparative Conclusions' in Bernhard A Koch and Helmut Koziol (eds), *Unification of Tort Law: Strict Liability* (Kluwer Law International 2002) 407–413.

48 cf, eg, sec 19 para 2 EKHG (Austrian Act on Liability for Railways and Motor Vehicles, *Eisenbahn- und Kraftfahrzeughaftpflichtgesetz*), sec 7 StVG (German Road Traffic Act, *Straßenverkehrsgesetz*).

49 This is even true for hackers attacking the digital infrastructure of the vehicle – while they are clearly liable for causing harm intentionally, they may simply be out of reach or lacking funds to compensate the losses they cause, which will trigger shifts towards secondary liabilities, eg for the vulnerability of the system towards such attacks. However, no producer of a digital product should be exposed to absolute liability for hacking as long as all standards available to shield it therefrom were obeyed. cf Gerhard Wagner (n 20) 727–728.

50 Recital 2 of the PLD.

insurance.[51] To the extent the risk attributed through this system overlaps with the production risk assigned to the manufacturer, we might continue to use solidary liability with recourse options as is already in force.[52]

VII. One Size Does Not Fit All

This may be even more convincing if we move from cars to items such as robots. Other products of AI or the IoT may not equally be embedded into a well-functioning system of liability insurance coupled with strict liability rules, which leaves the victim in a more vulnerable position than those hurt by self-driving cars. Unless there is a proven defect in the robot already existing at the time it left the factory, it seems more convincing to pursue the traditional approach of holding that person liable who benefits from the fact that using this technology is permissible despite inherent risks.

---

51 However, at least initially insurers may not yet be prepared to offer cover for novel risk scenarios, at least not for reasonable and actuarially correct premiums. After all, also they may not have sufficient experience-based data at hand to calculate the risk. This may incidentally also impact upon the time it will take to fully implement the new technology: cf Geistfeld (n 33) 1617–1618, who rightly argues that these uncertainties will already affect the price and therefore market acceptance of autonomous vehicles, since the manufacturer will have to calculate the price of her products with an eye to potential liabilities she will face: 'The rate at which the market converts from conventional to autonomous vehicles depends on the price that consumers must pay to adopt the new technology. For at least two reasons, systemic legal uncertainty about manufacturer liability increases the cost of an autonomous vehicle, thereby increasing price and reducing consumer demand for this technology.' Even if manufacturers try to mitigate these risks by taking out insurance, the premiums they will be charged will not necessarily reflect the actual risk due to lack of experience, and this 'systemic uncertainty about liability could significantly increase prices for autonomous vehicles and unduly delay their widespread deployment.' Furthermore, he argues that the unavailability of insurance might be speaking in favour of limiting liability: 'If manufacturers cannot procure liability insurance or if their liability exposure is sufficiently systemic such that it would otherwise unduly threaten bankruptcy, then there is a strong case for immunizing this type of malfunction from strict products liability.' Geistfeld (n 33) 1673.

52 cf Gerhard Wagner (n 20) 739: 'Besteht jedoch die Halterhaftung … für autonome Fahrzeuge fort, kommt die Produkthaftung ohnehin nur als Regressinstrument zwischen der Haftpflichtversicherung des Halters und der Produkthaftpflichtversicherung des Herstellers infrage.'.

However, even we limit ourselves to robots, there are so many varieties that a uniform liability solution applicable to all of them alike already at first sight may not offer an adequate distribution of the risks inherent in these products. Just think of automated lawn-mowers as compared to industry robots or smart kitchen devices compared to surgical robots. The risks attached to all these types of robots is obviously substantially different, starting with mobility: A self-learning lawn-mower may escape the garden for which it was bought through some malfunctioning and cause accidents on adjacent land or roads. An industrial robot which is part of an assembly line in a factory will most likely not escape the confines of that building, while a nanorobot will typically remain within the body of the patient. The damage caused by some household robot will be different from injuries inflicted by a surgical robot. When it comes to the latter, those potentially harmed will typically be in a contractual relationship with the hospital,[53] either as patients or as staff, which may not necessarily be true for possible victims of drones. Peculiar interests affiliated with military or emergency response robots may lead to yet another analysis.

These differences will not necessarily impact upon the rules governing the various bases of liability, but they will most likely lead to different results in the overall assessment of who should bear the loss in the big picture, either alone or jointly with others. The rules of product liability will presumably work for all these varieties, as long as the harm caused falls within the scope of the PLD. The safety to be expected in light of all circumstances will be substantially different, perhaps,[54] but that benchmark per se will work accordingly, as will defences such as the development risk or compliance with mandatory regulations, despite obvious differences between the latter. Still, the answer to the question whether product liability indeed leads to the afore-mentioned 'fair apportionment of the risks inherent' in these various types of robots may not be the same after all.

53 Unless the machine explodes, of course, in which case the radius of potential victims will be much larger, but that would not be a risk typical for robots, but for any machine.

54 See the example of robot vacuum cleaners vs self-driving cars given by Susanne Horner and Markus Kaulartz, 'Haftung 4.0 – Verschiebung des Sorgfaltsmaßstabs bei Herstellung und Nutzung autonomer Systeme' [2016] CR 7, 11, 14.

VIII. Liability of E-Persons?

Some argue that machines with artificial intelligence are so similar to humans that they themselves should be held liable and therefore call for the legal recognition of 'e-persons' or the like.[55] While we obviously already know legal personalities that are not human, the question here is moot as long as robots do not have assets of their own which would make it attractive and reasonable to pursue claims against them. Even if they had funds attributed to them, it is to be feared that this would merely be abused to introduce some artificial caps on liability through the backdoor,[56] which would invariably trigger the by far more complicated question of how to 'pierce the electronic veil' of this artificial creation of an e-person in order to pursue claims exceeding these allotted funds. In addition, we would have to introduce standards of 'conduct' for these e-persons in order to hold them liable individually, which could hardly be brought in line with negligence standards for humans. The idea of recognizing robots and other machines with artificial intelligence as legal persons should therefore not be pursued further.[57]

IX. Conclusions

Summing up, I think the PLD may indeed need some revision, but not a radical expansion. Yes, there is a need for fine-tuning, particularly when it comes to clarifying if and to what extent digital content fall within its scope (both as products and as objects of recoverable harm), and if not, how to justify liability of the manufacturer for a final product that includes flawed digital components, but not of the producer of the latter.

However, the expected complexity of scenarios in the age of the Internet and of robotics does not speak in favour of channelling liability for all potential risks onto the producer of the gadget. We have not done this in

55 Just see European Parliament resolution of 16 February 2017 with recommendations to the Commission on Civil Law Rules on Robotics, 2015/ 2103 (INL), para 59(f).

56 Eg Jochen Hanisch, 'Zivilrechtliche Haftungskonzepte für Robotik' in Eric Hilgendorf (ed), *Robotik im Kontext von Recht und Moral* (2014) 27, 39–40.

57 See also Horst Eidenmüller (n 30) 774–776; Melinda F Lohmann, 'Ein europäisches Roboterrecht – überfällig oder überflüssig?' [2017] ZEuP 168, 171; Gerald Spindler (n 20) 774–775.

the past with technologies that were new at the time, and we should not do it now either.[58]

Existing strict liability regimes can exist alongside product liability for the simple reason that they are based on different theories, and even the ECJ acknowledged that already more than 15 years ago.[59] The best examples are again cars – we have a well-functioning system of motor vehicle liability that can co-exist with product liability for cars because each is based on peculiar grounds, and the relationship between these liabilities is equally clarified. I therefore see no reason to desperately try to identify 'the one and only' regime of liability for artificial intelligence, since that would be artificial and certainly not intelligent.

58 Admittedly, though, the practical relevance of product liability may increase in a future where misconduct of humans plays a lesser role; cf, eg, Benjamin von Bodungen and Martin Hoffmann, 'Autonomes Fahren – Haftungsverschiebung entlang der Supply Chain?' [2016] NZV 449, 503, 508, and Gerhard Wagner (n 20) 708–709, who speaks of potential 'tektonische Verschiebungen innerhalb des etablierten Haftungssystems'.

59 Case C–52/ 00 *Commission v France* [2002] ECR I–3827, para 22.

Liability for Robotics: Current Rules, Challenges, and the Need for Innovative Concepts

*Ernst Karner**

I. Starting Point

Technological progress today allows for systems to undertake ever more complex series of actions. In no sense should we confine our thinking in this regard to 'self-driving' cars – we must also consider, for example, the use of robots for medical interventions or care activities, intelligent insulin pumps, and the so-called 'exoskeletons' used to help the paralysed move or to support workers undertaking difficult manual labour.

The following analysis will investigate the extent to which liability claims resulting from the activities of autonomous systems can already be resolved with conventional legal structures, and the extent to which legal innovation is required. In particular, it will consider fault liability, responsibility for auxiliaries, and risk-based and product liabilities.

II. Fault Liability

If someone is harmed by an autonomous system, then in all European jurisdictions it is first and foremost a fault liability which falls to be considered. In many cases, there exist differences in the construction of that liability,[1] but at its core the concern is always the same: the injurer is made

---

* Ernst Karner is the Director of the Institute for European Tort Law and the European Centre of Tort and Insurance Law and Professor of Civil Law at the University of Vienna. This paper is based on a lecture held on the occasion of the *4th Münster Colloquium on EU Law and the Digital Economy*, 12–13 April 2018. The lecture format has been retained, with footnotes added.

1 See Helmut Koziol, 'Comparative Conclusions' in Helmut Koziol (ed), *Basic Questions of Tort Law from a Comparative Perspective* (Jan Sramek 2015) 782ff; an in-depth analysis of the different concepts of fault-based liability within Europe was conducted in B Winiger, E Karner, and K Oliphant (eds), *Digest of European Tort Law. Volume 3: Essential Cases on Misconduct* (De Gruyter 2018).

liable where she has not behaved as an ordinary, careful actor and has thereby caused the relevant damage.

In the field of automated systems, a particular concern is to establish the relevant standards of care – for example, in respect of the level of monitoring necessary. Reference can be made in this context to the reform of the German Road Traffic Act (Straßenverkehrsgesetz, StVG) carried out in 2017,[2] whereby it has explicitly been provided that the user of an automated driving function is allowed to 'turn away' from the road and from steering the vehicle as long as she remains 'ready enough to perceive' a need to retake control of the steering at any given time.[3] However, given the rather indeterminate character of this provision, this rule has received quite some criticism from practitioners and academics alike.[4]

Generally, it may at least be said that the relevant standards of conduct are correlated to the state of development of the automation. The more autonomous the system is, the lower the requirements to take care.[5] Whilst for non-automated vehicles the driver bears full responsibility for control of the vehicle, the division of responsibilities increasingly slides along the scale towards the automated system with autonomous vehicles. For fully autonomous vehicles, the significance of fault liability will accordingly fall away almost completely.[6] Overall, the introduction of automated systems certainly leads to no demands which are qualitatively new. The adaptation of requirements of care to changed technical, economic or even social circumstances has in fact long since formed part of the jurist's craft.

---

2 German BGBl I 2017, 1648, 8; Gesetz zur Änderung des Straßenverkehrsgesetzes.

3 § 1b German Road Traffic Act (Straßenverkehrsgesetz, StVG).

4 See Schirmer, 'Augen auf beim automatisierten Fahren! Die StVG-Novelle ist ein Montagsstück' [2017] Neue Zeitschrift für Verkehrsrecht 254ff.

5 See also Julian Pehm, 'Haftung für den Betrieb autonomer Fahrzeuge: Eine komparative Sicht auf die Herausforderungen der Automatisierung' in Tagungsband XXVI. Karlsbader Juristentage 2018 (forthcoming).

6 See Gerhard Wagner, 'Produkthaftung für autonome Systeme' (2017) 217 AcP 707, 708.

III. Product Liability

Whilst fault liability will lose significance as automation progresses, the significance of the harmonised product liability regime will increase substantially.[7]

Of the many questions raised for product liability by automation, I would like to emphasise three:

- The question whether software is also to be understood as a product in the sense of the Product Liability Directive is highly controversial.[8] Given that the question cannot sensibly turn on whether the software is stored on a data carrier or not, this must be also be answered in the affirmative where the software is distributed through a Cloud or transferred otherwise than with a data storage medium.[9] In any event, however, a clarification is required to prevent legal uncertainty.
- Difficult questions are furthermore raised by the issue of a product defect and the standard to be imposed for the assessment of the same. As Wagner has convincingly demonstrated, there is much to be said for a system-related concept of defect here.[10]
- Specifically with software updates, there also arises the question of when a 're-manufacturing' occurs to trigger a separate liability.

Furthermore, thanks to automation, liability for services is again coming more strongly into view.[11] At times it is suggested that the concept of product liability should be expanded to services. In my opinion, it would seem more appropriate to reconsider a stricter liability for enterprises, as proposed by the Principles of European Tort Law (Art 4:202 PETL).[12]

---

7 cf Wagner, 'Produkthaftung für autonome Systeme' (n 6) 708.

8 See Duncan Fairgrieve et al, 'Product Liability Directive' in Piotr Machnikowski (ed), *European Product Liability. An Analysis of the State of the Art in the Era of New Technologies* (Intersentia 2016) 46f.

9 Wagner, 'Produkthaftung für autonome Systeme' (n 6) 719; see also Helmut Koziol, Peter Apathy, and Bernhard A Koch, *Österreichisches Haftpflichtrecht Band III* (3rd edn, Jan Sramek 2014) 453ff with further references.

10 Wagner, 'Produkthaftung für autonome Systeme' (n 6) 735f.

11 See Helmut Koziol, 'Product Liability: Conclusions from a Comparative Perspective' in Helmut Koziol, Michael D Green, Mark Lunney, Ken Oliphant, Yang Lixin (eds), *Product Liability. Fundamental Questions in a Comparative Perspective* (De Gruyter 2017) 538.

12 'Art 4:202. Enterprise Liability (1) A person pursuing a lasting enterprise for economic or professional purposes who uses auxiliaries or technical equipment is li-

IV. Machines as Auxiliaries

It is self-evident that one must answer for losses caused through automation-supported systems where these can be traced to careless human conduct and the same is true for operating and programming errors and failures in monitoring. A more interesting question is whether the activity of an autonomous system is also attributable to a human where there is a failure in the functioning of the system but no faulty human conduct. This very complicated question is certainly not new and was discussed as early as the 1980s in the context of automation-supported data processing. The question received an affirmative answer from weighty voices – Canaris, Spiro, and Koziol.[13] The key for attribution purposes lies in the analogical application of the rules on vicarious liability for auxiliaries, insofar as technological assistance functionally comparable to human labour is employed.[14] Though the approach appears revolutionary at first glance, there are – in Austria, for example – already now bases for supporting the proposition in positive law.[15] Moreover, the approach is entirely consistent with the general principles for attribution of the actions of auxiliaries. No one should be able to exclude the attribution provided for by vicarious liability provisions simply by employing technical means of support instead of human helpers.

At the European level, a two-part process could be recommended. In a first step, it would need to be clarified that the rules of vicarious liability are equally applicable to machines which replace human labour. A second, longer-term step would involve consideration of a harmonisation of existing vicarious liability rules in the various European jurisdictions.

---

able for any harm caused by a defect of such enterprise or of its output unless he proves that he has conformed to the required standard of conduct. (2) "Defect" is any deviation from standards that are reasonably to be expected from the enterprise or from its products or services.', Principles of European Tort Law, available online: <http://www.egtl.org> accessed 22 May 2018.

13 See Claus-Wilhelm Canaris, *Bankvertragsrecht I* (3rd edn, De Gruyter 1988) para 367; Karl Spiro, *Die Haftung für Erfüllungsgehilfen* (Stämpfli 1984) 209ff; Helmut Koziol, *Basic Questions of Tort Law from a Germanic Perspective* (Jan Sramek 2012) 228ff.

14 cf Eva Ondreasova, 'Haftung für technische Hilfsmittel de lege lata' [2015] Österreichische Juristenzeitung 444f.

15 Particularly §§ 89e and 91b para 6 Austrian Courts' Organisation Act (Gerichtsorganisationsgesetz, GOG); see Ondreasova, 'Haftung für technische Hilfsmittel' (n 14) 445ff.

V. Risk-based Liability

1. Self-driving cars against the background of existing non-contractual liability

In regards to liability for self-driving cars, reference can be made to what has been said already in respect of fault- and risk-based liabilities.[16] In the present context, a structural question appears to me to be more important; one which concerns the relationship between fault liability, risk-based liability and liability for products.

If a legal system – like German or Austrian law – provides for a comprehensive risk-based liability for motor vehicles, then liability for self-driving vehicles presents no new difficulty. If a software error leads to a traffic accident, then there is a defect in the quality of the vehicle for which its keeper will be liable.[17] As a producer is liable in solidum to an injured party in the case of a product defect, the keeper held liable has, in turn, a right of recourse against the producer. No legal uncertainty is generated, and no gaps in liability are produced, because the injured party can always claim against the keeper of the motor vehicle.[18] The same is true, mutatis mutandis, for a self-driving railway vehicle.

The position is very different, for example, in English law, which only recognises fault liability for motor vehicles.[19] With self-driving vehicles, this leads to serious gaps in protection. If someone is injured in a traffic accident through the faulty functioning of a self-driving car, then it is normally not possible for her to identify who should be the target of a claim:[20] The producer of the car because of the product defect? Or the possessor of the vehicle for not cleaning the vehicle sensors properly, for example? The injured party is left with no choice in these cases but to always bring two actions, one of which will surely be lost. A comparable issue arises in those jurisdictions in which risk-based liability only applies where the claimant was a non-motorised participant, and so is inapplicable to cases

---

16 See above II.

17 Tobias Hammel, *Haftung und Versicherung bei Personenkraftwagen mit Fahrassistenzsystemen* (VVW 2016) 206f; Maximilian Harnoncourt, 'Haftungsrechtliche Aspekte des autonomen Fahrens' [2016] Österreichische Zeitschrift für Verkehrsrecht 548f.

18 See also Wagner, 'Produkthaftung für autonome Systeme' (n 6) 758f.

19 cf Cees van Dam, *European Tort Law* (2nd edn, OUP 2013) 412ff.

20 See Wagner, 'Produkthaftung für autonome Systeme' (n 6) 760f.

of vehicle collision, like in Finland, the Netherlands and Poland,[21] or where only personal injury and not property damage is included, like in Belgium or Spain.[22] It is certainly now sometimes recognised that the very disadvantageous position thereby afforded to the injured party because of the procedural risks and evidential uncertainties is unsatisfying. Accordingly, in the UK a Bill has been introduced which grants direct claims against vehicle insurers to victims of accidents caused by a self-driving car[23] – an insurance solution which could lead to fairly similar results compared to a risk-based liability.

To avoid gaps in protection and value contradictions in the law, a comprehensive and unitary risk-based liability for vehicles, and also railways, is thus required at the European level.

2. *The need for a general rule for risk-based liability*

As already shown, problems in relation to liability for self-driving cars can be satisfactorily resolved where a comprehensive, risk-based liability for vehicles exists. In that regard, of course, it must not be overlooked that autonomous systems can manifest very different kinds of dangers, ranging from that exhibited by an automated lawnmower, to those involved with medical robots, to those attached to fully-automated means of transport, including motor vehicles, railways and aircraft.

In order to cope with those cases, sectoral rules on risk-based liabilities would be important for the most common applications. However, it is clear that even on the basis of the pace of technical development alone, it

---

21 cf for Finland: Manfred Hering, *Der Verkehrsunfall in Europa* (VVW 2012) 62; for the Netherlands: Michelle Slimmen and Willem van Boom, 'Road Traffic Liability in the Netherlands' (April 2017) available online: <https://ssrn.com/abstract=2975796> accessed 22 May 2018; for Poland: Miroslaw Nesterowicz and Ewa Baginska, 'Poland' in Bernhard A Koch and Helmut Koziol (eds), *Unification of Tort Law: Strict Liability* (Kluwer 2002) 267.

22 cf for Belgium: Herman Cousy and Dimitri Droshout, 'Belgium' in Bernhard A Koch and Helmut Koziol (eds), *Unification of Tort Law: Strict Liability* (Kluwer 2002) 51; for Spain: Dolores González Pacanowska, 'Development of Traffic Liability in Spain' in Wolfgang Ernst (ed), *The Development of Traffic Liability* (OUP 2010) 182; see also Ernst Karner, 'A Comparative Analysis of Traffic Accident Systems', Wake Forest L Rev (forthcoming 2018).

23 UK Automated and Electric Vehicles HL Bill (2017–19) 109.

is fruitless to rely solely on isolated, individual rules for various different autonomous systems. To prevent gaps in protection or value contradictions developing in the law, a general, strict liability rule structured according to levels of dangerousness is required as well. The draft reform for Austrian liability law could serve as an example for this.[24] This reform proposes a risk-based, strict liability for cases involving high levels of dangerousness, but, where dangerousness is merely higher than normal, liability is instead based simply on objective carelessness with a reversal of the burden of proof. As a first step at the European level, therefore, there is a need to produce sectoral, risk-based liability rules for specific autonomous systems of particular practical importance (eg motor vehicles and medical robots). A second step would see these sectoral rules expanded into a general liability rule based on risk, which would, as far as possible, exclude gaps in protection and value contradictions.

VI. A need for an e-person?

In legal discussions, a question is sometimes raised as to whether autonomous systems should be imbued with legal capacity, thus creating an 'electronic person'.[25] Such suggestions are flawed. On the one hand, the law serves to regulate conduct and thus only humans come into contemplation as the addressees of legal norms. On the other, it must be remembered that an electronic person would itself not possess any resources to satisfy a liability and would first have to be provided with the same. Ultimately, however, the introduction of an 'electronic person' capable of being held liable and holding assets would thus lead to deterioration in the position of the injured party, because the resources available for liability would be limited to the separate assets of the 'e-person'.[26] It therefore appears to be far more appropriate to rely on a risk-based liability of the system's keeper, for which compulsory liability insurance could be provided.

---

24 See Irmgard Griss, 'Gefährdungshaftung, Unternehmerhaftung, Eingriffshaftung' in Irmgard Griss, Georg Kathrein, and Helmut Koziol (eds), *Entwurf eines neuen österreichischen Schadenersatzrechts* (Springer 2006) 57ff.

25 On the debate see Susanne Beck, 'The Problem of Ascribing Legal Responsibility in the Case of Robotics' (2016) 31 AI & Society 478ff.

26 See also Jochen Hanisch, 'Zivilrechtliche Haftungskonzepte für Robotik' in Eric Hilgendorf (ed), *Robotik im Kontext von Recht und Moral* (Nomos 2014) 39f.

Discussion of an electronic person thus turns out to be a wrong turn, attributable not least to the fact that technological advances often bring with them unreflecting calls for special legal regulation. This tends to happen without there first having been a thorough analysis of the extent to which the existing legal frameworks allow for the development of solutions appropriate for the legal system.

VII. Summary

New technologies like autonomous systems certainly put existing liability regimes to the test. The current challenges do not, however, require a complete abandonment of pre-existing principles of tort law. Instead, they call — in my opinion — for a careful development of such principles against the backdrop of the vast field of emerging new applications.

1. There should be clarification that software is encompassed by product liability law and, indeed, that this is true regardless of whether the software is provided on a data storage medium or not.
2. If machines are employed like human auxiliaries, then the attributional rules of vicarious liability are to be applied to the machines. This too should be the subject of statutory clarification.
3. The problem of self-driving cars can be satisfactorily dealt with where there is provision made for a comprehensive, risk-based liability for vehicles which also encompasses property damage and vehicle collision cases.
4. Nevertheless, self-driving cars are not the only dangerous technologies. To avoid value contradictions and gaps in protection, risk-based liability rules should be introduced for areas of great practical importance, such as medical devices. Moreover, a general rule for risk-based liability is required. This should be structured to differentiate between various levels of dangerousness.
5. The further development of liability law indicated by autonomous systems must be conducted whilst taking into account the general rules of liability law and, thus, intrinsically.

User Liability and Strict Liability in the Internet of Things and for Robots

Gerald Spindler[*]

I. Introduction

As digitalization reaches every sector of our life and is not restricted to specific areas any more, risks and dangers of IT-products and –services also get more and more into the focus of the general debate on security and safety on the net. Global scandals like 'Wannacry'[1] or the massive attack on routers,[2] just to name a few, have risen the awareness to IT-risks that today affect every part of our daily life. In particular, the development of the 'Internet of Things', which refers to products of daily life that are constantly connected to services etc. on the Internet or of autonomous products such as self-driving cars, makes clear that IT-products or -services are not any more restricted to the industrial world or to processes which can only endanger wealth rather than physical assets or health.

Hence, product safety and liability for products has become more important than ever before. Even though IT-risks are basically not new, as the famous Year-2000 problem demonstrated[3], the new emerging technologies like artificial intelligence, the Internet of Things, and robots raise new

* Professor of Civil Law, Commercial and Economic Law, Comparative Law, Multimedia- and Telecommunication Law, University of Göttingen.

1 See for instance: Matt Hanson, 'Huge cyberattack leaves computers across the world reeling' <https://www.techradar.com/news/nhs-hospitals-in-england-hit-by-massive-cyberattack> accessed 14 June 2018.

2 See for instance: Eric Auchard, 'Deutsche Telekom attack part of global campaign on routers' <https://www.reuters.com/article/us-deutsche-telekom-outages-idUSKBN13O0X4> accessed 14 June 2018.

3 See for that Gerald Spindler, 'Das Jahr 2000 – Problem in der Produkthaftung: Pflichten der Hersteller und der Softwarenutzer' [1999] NJW 3737 with further references.

questions[4] which will be addressed in this article, beginning with a short review of the basic risks and challenges of new technologies (II.), briefly reviewing the state of the art concerning liability for IT-products and -services (III.), and then turning to new challenges and proposals to extend and modify liability rules (IV.). However, the scene would not be complete if we ignored the interplay with product security regulation (stemming from administrative law), including the role of technical standards and certifications.

II. Basic Risks

First, we have to recall the already known specific problems of IT-products when it comes to liability: IT-products, in particular software, are complex and can obviously never be 100% safe and secure. Moreover, they usually interact with other IT-products and digital environments which is evident for interactions between an operating system and specific applications, but also true for firmware and BIOS or specific graphic drivers etc. Further, given this interaction IT-products usually have to be maintained, in particular those connected to networks etc, in order to keep them updated with new developments, including new risks coming from unknown exploits in software. In addition, the business life cycle for IT-products is usually rather short, so that new software, new business models, and procedures are released in very short periods. Last but not least, IT-products are usually multiuse-products, in particular operating systems, so they are utilised for different needs of users what is sometimes hard to predict for producers (and even for retailers).

Whereas these risks are not 'new' in the sense of posing new challenges, the situation changes when we take the new features of autonomous systems and Internet of Things into account: The main feature of artificial intelligence (AI) (especially in the field of machine and deep learning) refers to the non-predictability of the behaviour of the system. As AI is able to learn and change the patterns of its program, it may adapt the system autonomously to new environmental conditions. Even though it is misleading to speak of 'intelligence' as the systems are not able to

4 See also the European Commissions approach to set ethical and legal frameworks for artificial intelligence, IP/18/3362 <http://europa.eu/rapid/press-release_IP-18-3362_en.htm> accessed 14 June 2018.

change their main goals and preference-settings, the autonomous re-programming is quite a remarkable step forward and towards real intelligence. However, this autonomous behaviour results in problems to legally qualify their behaviour or to assign actions of those systems to operators or producers.[5]

Even more, as AI is also used for robots, these machines may directly affect vital interests what is obvious for medical robots, but also for self-driving cars.

Overlapping with this phenomenon is the development known as 'Internet of Things' (IoT) referring to the connection of each product to services in the Internet (usually 'the cloud'). In extreme cases, the product (hardware) cannot be operated without a connection to a network, a so-called 'dummy client'. Usually, products are communicating with databases and other services in order to enhance functionalities of the product.[6] Thus, in contrast to former times a product cannot any more be described as something designed by a producer and then brought into the market; rather products today are designed in such a way that they depend on the availability of services on the (inter-)net in order to work in the desired way. Hence, here the already mentioned complex interaction between IT-products is even more strictly realized than ever before, as hardware cannot be operated without a network connection. Autonomous systems may also be designed in such a way that they communicate with each other or central servers.

The constant connectedness and complex interaction with other IT-products leads to another phenomenon which is pretty well known in financial markets: Systemic risks. In other terms, risks which, while being isolated, are not crucial for IT-systems, can result in enormous dangers if they interact with other risks stemming from other products. Moreover,

---

5 See for instance Susanne Wende, 'Haftungsrechtliche Verantwortung bei Weiterentwicklung des Produktes nach Inverkehrbringen, insbesondere bei maschinellem Lernen' in Thomas Sassenberg and Tobias Faber (eds), *Rechtshandbuch Industrie 4.0 und Internet of Things: Praxisfragen und Perspektiven der digitalen Zukunft* (Beck 2017) 82, 82.

6 For a basic overview on the Internet of Things see: Ioan Roxin and Aymeric Bouchereau, 'The Ecosystem of the Internet of Things' in Nasreddine Bouhaï Imad Saleh (ed), *Internet of Things – Evolutions and Innovations* (ISTE Ltd and John Wiley & Sons, Inc 2017) 21; Hwaiyu Geng, Internet of Things and Data – Analytics Handbook (John Wiley & Sons, Inc 2017).

risks may depend upon the specific digital environment into which one product is implemented.

Finally, user behaviour is more crucial for IT-risks than for other products: Mistakes while implementing software, misunderstandings of settings, refusal to accept necessary patches or just forgetting them etc. can hamper IT-security and any efforts of producers to reduce risks. Moreover, users themselves can contribute to endangering third parties if they use non secured systems or passwords which are easily hacked so that they become – unknowingly – part of huge bot net that uses their items in order to distribute malware etc.[7]

III. Traditional liability rules (briefly)

In order to assess liability gaps we have to briefly check the existing liability rules, be it on the European or on the national level.[8]

1. Product liability directive

On the European level, the product liability directive (PLD)[9] focusses on defect products as the trigger for liability. Only 'physical products' are covered by the PLD[10] – thus, excluding all kinds of services or information. As of now, software is not being considered a product as long as software is not embedded in hardware.[11] On the other hand, as 'Internet of

7 Regarding the human factor in IT-Security see for instance <https://www.kaspersky.com/blog/the-human-factor-in-it-security/> accessed 14 June 2016; also <http://www.verizonenterprise.com/resources/reports/2017_dbir_en_xg.pdf> accessed 14 June 2018.

8 Of course, a vaste comparative law approach would be the best way in order to distinguish several approaches – what, however, would need a larger scope of the study.

9 Council Directive of (EEC) 85/374 on the approximation of the laws, regulations and administrative provisions of the Member States concerning liability for defective products [1985] OJ L210/29.

10 Art 2 S. 1 PLD states: 'For the purpose of this Directive "product" means all movables'.

11 See for instance: *Produzentenhaftung*, no 3603, p. 8 (2/2017 August 2017); Sebastian Rockstroh and Hanno Kunkel, 'IT Sicherheit in Produktionsumgebungen' [2017] MMR 77, 82; Michael Lehmann, 'Produkt- und Produzentenhaftung für

Things' products usually embed software – even though they are connected to the cloud – the PLD applies to the full extent to IoT-products. However, what is still unresolved is the extent to which the PLD applies to such products as software may be based entirely in the cloud and is not provided by the producers of the IoT-product rather than by a third party (unbundling of components). Thus, remote control of the IoT-product without any software which is embedded in the IoT-product is outside of the scope of the PLD.

Moreover, the PLD does not address any intermediary problems – which could, however, be crucial for any connected product. Any interruption of connections could result – in the best case – in the turning off of the IoT-product, in the worst case in endangering third parties.

Liability under the PLD is mainly based on the concept of defect of a product, thus, excluding development risks. If a producer respects the state of the art – often, but not exclusively, defined by technical standards – he will be exempted from liability which is why many observers do not classify the PLD as a real strict liability.

Finally, systemic risks and causality problems of IT-products are not resolved by the PLD. Complex interaction of different products can only be covered by the PLD if the relevant (interacting) risks already existed when the product was introduced to the market; however, usually new risks emerge due to a change of digital environment in the post-sale phase, in other terms: when the product already has been designed und first introduced to the market.

2. Traditional liability rules – Negligence

On the national level, producers` liability in some jurisdictions, like the German jurisdiction, is based in tort law, here negligence. Once again, technical standards play a crucial role in determining negligence and lia-

---

Software' [1992] NJW 1721, 1723; Gerald Spindler, 'Verschuldensunabhängige Produkthaftung im Internet' [1998] MMR 119, 120; see also European Commission (COM) 1976/372/FINAL Proposal for a Directive concerning liability for defective products [1976] OJ C241/9; Although for the application of the PLD on software: Answer (Question No. 706/88) on behalf of the Commission [1989] OJ C114/42; K Alheit, 'The applicability of the ED Product Liability Directive to software' [2001] Comparative and International Law Journal of Southern Africa vol 34 issue 2 188, 194 with further references.

bility. Producers benefit, like under the PLD, from an exemption concerning development risks, if they have taken into account the state of the art concerning security and safety. However, in contrast to the PLD traditional negligence concepts also consider post-sale obligations such as monitoring products with reference to emerging risks and warning users against defective products. Moreover, in contrast to the PLD, every damaged party – be it consumer or commercial user – can file a claim against the producer in Germany except for just economic losses.

Further, whereas usually the damaged party has to show evidence for all preconditions of tort liability (such as negligence) courts have developed reversals of burden of proof concerning certain areas, such as compliance with state of the art in construction of products as well as quality monitoring of products when entering into the market. However, at least under German Law apart from negligence there is no general reversal of burden of proof, for instance not concerning causality.

To sum it up, producers` liability based on negligence is a rather flexible concept, which sometimes approaches strict liability in practice as courts interpret negligence standards in a very strict way.

3. Liability of Intermediaries

As mentioned, in particular IoT-products (as well as self-driving cars etc.) rely upon connection to cloud services. Hence, connectivity problems (of intermediaries) may as well result in damages like any other defect even though the IoT-product itself is not affected. Moreover, if networks are not secure they may be hacked by (criminal) third parties inserting malware, viruses, or any other kind of unsolicited content, thus also manipulating IoT-products.

However, intermediaries, in particular telecommunication providers, are grossly exempted from liability. In case of economic losses Sec. 44a of the German Telecommunication Act limits the liability for negligence to a maximum of 12 500 Euro per end user or 10 million Euro in total. Even if network problems led to injuries of life, body or health, for instance, if an IoT-product could not be controlled anymore, it is very problematic to assign liability to network providers as they cannot foresee damages caused by dysfunctionalities of their networks. It is highly probable that courts in such cases would not assign any liability based on negligence to network operators.

Nevertheless, Sec. 109 of the German Telecommunication Act requires network providers to implement safety and security measures – still it is not clear if those safety and security provisions also include civil liability for damaged third parties being affected by security breaches.[12]

Moreover, other intermediaries also benefit from a wide range of liability privileges, in particular the safe harbour privileges of the E-Commerce-Directive[13] enshrined in Art 12 – 15. Access providers are exempted from any liability and responsibility for the content and services they carry, even if they know the content is illicit. Host providers can only be held liable for third party content if they had knowledge or evidence that the content or service is illicit (notice-and-take-down). It is still unresolved if these providers also benefit from safe harbour privileges if hackers invade platforms or networks; from our perspective, in these cases safe harbour privileges cannot be applied.[14]

4. User/Operator liability

Furthermore, liability of users and operators also has to be taken into account. This is quite obvious for commercial operators using IoT-products or artificial intelligence. If they cannot control their product due to its unpredictable behaviour and if thus damages occur to third parties (or their clients) their liability is also at stake. First, contractual liability may be applied if damaged parties had been in contractual relationships with the operator, for instance in hospitals using medical AI-robots. Without any contractual relationship (so-called bystander) it depends on the activity of commercial operators if strict liability (such as for self-driving cars) or

12 Sec. 91ff. German Telecommunication Act are considered as protective statutes in sense of Sec. 823 (2) German Civil Code; Gerald Spindler, '§ 823 BGB Rn. 330' in *BeckOGK BGB* (C.H.Beck 2018).

13 Directive of the European Parliament and of the Council (EC) 2000/31 on certain legal aspects of information society services, in particular electronic commerce, in the Internal Market ('Directive on electronic commerce') [2000] OJ L178/1.

14 Gerald Spindler, 'Vor §§ 7 TMG, Rn. 32' in Spindler/Schmitz (eds), *Telemediengesetz* (C.H.Beck 2015) with further references; see also Andreas Dustmann, *Die privilegierten Provider* (Nomos 2001) 136; Jörg Podehl, 'Internetportale mit journalistisch-redaktionellen Inhalten Anbieterpflichten und Haftungsrisiken' [2001] MMR 17, 21.

negligence-based tort law would apply, for instance for any other kind of robot outside of strict liability areas.

Even consumers may be held liable if they cause damages to third parties, in particular if they neglect any safety measures like using secure passwords or implementing urgent patches. If they operate unsafe systems which enable third parties to hack their systems, thus implementing botnets or other kind of malware which attack other people, consumers may face civil liability. However, as of right now, there are no known court cases/decisions regarding that matter; it is highly probable that courts would declare consumers only liable if they acted with gross negligence or if they ignored warnings by their operators or public warnings.

The same would apply if consumers were using robots without reading instructions or updating their software; third parties affected may seek relief against them on the base of tort law concerning (gross) negligence. However, there is no strict liability for using robots by private parties so that effectiveness of traditional liability rules depend on what can be required of a consumer concerning negligence.

One of the major problems, however, which seems to be responsible for the lack of cases refers once again to causality. In contrast to dysfunctional robots in case of botnets causation is hard to be determined; usually, private parties are not forced to protocol and log everything on their devices so that evidence for causality is hard to provide.

5. *Impact of contractual provisions*

As mentioned already, IoT-products differ from traditional products in a crucial way as services and software may be operated from third parties 'outside' the product – or at least interact with software embedded in those products, for instance self-driving cars interacting with external databases and servers. Operators and users of these products usually have to enter into contractual relationships with these external providers, at least concerning End User License Agreements which on their side often contain clauses related to liability. Moreover, such contractual relations are not limited to copyright issues rather than to any kind of external service such as intermediaries, cloud providers, or databases like GPS-location based data. For instance, contracts with access providers (or telecommunication providers) often contain clauses which limit the availability of the networks to a certain amount, such as 90% availability.[15]

These liability limitations cannot exempt service and other providers from any kind of liability: Under the unfair contract terms directive[16] liability clauses restricting liability for injuries etc. are void concerning B2C-contracts. Concerning economic losses, EU law does not provide for harmonization on standard terms and conditions so that in most jurisdictions some sort of a cap or restriction for liability is allowed.[17]

Concerning liability clauses in B2B-contracts, most European jurisdictions do not apply – like the very strict German jurisdiction – the unfairness test of the directive so that liability clauses are permitted grosso modo.[18] Hence, for IoT-products used by commercial operators it is very likely that service providers (software, database etc.) are benefitting from liability restrictions. Moreover, usually End User License Agreements use choice-of-law clauses in B2B relationships – which in B2C-cases are not in general void but overruled by mandatory consumer protection provisions of the state where the consumer lives, Art 6 (1) Rom-I-Regulation.

A specific problem which also affects IoT-products refers to open source code, which is widely used in industry for designing IT-products. The GPL – as the globally most used license – restricts liability even in cases of intentional damaging;[19] even though such a clause is void under European contract law (also for B2B-contracts) it is acknowledged that Open Source Code is given away for free, thus benefitting from traditional

15 See for instance: 'General performance description, No. 2.4.1 (Deutsche Telekom)' <https://www.telekom.de/dlp/agb/pdf/44642.pdf> accessed 18 June 2018; 'General performance description, No. 9 (1&1)' <http://var.uicdn.net/pdfs/1und1_Leistungsbeschreibung_Mobilfunk.pdf> accessed 14 June 2018.

16 Council directive (EEC) 93/13 on unfair terms in consumer contracts [1993] OJ L95/29.

17 German jurisdiction only allows restrictions for non-foreseeable damages – in most cases, courts declare liability restrictions void.

18 For a comparative overview on the implementation of the unfair contract terms directive in Europe see: Hans Schulte-Nölke and others, 'EC Consumer Law Compendium – Comparative Analysis' (2007) 1 (341) <http://ec.europa.eu/consumers/archive/cons_int/safe_shop/acquis/comp_analysis_en.pdf> accessed 14 June 2018; also Elissavet Kapnopoulou, *Das Recht der missbräuchlichen Klauseln in der Europäischen Union* (Mohr Siebeck 1997).

19 'GNU General Public License (GPL) v. 3.0, Sec. 16' <https://www.gnu.org/licenses/gpl-3.0> accessed 14 June 2018.

reduction of liability in case of gratuitous contracts, such as restricting liability to gross negligence.

To sum it up, if operators (or even consumers) may be held liable for a defective IoT-product or a robot, they may be faced with severe problems to take redress against external providers of services, databases, or software if they used liability limitations. Hence, operators are left with the risks of using IoT-products with a large amount of external services; only if redress would mandatorily apply to those services and overrule contractual clauses, the risks would be allocated to producers (software providers etc.)

Even though the original directive proposal of the EU concerning digital content contracts (CSDC)[20] tried to address the problem of liability it is actually not part of the proposed directive any more, thus, completely leaving liability issues to the Member States.[21] Moreover, the proposed directive up until now excludes embedded software and alike products from its scope so that IoT-products may be hard to assess under the Digital Content Directive.

IV. Challenges for new regulations

1. Principles: The scale of regulation from product security to product liability

Given the mentioned pitfalls concerning liability for IT-products in general and IoT and autonomous systems in particular, a whole scale of regulatory options have to be considered, which refers to strict liability, liability based on negligence, as well as liability exemptions, combined with caps on liability or mandatory insurances. Moreover, liability for IT-products cannot be dealt with without taking into account product security (of administrative law) and technical standards specifying crucial notions such as defect or negligence. Both legal areas are closely intertwined with en-

---

20 European Commission, Proposal of a directive on certain aspects concerning contracts for the supply of digital content, COM (2015) 634 final, 2015/0287 (COD); for an overview see: Gerald Spindler, 'Contracts For the Supply of Digital Content – Scope of application and basic approach – Proposal of the Commission for a Directive on contracts for the supply of digital content' [2016] ERCL 12(3) 183.

21 See recital 43, 44 CSDC.

forcement issues, suffering from different pitfalls, be it small claims (if there are no class actions) or lack of sophisticated manpower (supervisory authorities). Thus, a regulatory approach should be taken as a mix of different legal instruments – just concentrating on one tool such as strict liability would probably not strike the right balance.

Concerning liability, we first have to sort out what the general principles are which should decide which regime of liability has to be chosen in order to cope with the mentioned issues. One of the leading principles based on institutional economics refers to the 'cheapest cost avoider'[22]: Those who are in the best position to control risks should also be the ones who are liable for damages occurred by third parties. Concerning strict liability, such a regime should be selected if the risk can be eliminated either by the injurer or the victim and the injurer is the cheapest cost avoider;[23] in contrast liability based on negligence is the best suited regulation if both parties – injurer and victim – are able to prevent the damages by (efficiently) taking due care.[24]

Hence, in general strict liability is preferable when the producer`s level of care cannot really influence the risks inherent to the product; in other terms, and mostly relevant for AI-products with more or less unpredictable behaviour: strict liability may be best suited if high risks and legal interests are involved and systems are not acting in a somehow deterministic environment any more.

Furthermore, it is arguable whether or not strict liability is always the best choice: Negligence based approaches or such, as the PLD, based on the notion of defects exempt industry from development risks, thus, enhancing technological progress. Whereas it is true that this exemption results in an – in principle undesirable – externalisation of risk to the detriment of third parties, it may turn out that such an externalisation is to some extent needed to not deter any developers. In other terms: perfect liability schemes may be ideal at a certain point of time in an ideal world but

---

22 See Steven Shavell, *Foundations of Economic Analysis of Law* (Belknap Press of Harvard University Press 2004), 189: 'least cost avoider'; also Hans Bernd Schäfer and Claus Ott, *Lehrbuch der ökonomischen Analyse des Zivilrechts* (5th edn, Springer Gabler 2012), 252.

23 See Steven Shavell (n 22) 190. However, in cases of reciprocal accidents the strict liability should be accompanied by the possibility of the defense of contributory negligence to induce also the victims to take appropriate precautions.

24 See Steven Shavell (n 22) 190.

are not the best solution when technologies evolve. How the balance has to be struck is hard to say; however, there are good reasons for strict liability stepping in after a certain time of product evolution if hazards are not too high and it is acceptable for society. Vice versa, strict liability should be used at the very beginning of a technology`s development when risks and involved potential damages are so high that society could not accept them, like for nuclear plants. Hence, a one-size-fits-all approach for strict liability does not seem to be appropriate but should be coupled with sector-specific assessments of risks and involved legal interests.

Here, product security regulation can be an important issue. As for pharmaceutical products (Sec. 84 (1) German Act on Pharmaceutical Products) shows safety regulation can integrate liability thus forming a holistic approach.

2. *Liability regimes*

a) *Producers of IoT- and AI-products*

aa) The case for strict liability for IoT and AI-products

Applying the afore mentioned principles there is a strong case for strict liability for those products which are steered by artificial intelligence. Likewise, in other technologies which hazards and risks cannot really be determined in advance IT-products with AI 'suffer' from unpredictable behaviour.

Technical standards may help to some extent concerning the traditional notion of defect; however, as these products modify themselves their software and their paradigms (but not the basic aims and preferences) technical standards can only be generic and management procedure orientated – as the whole product is dynamic. Hence, it seems to be more suitable that the producer should choose the level of activity and to give him strong incentives to design the product as safe and secure as possible than to rely upon the notion of 'defect'.[25] Strict liability also does not suffer from one

25 See Gerald Spindler, 'Roboter, Automation, künstliche Intelligenz, selbst-steuernde Kfz – Braucht das Recht neue Haftungskategorien?' (2015) CR, 766 (774); similiar Gerhard Wagner, 'Produkthaftung für autonome Systeme' (2017) AcP vol 217, 707 (762ff)

of most crucial problems of technical standards, the slowliness of developing and adopting technical standards (particular in the IT-sector). As liability does not depend on those standards and does not even require any expertise for assessing damages and responsibility it does not need to be adapted according to the technical progress.

Further, strict liability can cope better with multi-purpose products as it is simply irrelevant what the user's purpose of using the product is – in contrast to defect which is on one side not related to contractual relations, but refers to 'justified expectations of users in general', thus referring to normal purposes.

Last but not least, strict liability would not refer to management procedures or product monitoring etc.; as producers are liable for any hazard of the product at any time (within the boundaries of prescription) they should have a strong incentive to patch their products in order to keep them safe and secure in developing digital environments.

However, following an old tradition in strict liability it should be coupled with a cap, thus limiting liability to a certain extent. Caps can facilitate the job for insurers as producers are not faced with an incalculable liability. Moreover, caps for strict liability do not exclude damaged parties to claim further damages, then based on negligence or other liability provisions. The extent of the cap should be determined according to the sector in which the product is being used. Thus, the problem for the producer to calculate the risks[26] could be solved.

However, even though strict liability seems to solve a lot of problems some of them persist:

Strict liability would, like the PLD, still refer to the notion of 'producer'. Nevertheless, as it has been mentioned already, IoT-products often are 'unbundled' and not sold or brought into the market as a stand-alone-product any more, in other terms: which would work only in combination with services online. Hence, the 'producer' of such an IoT-product could only be held liable if services online etc. are qualified as suppliers' product. Thus, strict liability has to be extended to a new 'end-of-pipeline' principle: Whereas under existing PLD producers already are liable for every pre-product they integrate in their final product it has to be extended to software and services, which are part of the product being sold but provid-

26 For this reason rejecting strict liablity Borges 'Rechtliche Rahmenbedingungen für autonome Systeme' (2018) NJW 977 (981).

ed by third parties. Nonetheless, even though such an end-of-pipeline principle may work out for IoT-products it cannot resolve modifications of services and software after the product has been brought into the market – what is, however, quite typical. This unbundling process finally points to some sort of hybrid-situation between traditional product liability and contractual liability: if the user wants to sell his item to a third party he has to also transfer all service contracts etc. to the third party. Bystanders which are not part of contractual relationships may then benefit from some sort of third-party effects of contracts – as it is known under certain jurisdictions such as the German one.

To sum it up, this hybrid-solution already points out the general problem, that a perspective restricted to product liability would not really be fit for the modern networked industry and products.

bb) Negligence based liability

Beyond strict liability there is still ample room for negligence-based liability: If caps of strict liability are exceeded or strict liability is not applicable at all (due to lower risk which will be discussed later), negligence-based liability still is an important factor. Thus, the traditional role of technical standards to define the state of the art for products (and so negligence) continues to influence liability[27] – however, with all well-known problems as well (slowliness of the adoption of technical standards, prone to influences of stakeholders, not suited to individual hazards etc.).

Moreover, by means of technical standards management procedures can be required concerning the cycle of testing products, monitoring products (after-sale) and testing algorithms pre- and after-sale – following blue prints of quality management system already in place concerning product security. These management requirements can be combined with product security provisions also based on elements of (quality) management systems – such as the New Approach.

Furthermore, concerning burden of proof the damaged party should not be obliged to show evidence for negligence of the producer – according to court practice in some jurisdictions the producer should be required to prove that he has not acted negligent.

---

27 cf also Denga, 'Deliktische Haftung für künstliche Intelligenz' (2017) CR 69, 71ff.

cc) Causality

One of the problems which affect all kinds of liability regimes refers to causality, be it strict liability or liability based on negligence. As shown, it is hard to establish a causal link between an IT-product and the damage occurred. This is quite independent of the liability framework chosen as strict liability also requires a causality between the risks of the product and the damage. The problem of causality and the interaction of complex products can only be overcome by using an approach which is known from environmental liability provisions: the reversal of burden of proof concerning causality for emissions. As for environmental damages it is also hard to assess whether a specific problem (the 'emission') exactly caused the relevant damage (the 'immersion') or if the damage has just been caused by multiple factors (multiple 'emissions') which can be retraced after all or which only caused the damage in a cumulative way. Thus, to cope with this problem a joint liability with a reversal of the burden of proof has to be introduced – in the end coming very close to the market-share approach sometimes taken in the U.S. concerning environmental damages.[28]

Another way to cope with causality problems in particular concerning digital environments etc is to use technical means to document use of IT-products, in other terms: log files or event recorders like they are used as black boxes in air traffic in order to retrace influences on technical systems in case of accidents. Such an approach recently has been taken in the German Act on Road Traffic, Sec. 63a (1). However, such log files or event recorders also induce severe data protection problems: If third parties are allowed to read the memory of such recorders, they can easily inspect the whole digital environment of the affected party, thus deeply intruding their privacy sphere. The already mentioned proposal of the EU-commission concerning Digital Content contracts faces the same problem when it allows the retailer to inspect the digital environment of the client with regard to claims for defective products, Art 9 (3) CSDC.[29]

---

28 See also Gerald Spindler, 'Kausalität im Zivil- und Wirtschaftsrecht' (2016) AcP vol 208, 283 (296ff).

29 See Gerald Spindler, 'Contracts For the Supply of Digital Content – Scope of application and basic approach – Proposal of the Commission for a Directive on contracts for the supply of digital content' [2016] ERCL 12(3) 183 (203).

dd) Redress problems

IT-products, IoT-products in particular, are structured in a complex way and are mostly not crafted by just one producer; self-driving cars consisting of a variety of elements demonstrate this complexity in a perfect way. Hence, in order to effectively render producer liability – according to the cheapest cost avoider approach and internalization of risks/damages – the right of redress is crucial. However, contracts with suppliers may provide restrictions of liability so that producers cannot effectively take redress – which is quite probable in case of big IT-players with sufficient market power. Thus, product liability provisions should also provide for mandatory rights to redress in order to overcome such blocking of liability along the supply chain.

However, a particular problem concerning redress refers to the use of Open Source Code: As the GPL (and all other Open Source licenses) contains strict limitations of liability, producers cannot file claims (against whom?) based on defects of Open Source. Introducing a mandatory right to redress would contradict the basic idea of Open Source and backlash public interest in free available software. That is why such a mandatory right to redress has to be limited to commercially produced software.

ee) In sum: a concept for hybrid liability: Contracts – strict liability – negligence

To sum it up, the picture of liability is a complex one: it would be inefficient to only concentrate on strict liability of producers as modern IoT-products are embedded in complex networks and net-based services. Strict liability should be coupled with specific product regulation like for self-driving cars or medical robots where hazards are essential for society. Negligence based liability should be maintained in areas of middle or low risks giving leeway to the development of new technologies. Mandatory rights to redress should flank product liability.

b) User/Operators

Concerning users and operators of IoT-products, in particular autonomous systems, the same reasons as for producers apply concerning strict liability: If their products endanger their surrounding (bystanders, third parties) in a significant way, they should also be held liable on the basis of strict liability, in particular if the behaviour of their system in use cannot really be controlled and predicted. Blueprint for such liability regime are liability provisions for car keepers or pet owners, known in many jurisdictions such as the German one. Even for non-commercial users there is a strong case for liability if risks cannot be controlled – flanked by a cap concerning damages.

However, the traditional argument for strict liability – lowering level of activity according to the risks – cannot be easily transposed to IT-products as users have to rely upon these products as an essential part of their life. Without routers, for instance, users cannot access the Internet which has become a fundamental part of life.

Thus, mandatory insurances for users are necessary in order to relieve users of existential risks, also to ensure that third parties will be compensated for any damages. Moreover, mandatory insurances are more able to claim redress against producers as they gather information about casualties and dispose of more resources than (private) users.

As for producer`s liability, strict liability is not in all cases suited, particularly not when risks are low. Negligence standards can cope better with lacking resources or abilities of users to check safety and security of their products; on the other hand, liability based on negligence could induce users to take basic safety actions such as choosing secure passwords and patching their systems systematically. Also, negligence standards could be differentiated according to the status of the user, such as gross negligence for non-commercial users and normal negligence for commercial operators.

3. Intermediaries

Last but not least, the role of intermediaries has to be clarified, in particular if there is a need to change their liability regime or not. The starting point for discussion should be the 'neutrality' of networks – as codified recently by the EU-Regulation on Net Neutrality (Regulation (EU)

2015/2120)[30]; as mentioned, access providers and telecommunication providers usually do not have any information on what purposes their services are used for. Hence, they cannot calculate the risk and adopt their activity levels which justifies the broad liability exemptions. Unless it is a special network dedicated to just a class or one IoT-product, for instance car-networks for a fleet of cars (BMW-connect etc.), the operator of the network hardly has any knowledge about risks involved when his system is used.

Whereas there is a strong case for liability exemption or at least limiting liability in case of not foreseeable damages and disruptions of the service is it arguable if the same is true for damages occurred due to security breaches. Here, at least a negligence based approach would incentivize network operators to respect technical standards and minimum safety settings, in order to avoid any hacking or intrusion to their networks. Such a liability should be flanked by an obligation to notify security breaches – like in Art 33 GDPR[31] for data protection.

Finally, with regard to product security producers should be obliged to design their product in a user- and safety-friendly way. With regard to intermediaries, IoT-products should be designed in such a way that the product automatically shuts off if the connection is lost or – better – hand the control back to the user with a due warning.

4. *Interplay with Product Security*

As indicated, liability rules should not be designed separately from product security (administrative law). According to the risks, IoT-products with high risks should need an ex-ante permission, for instance for medical applications, whereas other IoT-products may benefit from lower regu-

30 Regulation (EU) 2015/2120 of the European Parliament and of the Council of 25 November 2015 laying down measures concerning open internet access an amending Directive 2002/22/EC on universal service and users' rights relating to electronic communications networks and services and Regulation (EU) No. 531/2012 on roaming on public mobile communications networks within the Union, OJ L310/1.

31 Regulation (EU) 2016/679 of the European Parliament and of the Council of 27 April 2016 on the protection of natural persons with regard to the processing of personal data and on the free movement of such data, and repealing Directive 95/46/EC (General Data Protection Regulation), OJ L 119/1.

lations such as an ex-post control of the supervisory authorities. In both cases, technical standards play a crucial role – even though they suffer from IT-specific problems such as quick business cycles and complex, highly variable uses of IT.[32]

IV. Conclusion

Liability for IT-products suffers from several problems that are due to specific characteristics of IT. Whereas these problems are not new (and for a longer time well-known), new IoT and the use of artificial intelligence in particular pose new problems that are due to the unpredictable behaviour of IoT-systems. Hence, it seems reasonable to introduce a strict liability regime for severe risks in order to avoid problems resulting of negligence-based liability provisions, such as slow adoption of technical standards and proof of defect etc. Such a strict liability, however, should be introduced sector-specific and according to high risks; not all IoT-products and artificial intelligence usages imply high risks. In addition, there may be good reason to allow development risks, at least for a certain time, in order to enhance new technologies. Hence, in some areas with less risk negligence based approaches to liability may still be sufficient. In addition, if IoT-products are 'unbundled' in hardware and services/software based on the cloud contractual liability becomes more important; hence, in addition to the unfair terms and conditions directive liability clauses should be banned beyond the existing state of the art. Moreover, mandatory rights to redress should be introduced.

The same reasoning concerning strict liability applies to commercial users in area with high risks, once again in the medical sector. These liability provisions should be flanked by mandatory insurances which can seek redress against producers with no way to contract around. For non-commercial users negligence-based liability provisions still are suited as they can only be blamed for basic safety measures such as secure passwords or constant patching.

Finally, product liability always has to be perceived together with product security regulation, including technical standards and certifications.

---

32 For a more thorough analysis cf Gerald Spindler, *Interplay of Technical Standards and Product Security and Liability* (forthcoming).

New Liability Concepts: the Potential of Insurance and Compensation Funds

Georg Borges[*]

I. Introduction

1. Autonomous systems and damage as an everyday occurrence

Autonomous systems have become embedded in the daily lives of humans. Autonomous cars, which are the autonomous systems currently attracting most public attention, have already been admitted to general road traffic in some US States.[1] In Germany, autonomous cars are being taken onto public streets in a rapidly increasing number of testing projects. The first international testing area for autonomous vehicles including German roads is has been established in Saarland, Lothringen and Luxemburg.[2] Autonomous vehicles are not the only form of autonomous system which are enjoying increased acceptance in today's society. Indeed, it could be said that the vacuum-cleaner robot is Germany's favourite child. Sales of vacuum-cleaner robots make up a quarter of all vacuum- cleaners in Germany and this trend is rising.[3]

---

* Professor of Law, Chair for Private Law, Legal Informatics, German and International Business Law, Legal Theory, Saarland University. The author gratefully acknowledges the valuable support by the chair's team, particularly by Caroline Hertwig and Andreas Sesing.

1 For details, see the overview of the legislation provided by the U.S. National Conference of State Legislatures (NCSL), <www.ncsl.org/research/transportation/autonomous-vehicles-self-driving-vehicles-enacted-legislation.aspx> accessed 20 July 2018.

2 Benjamin Auerbach, 'Zwischen Merzig und Metz entsteht digitale Teststrecke' (Springer Professional, 9 February 2017) <www.springerprofessional.de/automatisiertes-fahren/car-to-x/zwischen-merzig-und-metz-entsteht-digitale-teststrecke/12054984> accessed 20 July 2018.

3 'Die Roboter kommen: Staubsaugermarkt im Umbruch' (metoda blog, 21 November 2017) <http://blog.metoda.com/die-roboter-kommen-staubsaugermarkt-im-umbruch/> accessed 20 July 2018.

At the same time however, damage caused by autonomous systems arrive in daily life. Again, autonomous vehicles attract most public attention. In 2016, the first fatal accident involving a Tesla car driving autonomously caused worldwide consternation. In this case, the Tesla ran into a truck killing its driver. The car was equipped with an advanced driving assistant system of Level 2 according to SAE classification[4] which was, however, called 'autopilot' by its producer. As investigation of the accident reached the conclusion that the driver took this description too literally and relied upon using the car as a really 'autonomous' vehicle which the car however never was.[5]

In January 2018, the first claim was submitted against the manufacturer of an autonomous car in California. The claim alleged that the manufacturer was responsible for the accident.[6]

In February 2018, an Uber-car which was driving autonomously caused the death of a pedestrian.[7] The news of this event was greeted with shock and intensified the debate about the safety of autonomous cars.[8] It should be noted that, in this case, it is still unclear whether the accident was in

---

4 The classification issued by the US Society of Automotive Engineers (SAE) consists of six levels of automation (level 0 to 5) where level 0 is no automation, SAE, 'Taxonomy and Definitions for Terms Related to Driving Automation Systems for On-Road Motor Vehicles, J3016' (June 2018) 19 <www.sae.org/standards/content/j3016_201806/> accessed 20 July 2018.

5 See National Transportation Safety Board (NTSB), 'Official investigation report' (12 September 2017) Doc. No. HAR-17/02, 35ff <www.ntsb.gov/investigations/AccidentReports/Reports/HAR1702.pdf> accessed 20 July 2018.

6 Samuel Gibbs, 'GM sued by motorcyclist in first lawsuit to involve autonomous vehicle' (The Guardian, 24 January 2018) <www.theguardian.com/technology/2018/jan/24/general-motors-sued-motorcyclist-first-lawsuit-involve-autonomous-vehicle> accessed 20 July 2018.

7 Daisuke Wakabayashi, 'Self-Driving Uber Car Kills Pedestrian in Arizona, Where Robots Roam' (The New York Times, 19 March 2018) <www.nytimes.com/2018/03/19/technology/uber-driverless-fatality.html> accessed 20 July 2018.

8 Since then, several articles dealing with the safety have been published, see for example Dara Kerr, 'Are driverless cars safe? Uber fatality raises questions' (CNET, 21 March 2018) <www.cnet.com/news/uber-self-driving-car-fatality-in-arizona-has-people-asking-how-safe-are-driverless-cars/> accessed 20 July 2018; 'Driverless cars and the imperative of safety' (Financial Times, 20 March 2018) <www.ft.com/content/df4b266e-2c2f-11e8-9b4b-bc4b9f08f381> accessed 20 July 2018; Keith Naughton, 'Just How Safe Is Driverless Car Technology, Really?' (Bloomberg, 27 March 2018) <www.bloomberg.com/news/articles/2018-03-27/just-how-safe-is-driverless-car-technology-really-quicktake> accessed 20 July 2018; Bob O'Donnell,

fact caused by the pedestrian herself and thus unavoidable for both the 'driver' who was sitting in the car as well as for the car itself. An interim report on the investigation however showed that the system was not able to clearly identify the pedestrian.[9]

In March 2018, the second fatal accident involving the autopilot-function of a Tesla was reported, when the vehicle, driving in autopilot-mode drove its driver into a concrete wall and fatally injured him.[10]

2. *The role of insurance and compensation funds in the current discussion*

The reported accidents involving self-driving cars raise the question of whether society is actually ready for such systems. Consideration of whether current technical systems are sufficiently mature and whether the users are experienced enough to deal with them is required. From a legal perspective the key question is whether current legal systems are sufficiently prepared for autonomous systems or whether further development is required.

Through its Resolution of 16 February 2017 on Civil Law Rules on Robotics (the Resolution),[11] the European Parliament has stepped up the debate about the development of legal systems for the digital society. This Resolution focusses on responsibility for damage caused by autonomous systems.

'How safe should we expect self-driving cars to be?' (USA Today, 8 April 2018) <https://eu.usatoday.com/story/tech/columnist/2018/04/08/how-safe-should-we-expect-autonomous-cars/451494002/> accessed 20 July 2018.

9 See the findings of the report below II.2.

10 'Tesla in fatal California crash was on Autopilot' (BBC News, 31 March 2018) <www.bbc.com/news/world-us-canada-43604440> accessed 20 July 2018.

11 European Parliament Resolution of 16 February 2017 with recommendations to the Commission on Civil Law Rules on Robotics (2015/2103(INL)), A8-0005/2017, <www.europarl.europa.eu/sides/getDoc.do?pubRef=-//EP//NONSGML+TA+P8-TA-2017-0051+0+DOC+PDF+V0//EN> accessed 20 July 2018; also Georg Borges, 'Rechtliche Rahmenbedingungen für autonome Systeme' [2018] NJW 977ff; Jan-Philipp Günther, 'Europäische Regelungen im Bereich Robotik – alles noch Science Fiction?' [2017] DB 651; Oliver Keßler, 'Intelligente Roboter – neue Technologien im Einsatz' [2017] MMR 589; Melinda F. Lohmann, 'Ein europäisches Roboterrecht – überfällig oder überflüssig?' [2017] ZRP 168.

It is noteworthy that, in this context, the European Parliament places some emphasis on the idea of introducing compulsory insurance schemes and compensation funds for autonomous systems. Thus, the Resolution provides the impetus for a consideration of the potential of these instruments in the context of responsibility for autonomous systems.

II. Insurance

1. Insurance for autonomous systems in the current discussion

Insurance is a key factor in how society deals with damage caused by complex technical systems and it is undisputed that insurance will be an important element of the legal framework of autonomous systems.

Insurance covering damage caused by autonomous systems already exists: For example, the autonomous parking of cars is covered by compulsory third party vehicle insurance as well as by comprehensive insurance. However, it is clear from the Resolution that the European Parliament considers insurance to be an area with much bigger potential in the context of autonomous systems. The Resolution specifically proposes, in its Paragraph 59 a), the idea of establishing 'a compulsory insurance scheme […] whereby [...], producers, or owners of robots would be required to take out insurance cover for the damage potentially caused by their robots' as a possible solution.[12] The idea of introducing compulsory insurance is also explicitly mentioned in the concluding summary and its recommendations to the Commission's requested proposal.[13]

To summarise, the European Parliament proposes compulsory insurance for the users and manufactures of autonomous systems.

2. The liability system for autonomous systems

Compulsory insurance for users or manufacturers of autonomous systems is extrinsically linked to liability systems in general as insurance covering liability risks is only relevant to the extent that such liability risks exist. Thus, in order to be able to discuss compulsory insurance for autonomous

12 European Parliament Resolution (n 11) 15.
13 European Parliament Resolution (n 11) 18.

systems it will be necessary to make reference to existing liability systems.

The liability of users and manufacturers of autonomous systems has been widely discussed recently,[14] and different positions are taken in the question of whether the current liability system needs modification in the light of autonomous systems. As this debate cannot be outlined in this paper in detail, some theses on liability for autonomous systems will be set out below to serve as the basis for further reflection on the importance of insurance in the context of autonomous systems.

Thesis 1: the current liability system contains gaps.

The current legal system in Germany contains gaps in respect of liability for autonomous systems. By way of an example, there is no tortious liability for the user of a system, such as the driver of an autonomous car, when such system is operating autonomously because there is no obligation for the user to take any action.[15] To the extent that a car is permitted to drive autonomously, and in fact does so, the driver, who has, in effect,

---

14 Andreas Börding, Tim Jülicher,Charlotte Röttgen and Max von Schönfeld, 'Neue Herausforderungen der Digitalisierung für das deutsche Zivilrecht' [2017] CR 134ff; Borges (n 11) 980ff; Peter Bräutigam and Thomas Klindt, 'Industrie 4.0, das Internet der Dinge und das Recht' [2015] NJW 1137ff; Malte Grützmacher, 'Die deliktische Haftung für autonome Systeme – Industrie 4.0 als Herausforderung für das bestehende Recht?' [2016] CR 695ff; Jochen Hanisch, 'Zivilrechtliche Haftungskonzepte für Roboter' in Eric Hilgendorf and Jan-Philipp Günther (eds), *Robotik und Gesetzgebung* (Nomos 2013) 109ff; Susanne Horner and Markus Kaulartz, 'Verschiebung des Sorgfaltsmaßstabs bei Herstellung und Nutzung autonomer Systeme' [2016] CR 7ff; Renate Schaub, 'Interaktion von Mensch und Maschine' [2017] JZ 342, 343ff; Indra Spiecker gen. Döhmann, 'Zur Zukunft systemischer Digitalisierung – Erste Gedanken zur Haftungs- und Verantwortungszuschreibung bei informationstechnischen Systemen' [2016] CR 698ff; Gerald Spindler, 'Roboter, Automation, künstliche Intelligenz, selbststeuernde Kfz – Braucht das Recht neue Haftungskategorien?' [2015] CR 766ff.

15 Georg Borges, 'Haftung für selbstfahrende Autos' [2016] CR 272, 273; Paul T. Schrader, 'Haftungsrechtlicher Begriff des Fahrzeugführers bei zunehmender Automatisierung von Kraftfahrzeugen' [2015] NJW 3537, 3541; implicitly Volker M. Jänich, Paul T. Schrader and Vivian Reck, 'Rechtsprobleme des autonomen Fahrens' [2015] NZV 313, 316, who put their focus on the level of automation on which the system is currently working; similar for driving assistance systems Frank Albrecht, 'Die rechtlichen Rahmenbedingungen bei der Implementierung von Fahrerassistenzsystemen zur Geschwindigkeitsbeeinflussung' [2005] DAR 186, 190; Frank Albrecht, '"Fährt der Fahrer oder das System?" – Anmerkungen aus rechtlicher Sicht' [2005] SVR 373, 374; Ulrich Berz, Eva Dedy and Claudia

become a passenger in this car, cannot be found to have made a driving error. The same could be said to apply to tortious liability for the operators of autonomous systems.[16]

Strict liability of the operator only exists in certain situations. In the case of autonomous cars, it exists in the form of the liability of the registered keeper of the vehicle pursuant to the German Road Traffic Act (StVG). In other situations, there is a lack of statutory basis.[17]

The liability of the manufacturer contains gaps as compensation pursuant to Product Liability law will frequently not be available in the case of autonomous systems.[18] The reason for this is two-fold. Firstly, the requirement that the product be defective is a significant barrier to liability and secondly, and perhaps more importantly, the procedural requirement to prove the existence of a defect in a lawsuit can be an impediment to successfully claim compensation.

This can be illustrated by reference to the most recent accidents involving self-driving cars mentioned above. It has not yet been clarified whether the pedestrian was killed as a result of a product defect of the self-driving Uber-car.

This accident is being examined by the US National Transportation Safety Board. In an interim report on the investigation the board publishes its findings on the car's function before the accident: 'According to data obtained from the self-driving system, the system first registered radar and LIDAR observations of the pedestrian about 6 seconds before impact, when the vehicle was traveling at 43 mph. As the vehicle and pedestrian paths converged, the self-driving system software classified the pedestrian as an unknown object, as a vehicle, and then as a bicycle with varying expectations of future travel path. At 1.3 seconds before impact, the self-

---

Granich, 'Haftungsfragen bei dem Einsatz von Telematik-Systemen im Straßenverkehr' [2000] DAR 545, 547; Wolfgang Vogt, 'Fahrerassistenzsysteme: Neue Technik – Neue Rechtsfragen?' [2003] NZV 153, 156.

16 cf Horner and Kaulartz (n 14) 8; Thomas Riehm, 'Von Drohnen, Google-Cars und Software-Agenten' [2014] ITRB 113, 114; Thomas Schulz, *Verantwortlichkeit bei autonom agierenden Systemen* (Nomos 2015) 143ff; Spindler (n 14) 768.

17 Borges (n 11) 982.

18 cf Grützmacher (n 14) 696; Claus D. Müller-Hengstenberg and Stefan Kirn, 'Intelligente (Software-)Agenten: Eine neue Herausforderung unseres Rechtssystems' [2014] MMR 307, 313; Schaub (n 14) 343.

driving system determined that an emergency braking maneuver was needed to mitigate a collision (see figure 2).'[19]

In the case of the first fatal Tesla accident mentioned above, the US National Transportation Safety Board concluded, in its final investigation report, that the accident was caused by the combined effect and collaboration of several separate causes.[20]

Pursuant to German law, even with the information gathered by the investigation, it is unclear if and to what extent the manufacturer of the vehicle could be held liable for the damage caused by the accidents. It is also clear that, without such information, there would be no realistic chance of holding the manufacturer of the vehicle liable in either of these abovementioned cases.

Thesis 2:generalised strict liability of the operator of an autonomous system is not appropriate

The introduction of generalised strict liability for the operators of autonomous systems could be achieved, for example, by way of a legal provision similar to that which exists for the keeping of luxury animals pursuant to section 833 of the German Civil Code. Although such a provision would appear to be easy to draft, it is doubtful whether this would be a convincing solution.[21] The introduction of objective liability would only be appropriate if the risk is controllable by the person who is being held liable.[22] In the case of autonomous cars, the manufacturer fulfils this requirement. However, in many other situations, this would not be the case.

---

19 National Transportation Safety Board (NTSB), *Preliminary Report Highway HWY18MH010*, (2018) 2 <www.ntsb.gov/investigations/AccidentReports/Reports/HWY18MH010-prelim.pdf> accessed 20 July 2018.

20 NTSB *Investigation report* (n 5) 42.

21 This idea is discussed and rejected by Borges (n 11) 981; Grützmacher (n 14) 698.

22 The controllability of the risk is a leading idea for the introduction of objective liability, see Borges (n 15) 278; also for an explanation of the term strict liability in the sense of the liability model described as objective liability Gert Brüggemeier, *Deliktsrecht* (Nomos 1986) para 30; Susanne Hehl, *Das Verhältnis von Verschuldens- und Gefährdungshaftung* (Roderer 1999) 90; Karl Larenz, 'Die Prinzipien der Schadenszurechnung. Ihr Zusammenspiel im modernen Schuldrecht' [1965] JuS 373, 374; Rudolf Müller-Erzbach, 'Gefährdungshaftung und Gefahrtragung' [1910] AcP vol 106, 309, 413; Max Rümelin, *Schadensersatz ohne Verschulden* (Mohr 1910) 46; contradictory opinions expressed by Andreas Blaschczok, *Gefährdungshaftung und Risikozuweisung* (Carl Heymanns 1993) 66; Johannes Köndgen, *Haftpflichtfunktionen und Immaterialschaden am Beispiel von Schmerzensgeld bei Gefährdungshaftung* (Duncker & Humblot 1976) 32.

Therefore, one can assume that only in some cases imposing strict liability on the operator would be the most appropriate approach as it is often the operator who is best placed to control the risks arising from the use of the autonomous system. The key challenge for an effective liability system is therefore the definition of the field of application of such strict liability.
Thesis 3: generalised strict liability of the manufacturer is not appropriate.

The same reasoning could also be adopted to justify the rejection of the idea of generalised strict liability of the manufacturers of autonomous systems.[23]

Such generalised strict liability would make sense in some individual cases, for example, in the case of autonomous cars,[24] but would not be convincing as a general concept.[25]

In relation to both the strict liability of the operator as well as that of the manufacturer, it is clear that a differentiated solution is required which, for example in the case of autonomous cars, could lead to an appropriate apportionment of the damage between these parties.[26] Again, a central challenge for an effective liability system is therefore the definition of the field of application of such strict liability.
Thesis 4:Liability law should be supplemented by a concept of registration and classification of autonomous systems.

It is implicit in the idea of a differentiating liability regime that the liability system for autonomous systems would have further requirements.

---

23 See for the discussion Benjamin von Bodungen and Martin Hoffmann, 'Autonomes Fahren – Haftungsverschiebung entlang der Supply Chain? (2. Teil)' [2016] NZV 503, 508; Borges (n 11) 977ff; Sabine Gless and Ruth Janal, 'Hochautomatisiertes und autonomes Autofahren – Risiko und rechtliche Verantwortung' [2016] JR 561, 574; Schaub (n 14) 348; Olaf Sosnitza, 'Das Internet der Dinge – Herausforderung oder gewohntes Terrain für das Zivilrecht?' [2016] CR 764, 772; Bernd Wagner and Thilo Goeble, 'Freie Fahrt für das Auto der Zukunft?' [2017] ZD 263, 266.

24 Borges (n 15) 277ff; Georg Borges, 'Herstellerhaftung für selbstfahrende Autos' in Erich Schweighofer and Franz Kummer and Walter Hötzendorfer (eds), *Netzwerke/Networks, Tagungsband des 19. Internationalen Rechtsinformatik Symposions (IRIS)* (Weblaw 2016) 611, 617ff; Merih Kütük-Markendorf, 'Die hoch- oder vollautomatisierte Fahrfunktion als Vorstufe zum autonomen Fahren' [2017] CR 349, 354.

25 Borges (n 11) 981; similar Bodungen and Hoffmann (n 23); Schaub (n 14) 348; Sosnitza (n 23).

26 Borges (n 11) 981.

Indeed, the European Parliament has already recognised this and correctly referred to the necessity of developing and implementing a concept of the registration of autonomous systems.[27]

However, registration itself is not sufficient and more important than the act of registration is the classification of the autonomous system according to its risk potential. Such classification, the criteria for which still need to be developed, must relate to the specific risks of the autonomous systems and can be used as the basis for the compulsory registration and insurance as well as the creation of compensation funds.

The above-mentioned theses lead to the conclusion that development of a liability system for autonomous systems is required and that this liability system should contain differentiated implementation of strict liability as well as additional elements such as the registration of autonomous systems and classification of such systems according to their risk potential.

3. Compulsory insurance for autonomous systems?

The importance of insurance in connection with autonomous systems is an extremely wide-ranging topic and a discussion of this issue in general terms is beyond the scope of this paper. However, this paper deals with one aspect, namely, the question of whether compulsory third party insurance for autonomous systems should be introduced.

a) Purpose of compulsory insurance

Compulsory third party insurance is, in many legal systems including Germany, an established instrument which is utilised in many different branches of the law.[28] An illustration of such a use is the compulsory insurance for the operators of machines where, by way of example, compulso-

---

27 European Parliament Resolution (n 11) 15, 18.

28 A detailed explanation of compulsory third party insurance under German law can be found, for example, from Roland Michael Beckmann, 'Anh. Vor §§ 113–124' in Ernst Bruck and Hans Möller (eds), *Großkommentar zum VVG* (De Gruyter 2014) paras 2ff; Oliver Brand, 'Vorbem. §§ 113–124' in Theo Langheid and Manfred Wandt (eds), *Münchener Kommentar zum VVG* (C.H. Beck 2017) paras 17ff.

ry insurance is required by the registered keepers of vehicles[29], railways[30] as well as aircraft[31] and, in some cases, the use of dangerous installations such as nuclear power stations.[32]

In the area of compulsory insurance for the keepers of animals, the legal framework is manifold. In particular, the compulsory insurance for dog-owners, which each Federal State in Germany regulates itself, impressively demonstrates how it is possible to regulate one legal issue in a number of different ways.[33] Compulsory insurance can also be found in fault-based liability with examples of such insurance being the compulsory insurance of lawyers,[34] architects[35] and tax advisors.[36] On the other hand, the activities of doctors are not subject to any appropriate insurance obligations and no systematic reasons for this are apparent.[37] The legal position in relation to manufacturers of machines is very similar and it is again the case here that no compulsory insurances exist to date.[38]

In summary, it is clear that compulsory insurance is not bound to any particular role. Compulsory insurance is a requirement for operators, for example, those who keep machines and animals, as well as for persons acting in a specific way such as lawyers or tax advisors. It is also not

29 See § 1 PflVG.

30 § 14 para 1 AEG.

31 Insurance obligations exist for both aircraft operators (§§ 2 para 1 No 3, 43 para 2 cl 1 LuftVG) as well as for air carriers (§ 50 para 2 LuftVG).

32 Atomic law, for example, recognises the obligation to provide coverage (§ 13 AtG), which can, amongst other ways, be satisfied through proof of the existence compulsory insurance (§ 14 AtG).

33 See the compilation of the rules on the compulsory insurance for the keepers of dogs by Brand (n 28) para 20.

34 § 51 para 1 cl 1 BRAO.

35 Here, the duty to insure is a matter of State law. See eg § 2a para 3 ArchG BW; §§ 4 para 6 No 5, 17 para 1 No 8 HASG; § 30 ArchIngG M-V; § 22 para 2 No 2 BauKaG NRW; § 2 para 1 No 7 ArchG R-Pf; § 43 para 1 No 5 SAIG; § 3 para 2 No 2 SächsArchG.

36 See § 67 StBerG.

37 In the case of doctors, regulation of mandatory third party insurance of the associated occupational risks is, as a rule, only found in the bylaws of the relevant professional bodies which, in the absence of appropriate legal integration, does not constitute a statutory obligation for compulsory third party insurance. For an overview of the regulation in the Federal States see Brand (n 28) para 21. The only exception would seem to be the statutory authorisation of regulation of occupational duties in Saxon state law (§ 17 para 1 No 9 SächsHKaG).

38 Brand (n 28) para 4 (no compulsory insurance for manufacturers in general).

bound to a particular liability concept as compulsory insurance is as applicable to strict liability as it is to fault-based liability.[39]

The aim of compulsory third party insurance is unanimously accepted as being the safeguarding of compensation for the benefit of the injured party,[40] despite it being applied in numerous different areas. Put succinctly, compulsory insurance deals with the problem of the solvency of the party causing the damage[41] as well as with the risk of a lack of financial provision by the damaging party.[42] Therefore, it is clear that, in some cases, there will be a duty to provide financial security rather than compulsory insurance. This can be achieved through insurance. In addition, it is expressly emphasised that the party causing the damage is also protected from the existential threatening consequences of negligent misconduct.[43]

This paper considers whether the general goals of compulsory insurance call for the introduction of such a duty in the case of operators and manufacturers of autonomous systems.

---

39 Brand (n 28) para 4; Manfred Deiters, 'Die Erfüllung öffentlicher Aufgaben durch privatrechtliche Pflichtversicherungen' in Fritz Reichert-Facilides (ed), *Festschrift für Reimer Schmidt* (Versicherungswirtschaft 1976) 379, 393; Peter Reiff, 'Sinn und Bedeutung von Pflichthaftpflichtversicherungen' [2006] TranspR 15, 20. Karl Sieg, *Ausstrahlungen der Haftpflichtversicherung* (Versicherungswiss. Verein 1952) 269ff takes a different position and considers compulsory insurance only to be appropriate within the framework of strict liability.

40 Reasons for the governmental draft of a law to reform the law on insurance contracts, BT-Drucks. 16/3945, 50; Brand (n 28) para 6; Dominik Klimke, 'Vorbem. zu §§ 113–124' in Jürgen Prölss and Anton Martin, VVG (C.H. Beck 2018) para 1; Reiff (n 39) 18ff; also Georg Büchner, *Zur Theorie der obligatorischen Haftpflichtversicherung* (Versicherungswirtschaft 1970) 33; however, the German Federal Supreme Court takes a different position, BGH, Judgement of 9 November 2004 – VI ZR 311/03 [2005] NZV 190, 191 (no third party protection within the meaning of§ 823 para 2 BGB through compulsory insurance for freight transportation companies according to § 7a GüKG).

41 Brand (n 28) para 4; Ulrich Magnus, 'Ökonomische Analyse des Rechts' in Hamburger Gesellschaft zur Förderung des Versicherungswesens (ed), *Pflichtversicherung – Segnung oder Sündenfall* (Versicherungswirtschaft 2005) 102, 108; Reiff (n 39) 16.

42 cf Hans-Peter Schwintowski, 'Pflichtversicherungen – aus Sicht der Verbraucher' in Hamburger Gesellschaft zur Förderung des Versicherungswesens (ed), *Pflichtversicherung – Segnung oder Sündenfall* (Versicherungswirtschaft 2005) 48, 59ff and esp. 69.

43 Brand (n 28) para 5; Büchner (n 40) 35; Klimke (n 40) 2; Reiff (n 39) 17.

b) Compulsory insurance for the operator of autonomous systems

The operator of an autonomous system is a key addressee of liability for damage caused by such autonomous systems. As noted above, the starting point for the classical purpose of compulsory insurance is whether or not a solvency risk actually exists. This starting point is equally applicable in the case of an autonomous system.

The existence of a solvency risk must be assumed in principle. The acquisition of a dangerous dog is not necessarily linked to a sufficient ability to pay damages and nor is the acquisition of an autonomous system. Essentially, the key question asks in which cases such a risk of insufficient solvency exists. This is to be presumed in circumstances where, in case of damage, there is the risk that the amount of damage caused is particularly high, and thus the keeper of the system would be overburdened financially. This would, to the extent that consumers are in the position of operators, often be the situation where there is a risk of significant personal injury as is the case in traffic accidents. Generally, the risk of a rare but substantial amount of damage caused by the use of an autonomous system, could be a suitable case for the consideration of compulsory insurance.

The classification of autonomous systems set out above could assist in identifying such areas. Such classification, combined with registration, could be linked to compulsory insurance for the operators of autonomous systems and such compulsory insurance could certainly be a requirement in the future.

c) Compulsory insurance for the manufacturers of autonomous systems

Whether, under current law, there is a need for compulsory insurance for the manufacturers of autonomous systems is certainly doubtful, particularly in light of the lack of clarity in respect of the manufacturer's liability. There is no doubt that compulsory insurance is not only possible in the area of strict liability but also has a role to play in the area of fault-based liability. However, clear liability risks are necessary in order to be able to justify imposing a requirement for compulsory insurance.

In this regard, it should be noted that the European Parliament's Resolution not only refers to compulsory insurance but also calls for the introduction of strict liability of manufacturers. It is therefore necessary to consider whether there is a risk that manufacturers will lack solvency.

Whilst the existence of such a risk would initially seem to be questionable given the nature of the manufacturer of autonomous vehicles, it is to be expected that the insolvency risk will increase in importance as soon as smaller manufacturers start offering autonomous systems with increased risk potential. In particular, it is not a given that an importer of autonomous systems, who will also be subject to product liability and should be subject to future liability rules, will be solvent enough to pay compensation.

Product liability law treats the importer and the manufacturer equally and does so for good reason. The liability position of the domestic damaged party is hereby secured[44] and competition disadvantages for domestic manufacturers can be avoided.[45] The same deliberations are also relevant to compulsory insurance. The need to guarantee compensation for damage as well as the need to protect competition both point to the introduction of compulsory insurance for the manufacturer and importer of autonomous systems.

As a result, it is necessary to at least consider the introduction of compulsory insurance for manufacturers in the case of liability relating to autonomous systems.

---

44 Jürgen Oechsler, '§ 4 ProdHaftG' in Julius von Staudinger, *BGB* (Sellier – De Guyter 2014) para 68. In this respect, references are often made to consumer protection (Reasons for the governmental draft of a law on § 4 ProdHaftG, BT-Drs. 11/2447, 20; criticism in Peter H. Schlechtriem, 'Angleichung der Produkthaftung in der EG – Zur Richtlinie des Rates der Europäischen Gemeinschaft vom 25.7.1985' [1986] VersR 1033, 1040), if, at the same time, there is also reference to the simplification of the enforceability of claims for the damaged party in international business dealings (Gunther Hess, '§ 12' in Michael Martinek, Franz-Jörg Semler and Eckhard Flohr (eds), *Handbuch des Vertriebsrechts* (C.H. Beck 2016) para 117; Gerhard Wagner, '§ 4 ProdHaftG' in Jürgen Säcker, Roland Rixecker, Hartmut Oetker and Bettina Limperg (eds), *Münchener Kommentar zum Bürgerlichen Gesetzbuch* (C.H. Beck 2017) para 35).

45 Some authors support the view that the harmonisation of product liability law on an EU level should be seen as an instrument to correct competition disadvantage as the producers, who are subject to more stringent liability, are threatened by competition disadvantages; cf eg Ulrich Magnus, 'Elemente eines europäischen Deliktsrechts' [1998] ZEuP 602, 606; dissenting Renate Schaub, 'Abschied vom nationalen Produkthaftungsrecht? Anspruch und Wirklichkeit der EG-Produkthaftung' [2003] ZEuP 562, 586 (Harm to competition seems to be 'less significant' in the context of strict liability).

III. Compensation funds

1. Compensation funds in the Resolution

In the Resolution, the European Parliament pushes strongly for the introduction of compensation funds. In paragraph 58, the Resolution describes how the insurance system could be supplemented by funds in order to ensure that reparation can be made for damage in cases where no insurance cover exists.

In the following paragraph 59, the European Parliament stresses that compensation funds should not only be used to cover damage where there is no insurance coverage. (Paragraph 59 b). Further, the European Parliament links liability and compensation funds by considering that the contribution to a compensation fund could lead to a limitation of liability (Paragraph 59 c.) The European Parliament also links the compensation fund with the registration of robots. (Paragraph 59 e.)

The Resolution sets out several different concepts in relation to compensation funds. This paper deals with two of the concepts, namely, compensation funds in the context of compulsory insurance and compensation funds as an alternative, or indeed rival, to liability.

2. Compensation funds for lack of insurance cover

One purpose of compensation funds could be to guarantee the compensation of damage in situations where there is no insurance cover. An example of this can be found in Section 12ff of the German Compulsory Insurance Act (PflichtVG) which regulates compensation funds for damage arising from vehicular accidents.[46] Pursuant to this, the injured party can seek damages from the compensation fund if his claim for damages against the registered keeper or driver cannot be enforced for certain reasons,[47] such as a failure to establish the vehicle which caused the damage or a lack of the third party insurance required by law. The principal pur-

46 cf Thomas Münkel, '13. Ch.' in Reinhart Geigel, *Der Haftpflichtprozess* (C.H. Beck 2015) para 71 (the lack of opportunity to seek recourse from the insurer is 'unreasonable').

47 The reasons stated in § 12 para 1 PflVG are exhaustive, Münkel (n 46).

pose of this concept is to close the gaps in the compulsory insurance system.[48]

Such a concept, which is referred to in paragraph 58 of the Resolution, could be applied to autonomous systems. It would serve to ensure comprehensive protection through compulsory insurance for the benefit of the injured party.

3. Compensation funds as an alternative to liability

However, compensation funds can serve other purposes which go far beyond supplementing compulsory third party insurance. In effect, compensation funds can act as an alternative to liability. In paragraph 59 b) of the Resolution, the European Parliament seems to indicate that this is the case. It expressly notes that compensation funds would not only serve the purpose of guaranteeing compensation if the damage was not covered by insurance and, in paragraph 59 c), it describes how liability can be limited through the contribution to a compensation fund.

a) Possible advantages of a compensation system

The replacement of a liability system by a compensation system would seem to have a number of distinct advantages: Such compensation system could be much more comprehensive than a liability system and thus gaps in liability could be avoided. Financial contributions to a compensation system can come from many different sources. These include the person causing the damage, the operator and owner of a system who can potentially obtain benefits from that system as well as a third party such as the State.[49] Finally, a notable advantage of a compensation system is that it

---

48 cf Münkel (n 46); this also follows from the subsidiarity restrictions § 12 para 1 cl 2 PflVG, cf Manuel Baroch Castellvi, '§ 12 PflVG' in Wilfried Rüffer, Dirk Halbach and Peter Schimikowski (eds), *Versicherungsvertragsgesetz* (Nomos 2015) para 1; Jürgen Jahnke, '§ 12 PflVG' in Ernst Stiefel and Karl Maier, *Kraftfahrtversicherung: AKB-Kommentar* (C.H. Beck 2017) para 121.

49 An example of this is the case of the charity 'Humanitäre Hilfe für durch Blutprodukte HIV-infizierte Personen' (humanitarian aid for people infected by HIV through infected blood products), which was established by § 3 para 1 HIVHG and

would no longer be necessary to prove the requirements needed to establish liability.

As mentioned above, the establishment of responsibility can be particularly problematic and the most recent cases of accidents with autonomous cars are not the only clear evidence of this. More serious is the weakness of Product Liability law which arises from the problems with proving a product defect.

The tempting idea in support of such a compensation fund regime is that vast amounts of money which, under the current system, would have to be invested in litigation could be saved and instead invested in the compensation of damage.

b) Communitisation of the risks through compensation funds

As a general principle, compensation funds can be used to achieve communitisation of risk independently from the civil law system of liability. In the context of autonomous systems, the idea of such communitisation would seem to bring particular benefits, especially if one were to adopt the view that the risks arising from manufacture and the operation of autonomous systems are risks to society as a whole and must be borne by society as a whole.

An important consideration is therefore whether the introduction of autonomous systems should be seen as a task for society as a whole in the same way health care and education are. The comprehensive use of autonomous systems is a key element of the emerging digital society and it forms a significant part of the transformation process. There is no doubt that this transformation process will require enormous effort which can be regarded as an investment in the development of a digital society. It is necessary to consider who should bear the costs of this transformation process.

The fundamental question of whether society is mature enough for autonomous systems cannot easily be answered in the affirmative. The examples of the first Tesla accident where the driver grossly overestimated the car's ability to drive autonomously illustrates for unprofessional users

---

which received initial funding of 150 million DM, 60 % of which came from public funds (cf § 2 HIVHG).

of autonomous systems to adequately assess the risks. Also, in the case of the Uber car accident, it if questionable whether the parties involved correctly understood the risks: Uber deactivated the emergency braking maneuver system in order reduce erratic vehicle behaviour[50] thus shifting the whole task of preventing accidents to the 'driver' and her ability in recognising danger and overriding the system adequately. It is not even clear from the interim report whether the driver was informed about this fact.

The same is true for the question of whether only the manufacturers and operators of autonomous systems should bear the cost of the transformation process. It can be assumed that damage from the use of autonomous systems has the potential to occur not just through unsuitable manufacture and supervision but also through unsuitable reactions from an environment which has not adapted adequately to such systems.

This raises the question of whether the cost of damage which occurs during the transformation process should be borne solely by those participants who are addressed by the liability system, namely the injured party to the extent that he is denied compensation, or also by the operators and manufacturers of the autonomous systems.

The concept of strict liability is traditionally justified with the reasoning that this stringent liability leads to the costs resulting from the use of the system, including damage suffered by a third party, being borne by the user of the system as it is the user who draws a benefit from such system.[51] The liability of the manufacturer, who is able to factor the costs of liability into his pricing, can also be partially included in this system.[52] The merit of strict liability in relieving the burden on the damaged party and having

50 NTSB *Preliminary Report* (n 19).

51 Börding, Jülicher, Röttgen and von Schönfeld (n 14); Bräutigam and Klindt (n 14) 1139; Hans Brox and Wolf-Dietrich Walker, *Besonderes Schuldrecht* (C.H. Beck 2018) § 54 para 2; Nico Brunotte, 'Virtuelle Assistenten – Digitale Helfer in der Kundenkommunikation' [2017] CR 583, 585; Erwin Deutsch, 'Das neue System der Gefährdungshaftungen' [1992] NJW 73, 74; Manfred Wandt, Gesetzliche Schuldverhältnisse (Vahlen 2017) § 22 para 1; also Christian Armbrüster, 'Automatisiertes Fahren – Paradigmenwechsel im Straßenverkehrsrecht?' [2017] ZRP 83, 85.

52 Deutsch (n 51); Mathias Rohe, 'Gründe und Grenzen deliktischer Haftung – die Ordnungsaufgaben des Deliktsrechts (einschließlich der Haftung ohne Verschulden) in rechtsvergleichender Betrachtung' [2001] AcP vol 201, 117, 142; cf Spindler (n 14) 775.

the user of the system bear the risks of the use of such system will lead substantially to a concentration of the risks on the user.

There are two important considerations which go against extensive strict liability: Firstly, the direct operators of autonomous systems and the person who happens to be injured are not the only beneficiaries of the transformation process. Society as a whole also benefits from it. Secondly, it is difficult to accurately predict the level of transformation costs because the amount of damages which will be payable as a result of the introduction of autonomous systems is unclear and therefore cannot be factored into cost calculations with any degree of accuracy. If the estimate of these costs is too low, this could lead to externalisation. However, an estimate which is too high could result in the feared chilling effect.

c) The disadvantages of compensation funds replacing liability

A certain degree of communitisation of the risks arising from the transformation task might prove to be an adequate popular approach. However, the risks of communitisation must not be ignored. One such risk is that, to the extent that compensation funds are laid over the liability system or even displace it, the steering effect of liability would be lost.[53]

Further, the administration of compensation funds will also require a great deal of effort.[54] It will be necessary to collect contributions, set the amount of damages payable and to distribute the damages. The effort involved is not likely to be less than it would have been in the case of liability. In particular, a complex set of rules governing compensation funds must be developed. These must establish what the scope of application of the fund is and the conditions under which it should intervene. It is also clear that the effort involved is not likely to be less than the effort of developing suitable liability rules.

---

53 cf RoboLaw, *Guidelines on Regulating Robots* (2014) 65 on the Swedish system of a generalisation of the liability question which is segregated from insurance for damage in road traffic accidents.

54 Criticism of the introduction of compensation funds therefore also by Christian von Bar, *Verhandlungen des 62 Deutschen Juristentages Bremen 1998 Band I: Gutachten* (C.H. Beck 1998) A 73.

The result would be that a compensation fund which is laid over the civil law liability system with regards to autonomous systems, or even displaces it completely, cannot be a convincing solution.

d) *Potential of compensation funds in the transformation process*

However, the necessity to avoid chilling effects whilst not burdening injured parties with the cost of the transformation process must still be addressed. How this should be done and what role compensation funds will play in this, cannot be comprehensively dealt with in this paper. However, one potential solution could be the introduction of limits on liability in order facilitate insurance and avoid chilling effects. Compensation funds could be used in such situations to close gaps in liability.

It is clear that the discussion about the purpose of compensation funds in connection with autonomous systems has only just begun and further research is essential.

IV. Conclusion

A number of conclusions can be drawn.

Firstly, there is no doubt that the existing liability system contains gaps and must be developed further. In doing so, a differentiated introduction of strict liability for operators and manufacturers is as important as the registration of autonomous systems. It is particularly important to classify autonomous systems according to their risk potential.

Secondly, insurance is an important instrument in controlling the allocation of risk in connection with autonomous systems. Compulsory third party insurance is an appropriate instrument in achieving this and should be utilised. However, further research is required to decide exactly how and in which circumstances it should be applied.

Finally, compensation funds can supplement compulsory third party insurance and should be implemented in this area. In addition, they could perhaps be used to cushion the transformation risks in the development of our transforming society. However, a great deal more research is required in this area.

Multilayered (Accountable) Liability for Artificial Intelligence

*Giovanni Comandé**

I. The networking society and the internet of humans: an introduction

Today's technologies enable unprecedented exploitation of information, be it small or big data, for any thinkable purpose ensuing thus juridical and ethical anxieties. Algorithms are regularly used for mining data, offering unexplored patterns and deep non-causal analyses to those able to exploit these advances. Yet, these innovations need to be properly framed in the existing legal framework, fit in to the existing set of constitutional guarantees of fundamental rights and freedoms, and coherently related to existing policies in order to enable our societies to reap the richness of big and open data while equally empowering all players.

By referring to algorithms as a pivotal element of 'new technologies', we hereby summarize for the sake of brevity reference to the use of the so-called machine learning to produce: 1) new unexpected solutions; 2) the ability to exploit the interconnectedness of things and of humans; 3) the embedding of Artificial Intelligence – AI (autonomous more than automatic) based decision making in robots or the AI deployment as a software; and, 4) algorithms' implications in the use of 3D printing[1].

In short, today we live in a continuously expanding explosion of data production and data use. Our life is permanently connected to internet both via the direct access we have to it or by the use we make of connected objects and tools in our daily activities. Both our connections avenues

---

* Full Professor of Private Comparative Law, Scuola Superiore Sant'Anna, Pisa.

1 Anton Vedder and Laurens Naudts argue that 'Algorithmic accountability does not only require the examination of algorithms or the code as such but also an examination of how algorithms are deployed within different areas and what the tasks are that they perform' and that 'The potential interconnectedness of algorithms and of algorithmic decisions also seriously restricts the means of algorithmic decision makers to give an account of the decisions they make'. Anton Vedder and Laurens Naudts, 'Accountability for the use of algorithms in a big data environment' (2017) 31 International Review of Law, Computers & Technology 206, 209.

to internet use data (personal and non-personal ones) and generate new data, which in turn a number of entities analyse and often monetise.

Note from the outset that almost any liability regime that can be envisaged for these technologies would require for (technological) reasons the 'help' of the very same technologies it is regulating to make effective its legal rules. Thus, the emerging regulatory approach must necessarily blend various legal, technological, and economic strategies for which the time frame is of crucial importance.

Algorithms, big data, and the large computing ability that connect them do not necessarily follow causal patterns and are even able to identify information unknown to the human individual they refer to. These elements deeply alter the notion of causality employable by any chosen liability regime[2].

Datasets are actively constructed and data do not necessarily come from the same sources, increasing the risks related to de-contextualization. Moreover, since an analyst must define the parameters of the search (and of the dataset to be searched), human biases can be 'built in' to the analytical tools (even unwillingly) with the additional effect of their progressive replication and expansion once machine learning is applied. Indeed, if the machine learning process is classified as 'non-interpretable' (by humans), for instance because the machine learned scheme is assessing thousands of variables, there will not be human intervention or a meaningful explanation of why a specific outcome is reached.

In the case of interpretable processes (translatable in human understandable language), a layer of human intervention is possible (although not necessary). Again, this possibility is a double-edged sword since human intervention can either correct biases or insert new ones by interfering with the code, setting aside or inserting factors. In any event, the technological features will necessarily affect the selected liability rules in various ways.

The lack of (legal and ethical) protocols to drive human action in designing and revising algorithms clearly calls for their creation, but requires a common setting of values and rules, since algorithms are basically enjoying a-territoriality in the sense that they are not necessarily used in one given physical jurisdiction. Moreover, the expansion of the autonomous

2 Giovanni Comandé, 'The Rotting Meat Error: From Galileo to Aristotle in Data Mining? (2018) 4 European Data Protection Law Review 270–277.

generation of algorithms calls for building similar legal and ethical protocols to drive the machine generation of models. In both cases, there is also a need for technological verifiability of the effectiveness of the legal and ethical protocols making human readable at least the results of the application of the model when the model itself is not readable by humans.

Data and the ability of making use of them is the key for both developing new informatics tools, such as analytics and predictive coding, and feeding the creation of artificial intelligence (AI) and its actual operation.

As in the relationship between the human body and its brain, the brain plays the most relevant part. Similarly, in the emerging use of robotics the kingmaker is not the robot itself, but the AI enabling its performance. In a word, disruption does not come from Robotics or IoT as such. It comes from the embedding and expansion of Artificial Intelligence in products. Robots as such do not differ much from things, employees, and collaborators. This is why, until AI moved out from science fiction to appear in the real world, liability of robots themselves was not on the table.[3] However, there are several semantic misunderstandings both in the use of the word 'intelligence' and in several connected elements that need clarification before tackling the issue of liability more in detail.

What do we mean by Artificial Intelligence? AI is intelligence exhibited by machines. In computer science, the field of AI research defines itself as the study of 'intelligent agents': any device that perceives its environment and takes actions that maximize its chance of success at some goal. This definition already illustrates that artificial intelligence is mostly vertical: it is excellent in doing one thing as compared to the versatility of the human intelligence that we could call horizontal and apt to a manifold of tasks. The AI animating our cleaning robot can enable it to clean better and longer than a human can but cannot perform at all any other 'intelligent' task the worst human cleaner can perform sufficiently well.

AI largely builds on Machine Learning: the subfield of computer science that, according to Arthur Samuel, gives computers the ability to learn

3 For a literature review on the attribution of legal personhood and liability to non-human entities operating at an increasing distance from the physical persons, such as pseudonyms, avatars, and software agents, see Bert-Jaap Koops, Mireille Hildebrandt and David Olivier Jaquet-Chiffelle, 'Bridging the Accountability Gap: Rights for New Entities in the Information Society' (2010) 11 Minnesota Journal of Law, Science & Technology 497.

without being explicitly programmed.[4] It is Big Data to make possible Machine Learning. Big data is a term for data sets that are so large or complex that traditional data processing application software is inadequate to deal with them. Big data are continuously generated by sensors, humans, algorithms, computers, things, etc, and increase unceasingly.

In turn, Big Data enables AI to develop degrees of 'Autonomy' (mostly vertical as the described cleaning robot): autonomy is not of a moral character but rather has to be expressed in terms of relative absence of human control. It offers unpredictable or at least unpredicted behaviors that might entail a reduction or shifting of liability from the moral (human) agent involved in the production, deployment, use of the system using the 'autonomous' AI.[5]

II. Automation, autonomy and unpredictable behaviours

This further step requires a clarification as well. We need to distinguish between 'automation' that has been with us since a very long time (think of any first industrial revolution factory, for instance) and 'autonomy' of things that is the real novelty in terms of triggering new issues in liability (think of a fully autonomous vehicle as a well-known example).

The borderlines between automated (Airports' transfer trains, for instance) and autonomous systems (fully autonomous vehicles) are progressively blurring for several reasons we cannot discuss here. Suffice is to say that autonomy depends on the margins of 'liberty' AI has in its choices. Their degrees of liberty are often guided by the information they can gather and process in their own automated decision-making processes; similarly to what humans do but at a much wider level and at higher computational speed.

Equally to humans, AI systems can operate in unstructured environments, making them dependent on sensor data and information or on the

4 Arthur L Samuel, 'Some Studies in Machine Learning Using the Game of Checkers' (1959) 3 IBM Journal of Research and Development 210.

5 Yet the limitation of criminal liability, for instance of self-driving cars operators, to situations where they neglect to undertake reasonable measures to control the risks emanating from robots has been suggested. In this regard, see Sabine Gless, Emily Silverman and Thomas Weigend, 'If robots cause harm, who is to blame? Self-driving cars and criminal liability' (2016) 19 New Criminal Law Review 412.

using of random/stochastic approaches to expand their problem-solving capability and eventually maintain their learning ability (autonomy, again). The former triggers the issue of liability of the data producer or of the network, feeding the data to the AI, which can have problems affecting the AI decision making process severely. The latter, might trigger eventual liability of the programmer or of the producer embedding the AI.[6]

Thus, unpredictable behaviours are the real game changer in the issue of liability attached to the use of AI. A new notion (Emergence Intelligence) has been created to refer to the ability of the system to engage in unpredictable behaviours still deemed useful despite (or because of) their unpredictability.[7]

Moreover, AI to remain 'intelligent' should maintain some form of continuous learning that constantly updates and changes the algorithm. For liability allocation this requires to target the 'right' algorithm involved in the specific decision-making process under scrutiny for liability. It requires accountability in the computational technical sense and a holistic approach.[8]

An example (the so-called 'runway trolley' scenario) in the AI setting (e.g. of biased decisions) will illustrate it. Suppose an autonomous vehicle is presented with the following alternatives: 1) to divert its path to save a busload of schoolchildren, but kill the vehicle's occupants in the process by colliding with a tree; or 2) to save the occupant, but let all the children

---

6 The consequences are manifold. For instance, KC Webb suggests that manufacturers must seek liability protection via legislation, leading the way to establish a national insurance fund, and develop training modules for buyers as part of purchase and lease agreements. KC Webb, 'Products liability and autonomous vehicles: who's driving whom' (2017) 23 Richmond Journal of Law and Technology 1.

7 Ryan Calo, 'Robotics and the Lessons of Cyberlaw' (2015) 103 California Law Review 513.

8 Jack Balkin clearly illustrates this need of a holistic approach: 'The laws of robotics that we need in our age are laws that control and direct human beings who create, design, and employ robots, AI agents, and algorithms. And because algorithms without data are empty, these are also the laws that control the collection, collation, use, distribution and sale of the data that make these algorithms work. […] So the laws we need are obligations of fair dealing, non-manipulation, and non-domination between those who make and use the algorithms and those who are governed by them'. Jack M. Balkin, 'The Three Laws of Robotics in the Age of Big Data' (2017) Yale Law School Faculty Scholarship Series 5159. Available at <http://digitalcommons.law.yale.edu/fss_papers/5159> accessed 28 July 2018.

die. Assume further that the AI 'driving' the vehicle learned what to do and decides autonomously its course.

Suppose something its machine-learned /was taught (the alternatives have different implications for liability we cannot discuss here in detail) is to reduce social cost (also in terms of compensation needed for victims following actual tort rules). Accordingly, it decides to kill the children because the loss of earnings of the vehicle occupant outweighs compensation for the children.

Under this exemplary scenario, we should ask ourselves whether there is a cause of action. And against whom? The non-existent programmer? The user of the car 'selecting' the tort interpretation to follow? The producer? Would it be different if a programmer actually taught (programmed) the rules to follow or the AI just learned them by 'reading' the case law provided for its training? Last but not least, we should investigate whether or not the algorithm should be tweaked to solve the problem? With which implications and by whom?

III. First policy implications

These very preliminary and simplified considerations already highlight, for law and policymakers, some key changes that stem from algorithmic decision-making used in AI and are extremely relevant for defining liability regimes:

1. Choices of algorithms embed specific policy choices and algorithms automatically enforce them.
2. Yet algorithms can permit direct accountability to the public, or other third parties (e.g. users, bystanders, producers, etc.) using the technological and legal frameworks already in place by providing analysable evidence of decision making processes, at least under some circumstances that can be programmed for scrutiny in an adjudication process;
3. Full transparency does not automatically help deciding liability issues;
4. Full Transparency is neither sufficient nor necessary (solving many IP and competition roadblocks in regulating AI related liability) for accountability and does not automatically help deciding liability issues;
5. Algorithms learn/are taught to (and in any event, they do) enforce their own interpretations of law and standards. It is for example the case,

stressed in literature[9] for algorithms automatically and autonomously 'enforcing' IP rights by sending notifications to (assumed) infringers.

6. Thus:
   a) In the absence of a clear regulatory framework algorithms might effectively advance the intermediaries' own interpretation of legal norms (instead of the legislator intended ones);
   b) The individual costs of reversing these interpretations might be so high (as opposed to their actual merit) to entirely beg the policy goals of the regulation.
   c) They risk self-setting the standard to abide to (requiring cautions in using soft law and self-regulation mechanisms).
   d) They might learn and reinforce wrong standards (e.g. with the task of minimising the costs of an accident, in the trolley car scenario they might decide to sacrifice a higher income individual instead of a lower income one or *vice versa*).

Regulators should take into account all these issues in reviewing the current debate on AI liability, a debate that might be driven too much by the examples of driverless vehicles since many valuable artificial intelligent agents are already employed in many fields and fully autonomous vehicles are not. Notwithstanding, surveying the autonomous cars liability debate enables to set the scenario for a more thoughtful intervention that considers liability in a wider legal and policy framework, a holistic approach that considers competition, IP, data protection, etc. After all in the common perception autonomous vehicles represent a sort of archetype of autonomous products in the meaning we clarified earlier.

IV. The debate on Autonomous vehicles as an example of an insufficient path.

Paradoxically as it might be, we do not have fully autonomous car traffic yet, but there is already extensive literature addressing the issue of liability in case of accidents caused by autonomous vehicles. We can quickly summarise the various positions with their arguments as follows.

9 Maayan Perel and Niva Elkin-Koren, 'Accountability in Algorithmic Copyright Enforcement' (2016) 19 Stanford Technology Law Review 473.

A number of authors sustain products liability or autonomous liability regimes based on strict liability. For instance, David Vladeck[10] claims that in the case liability concerns with the vehicle are the result of human (but not driver) errors, the products liability settled principles should be adopted to govern artificial intelligent machines, such as driverless cars. In other words, for the classical product liability defects (design, manufacturing and information defects failing to instruct humans on the safe and appropriate use of the product) a plain application of products liability rules would suffice, since there would not be a justification for treating even autonomous thinking machines differently than any other machine or tool a human may use; except, perhaps, holding them to a higher standard of care.[11]

In the case these machines cause injury in ways wholly untraceable and unattributable to the hand of man, i.e., that cannot fairly be attributed to a design, manufacturing, or programming defect, and where even an inference of defect may be hard to justify, the only feasible approach (it is suggested) would be to infer a defect of some kind on the theory that the accident itself is proof of defect, even if there is compelling evidence that cuts against a defect theory, as a simply restatement of *res ipsa loquitur* theory.

Leaving aside the problems and objections an interpretative approach fully based on *res ipsa loquitur* arguments would rise, the shortcomings of this reading appear evident by merely considering the role machine learning has in developing the driving algorithms and the implication the inability to understand the reasoning of them when they are black-box ones (unreadable to humans)[12].

Other authors[13] claim that autonomous vehicles should be treated like non-automobile products that have similar features, like elevators or autopilot technology (such as autopilot in ships and aeroplanes). Therefore, automobile liability regime should not be applicable to autonomous vehicles because they are 'too far removed from current automobiles both in

10 David C Vladeck, 'Machines without principals: liability rules and artificial intelligence' (2014) 89 Washington Law Review 117.

11 ibid 127.

12 As mentioned, when only their inputs and outputs are known it is not possible to have any knowledge of its internal workings even for its producer.

13 Jeffrey R Zohn, 'When robots attack: how should the Law handle self-driving cars that cause damages' (2015) 2 Journal of Law, Technology and Policy 461.

function and likely cause of injury'.[14] In the first case, 'autonomous cars can follow the evolution of elevator liability by beginning with a more standard negligent principle and then evolving to a more stringent and higher standard on the manufacturers over time and as the product continues to improve'.[15] In the case of autopilot technology, liability is attached to the manufacturer unless there has been negligence by the user.[16] Here the main shortcoming relates to the notion of 'autonomy' we discussed earlier. An elevator or a self-pilot in an aeroplane does not enjoy the same degrees of liberty and unpredictability a truly autonomous AI does.

A different approach[17] considers AI as software arguing that liability rules should follow those applicable to software because 'we cannot treat Al as legal entity [...] since they do not bear own consciousness nor have independent property.'[18] However, 'Al can make a valid contract or do other legally binding declarations through its individual decisions but these are binding the represented person.'[19] By considering AI as software, these authors analyse the different paths in terms of liability rules and attribution of responsibility arising from this premise. Reference, for example, is made to Giovanni Sartor's arguments to explain that in the case of software we can count on more legal entities from the viewpoint of legal responsibility. According to Sartor, parts of the software agent could have separated legal fate. If the agent contains copyright protected software (as in most situations), the author could bear liability for programming mistakes. If the agent contains some kind of database, then the producer of the database could bear the liability for database mistakes. If the agent processes personal data, – from a data protection point of view – the data controller is responsible for legitimate data processing. If the agent is being operated by a certain user for own purposes, the user is liable for its operations. According to Sartor, since the usage of the software agent could have such aspects on which the given legal entity cannot exercise control, therefore the operator should not be held liable for such damages.

14 ibid 484.
15 ibid 483.
16 ibid 481.
17 D Eszteri, 'Liability and damages caused by artificial intelligence – with a short outlook to online games' (2015) 153 Studia Iuridica Auctoritate Universitatis Pecs Publicata 57.
18 ibid 65.
19 ibid 66.

For example: the user should not be liable for damages caused by Al software when the wrongful act originates from the programming mistakes of the software and the user is not allowed to access the source code or either to decrypt it.[20]

These authors clearly argue for a reasoned extension of existing legal rules and Sartor illustrates how different legal rules can deal with various instances of AI related liability paving the way to what we could call a multilayered approach.

A number of authors advocate a more radical shift from fault liability to strict liability based on defective products theories. For instance, some authors,[21] analysing the liability for damages caused by autonomous vehicles according to Belgian Law, argue that the fault-based regime entails several problems because: 1) it is unlikely that a victim will be able to prove that the user of the vehicle acted negligently because of the unpredictability of software systems and the rigid interaction with users make it harder to assess the reasonable foreseeability and avoidability of the harm, which is an essential element for a negligence claim[22]; and 2) it is unlikely that a human would be able to avoid damages that a computer cannot.

Accordingly, the solution would be to evolve from fault-based to strict liability in traffic-related matters. In this regard, autonomous vehicles that caused damage due to a dysfunction in their software or hardware will be seen as a defective product and claims could be filed either against the manufacturer of the vehicle or the software producer depending on the factual situation. In any case, according to Belgian Law it is unsure whether the software producer could be held liable. Some improvements on defective products regime would remain necessary.

Other authors propose a different strict liability test (reasonable car standard test) adapted to autonomous vehicles. This test should be applicable in the strict liability products regime and would hold a car manufacturer liable only when the car does not act in a way that another reasonable autonomous vehicle would act. Accordingly, the test would be 'determining how a reasonable AV would act and comparing it to an allegedly deviant AV would be far less invasive and expensive for the parties than liti-

---

20 Giovanni Sartor, 'Cognitive automata and the law: electronic contracting and the intentionality of software agents' (2009) 17 Artificial Intelligence and Law 253.

21 J De Bruyne and J Tangue, 'Liability for Damage Caused by Autonomous Vehicles: a Belgian Perspective' (2017) 8 Journal of European Tort Law 324.

22 ibid 346 and 371.

gating whether a safer alternative design would be implemented by comparing lines of computer code.'[23]

Feasible or not such an approach illustrates again the need to move from existing liability regimes (product liability remaining one among the others) and adapt them to the novelties brought about by AI. Yet, the key issues on the adaptation of the existing liability regimes (or the creation of new ones for what it matters) are not fully tackled: above all, the way the different regimes should interact among them; what we could call the problem of splitting the bill among the different potential tortfeasors.

Finally, yet importantly, there are authors who propose strict liability rules in the field of AI, by analogy with a party's responsibility for the behaviour of animals, children, employees or even ultra-hazardous activity. These authors' approaches vary extensively. For instance, some consider AI systems as a tool using the general principle contained in article 12 of the United Nations Convention on the Use of Electronic Communications in International Contracts. According to this principle, 'the principal of a tool is responsible for the results obtained by the use of that tool since the tool has no independent volition of its own'[24]. Accordingly, they propose strict liability rules by analogy with a party's responsibility for the behaviour of children and employees (vicarious liability). Applying this regime for the case of AI 'means that liability for the actions of AI should rest with their owners or the users.'[25] Therefore, liability is imposed on the person, not because of his/her own wrongful act, but due to his/her relationship with the tortfeasor AI.[26]

In the case the AI is a source of danger they suggest treating AI liability as that applicable to certain types of activities associated with greater danger to others. Therefore, in these situations, the AI developer should be held liable for creating this greater source of danger, and, liability arises without fault by using the '*Cuius commoda eius et incommoda*' theory, 'which means that a person engaged in dangerous activities that are profitable and useful to the society should compensate for damage caused to society from the profit gained'.[27] This person can be the AI producer or

23 KC Webb, 'Products liability and autonomous vehicles: who's driving whom' (2017) 23 Richmond Journal of Law and Technology 1.

24 Bruyne and Tangue (n 20) 386.

25 Bruyne and Tangue (n 20) 385.

26 Bruyne and Tangue (n 20) 387.

27 Bruyne and Tangue (n 20) 386.

programmer, who should be required to insure against civil liability as a guarantee for their hazardous activities. Another possibility would be to use the Common Enterprise Doctrine, adapted to a new strict liability regime.[28]

These final examples are a clear illustration of the potentials and limits of mere extending the existing legal rules to the unsettling elements of AI related liability. A deeper analysis of other factual examples, for instance referring to robotics or IoT[29] demonstrates that any liability regime (extended from existing rules or created anew) is but one (insufficient) layer in the multilayered liability environment the complexity of these new technologies require.

We will briefly argue that a multilayered liability system based on accountability would prove more apt to solve the emerging legal issues and will help solving the allocation of costs among the possible liable entities (the split the bill – among tortfeasors-problem).

V. Towards a multilayered liability approach based on accountability

Before providing more details on the role of the concept of accountability, it is useful to summarise the most fundamental questions not answered by interventions on applying liability rules to Robotics, IoT and AI in general.

How to deal with the issues raised by AI (e.g. black boxes issues and the 'defects' produced by machine learning)? How to allocate costs among the various players in the development, deployment, use of AI? (e.g. algorithm developers, products producers, connection providers, data providers, data brokers, users, the State, bystanders, infrastructure maintenance, sensor producers, …).

Even when duly adapted, traditional tort liability rules are ineffective in sorting the allocation of liability and costs related to AI (recourse, contribution, joint and several liability, etc.). For distributing the costs among

---

28 Bruyne and Tangue (n 20) 387.

29 See Goldman Sachs, 'The Internet of Things: Making sense of the next megatrend' (2014) *Iot Primer*, available at <https://www.goldmansachs.com/our-thinking/outlook/internet-of-things/iot-report.pdf> accessed 28 July 2018; Mauricio Paez and Mike La Marca, 'The Internet of Things: Emerging Legal Issues for Businesses' (2016) 43 Northern Kentucky Law Review 29.

the mentioned players, the public and the insurance market (to address the 'split the bill problem') accountability would still be needed to allocate effectively liability. Indeed, whatever liability basis is chosen (fault, strict liability, vicarious liability, no-fault, funds, AI direct liability, etc.) legal and computational accountability mechanisms effectively help splitting the bill in 'automated' and 'verifiable' ways at virtual no costs.

A simple example will illustrate this point. Any selected liability regime would set a 'required standard of conduct' that would request to establish a number of causal connections between the actions/omissions targeted as it triggers of liability to the 'required standard of conduct'. However, most of the time, it would be necessary to ascertain these causal links notions of computational accountability applied to the legal issues in discussion.

What we are suggesting is that AI requires a gradual layered approach to liability grounded on accountability principles (already embedded in the EU legal system). AI requires the use of technology itself to unfold a multilayered accountable liability system and solve the 'splitting the bill problem'.

The need to embed technologies in liability rules and not only attach liability to technology is illustrated by the example of the required standard of conduct. While the deviation from the standard conduct by humans is assessable by humans, the deviation from the standard of conduct by AI is assessable only with the help of 'technologies' with the characteristics required by the accountability principle.

The almost automatic verification of the causal reasons for AI's actions might then trigger different layers of the multilayered liability system.For example, verification of full compliance with the set of rules coded in the AI and made available could trigger the application of compensation funds or a reversal of the burden of proof in a given liability regime, channelling liability on different individuals, a stricter or more lenient regulatory system, various kinds of insurance, the ability to contract around liability, the shift of liability on users, and so on.

In a word, any path suggested by the European Parliament resolution on liability of robots[30] or the European Commission on building a European data economy requires this approach.

30 European Parliament Resolution of 16 February 2017 with recommendations to the Commission on Civil Law Rules on Robotics (2015/2103(INL)).

VI. For a theory of layered liability: accountable multilevel liability

As the brief discussion of the literature on driverless car liability illustrates, as a baseline in defining the liability regimes applicable to Robotics, IoT and their AI we should acknowledge that we do have liability rules and principles theoretically applicable to them. As illustrated, the debate swings between a choice of fault, no-fault, strict liability, vicarious liability, on the one hand, and the attribution of liability on the AI agent itself on the other. Normally, the application of existing rules and principles is only a matter of interpretation and asks simple yet relevant questions jurists are used to answer using the traditional hermeneutical tools. Reinterpretation, however, presents its own limits and certainly cannot cover every facet of the changes fostered by the tackled technologies.

In relation to liability applicable to AI and autonomous systems, there is a frequent criticism pointing to the fact that the use of AI and autonomous systems could create responsibility gaps rendering impossible to attribute legal liability to anyone for harms caused by the autonomous operation of these technologies. This is the case for instance because neither designers nor users would be at fault with regard to errors and harms which are unknown and undiscoverable at the time the product is placed on the market and therefore could not be anticipated or remedied given the existing technological knowledge.[31] Nevertheless, legal scholars have been trying to overcome this gap by applying and adapting traditional civil liability rules to damages caused by artificial intelligence. Accordingly, authors have proposed different solutions for the prospective scenarios they envisage. These solutions are usually based either on the strict liability regime of party's responsibility for the behaviour of people or animals under their responsibility or on the strict liability regime for products, abnormally dangerous activities or wild animals, both of them with some adaptations. Moreover, traditional civil liability rules also provide for special regimes that attribute responsibility to persons not actually responsible for perpetrating a wrongful act due to their relationship with the perpetrator, as in the case of liability of owners of guardians or vicarious liability.

As anticipated, among the proposal on the floor seriously considered at the EU level is to attribute liability directly to the AI (*rectius*: in the pro-

---

31 Giovanni Sartor and Andrea Omicini, 'The autonomy of technological systems and responsibilities for their use' in Nehal Bhuta et al (eds), *Autonomous Weapons Systems: Law, Ethics, Policy* (Cambridge University Press 2016).

posal to the robot using the AI).[32] However, also this proposal does not answer the key issues and cannot work properly. For reasons we cannot explain here liability of the autonomous agent systems might create more problems than solving ones.

The idea that AI can have autonomy and should trigger the liability of the AI itself might sound naïve or futuristic. However, for centuries we have been attributing liability on non-humans, shielding humans consequently from liability. Liability of legal persons (e.g. corporations) is a suitable example of this approach. Yet, the similitude would work upon the condition that we confer a sufficient patrimony to the AI to fulfil eventual compensation duties. However, it is easy to see the actual risk of creating AI entities with limited assets to the exclusive aim of reducing liability for their creators/users.

As anticipated, the borderlines between automated and autonomous[33] systems are progressively blurring for several reasons. It is worth remembering that even automated systems increasingly employ AI with embedding machine learning that makes opaque the way the AI operates and difficult the understanding of the role data (both training and sensor data) play in the operation itself. Moreover, they can operate in unstructured environments, making them dependent on sensor data and information, and using random/stochastic approaches to expand their problem-solving capability and eventually maintaining their learning ability. Here, again, autonomy is not of a moral character but rather a degree of relative absence of control triggering various degrees of liability in using the 'autonomous' AI.

As already acknowledged in most jurisdictions the principles of *respondeat superior*, *ubi commoda et eius incommoda* in vicarious liability see rules limiting (e.g. defences or recourse actions) liability of the *prima facie* responsible agent (employers, users, producers). This happens, for instance, when the collaborator violates the instructions or rules set by the person who avails herself of the collaborator. We might be tempted to consider AI (at least one showing autonomous decision-making) as we consider collaborators. Yet, the opacity of the AI decision-making process or its biased evolution requires the use of technology itself to guarantee a

---

32 European Parliament Resolution (n 29.)

33 For a caution not to confuse autonomy in philosophical and in robotic terms see Noel Sharkey, 'Saying "No!" to Lethal Autonomous Targeting' (2010) 9 Journal of Military Ethics 369.

correct assessment of the deviation from the expected/commanded conduct.

In other words, while the deviation from the standard of conduct by humans is assessable by humans, the deviation from the standard of conduct by AI is assessable only with the help of software with the characteristics required by the accountability principle. It is technically possible to a significant extent that computer science itself enables the almost automatic verification of the causal reasons for AI's actions in a number of instances. This might then trigger different layers of a multilevel liability system. For example, full compliance with the set of rules coded and made available could trigger the application of compensation funds, a reversal of the burden of proof, channelling liability on different individuals…

In addition, the same mechanisms, guaranteed by making AI accountable, would help apportioning the costs among various stakeholders and across different liability regimes that would probably coexist at least for some time.

VII. Blending liability and accountability for selecting AI liability regimes

It is now time to understand better the meaning and role of accountability. It has precise (although varied) meanings in both computer science and law.

In law 'Accountability refers to the extent to which decision-makers are expected to justify their choices to those affected by these choices, be held answerable for their actions, and be held responsible for their failures and wrongdoings'.[34] Thus, relevant literature already acknowledged that accountability indicates liability to account for and answer for one's conduct, the obligation to provide a satisfactory answer to an external oversight

---

34 Maayan Perel and Niva Elkin-Koren (n 8). See also Michael D Dowdle, 'Public Accountability: Conceptual, Historical, and Epistemic Mappings' in Michael D Dowdle (ed), *Public accountability: Designs, dilemmas and experiences* (Cambridge University Press 2006) ('persons with public responsibilities should be answerable to "the people"' for the performance of their duties.'); Danielle Keats Citron and Frank Pasquale, 'Network Accountability for the Domestic Intelligence Apparatus' (2011) 62 Hastings L.J.1441 (focusing on accountability as a measure to cure the problems generated by the growing use of Fusion Centers); Tal Zarsky, 'Transparent Predictions' (2013) U. Ill. L. Rev. 1530.

agent. A notion well known also in our legal systems as clearly exemplified by the EU General Data Protection Regulation.

This notion of accountability has a counterpart in computational disciplines. Here it is defined as 'set of mechanisms, practices and attributes that sum to a governance structure […] for processing, storing, sharing, deleting and otherwise using [personal and/or confidential] data according to contractual and legal requirements. Accountability involves committing to legal and ethical obligations, policies, procedures and mechanism, explaining and demonstrating ethical implementation to internal and external stakeholders and remedying any failure to act properly'.[35] Surprisingly enough computer scientists are more aware of the links between computational accountability and law than jurists are.

As already illustrated in literature[36] accountability can have a procedural and a substantive meaning. In the former, it indicates a sort of procedural regularity ensuring each individual that the same procedure is applied to them and that the procedure was not designed in a way that disadvantages them specifically. In substantive terms, accountability imposes that the policy furthers fundamental goals or principles addressing legal and ethical questions: does the rule implemented correspond to moral, legal, and ethical criteria. Is it actual operation faithful to these substantive choices?

Along these premises, we can develop a threefold notion of accountability for AI (a notion which is already implemented in the GDPR, for instance):

1. The obligation to report back to someone (*rendre le compte*) to show how responsibility is exercised and making this verifiable;
2. Enabling the 'Audience' (stakeholders, victims, authorities) to interrogate and question the accountable entity thus producing 'their own accounts';
3. Providing for various levels of 'Sanctions' when a violation of accountability occurs (inaction or bad actions).

This threefold notion of accountability requires 'demonstration' mechanisms and criteria to assess them: enabling more than correlation in compu-

35 IEEE, *A Glossary for Discussion of Ethics of Autonomous and Intelligent Systems*, available at <https://standards.ieee.org/develop/indconn/ec/eadv 2_glossary.pdf> accessed 8 August 2018.

36 Joshua A Kroll et al, 'Accountable Algorithms' (2017) 165 U Pa L Rev 633.

tation, giving certainty to legal standards. Accountability is an *ex-post* instrument that requires *ex ante* actions (an already emerging regulatory framework) to enable the provision of evidence in an adjudication process.

Finally, accountability enables different layers of liability: reversal of the burden of proof, compulsory insurance, funds, regulatory constraints, criminal sanctions. These are made more easily applicable and scalable using algorithm (procedural and substantive) accountability for liability purposes.

It is important to note that technology is today able to offer a number of tools to implement effectively algorithm (procedural and substantive) accountability for liability purposes.[37] Although we do not have here the possibility to illustrate it in detail, the accountability principle coupled with a proper use of technology enable to assess and show, for instance, that the deviation from the expected conduct is triggered by the specific use to which the AI has been put in use for or that the deviation from the expected conduct is triggered by the dataset originally used in the machine training of the AI. Intuitively, this ability to allocate factual causality would prove essential in the allocation of liability among potential multiple tortfeasors/stakeholders. It is a possible way to solve the split the bill problem.

Of course, we are aware that there are technical restrictions to the use of such technologies. For instance, the potential interconnectedness of algorithms and of algorithmic decisions seriously restricts the means of algorithmic decision-makers to give an account of the decisions they make.

---

37 Among these techniques are Software verification (on this subject see Jean Souyris et al, 'Formal verification of avionics software products' in Ana Cavalcanti and Dennis Dams (eds), *FM 2009: Formal Methods* (Springer 2009) 532, Norbert Völker and Bernd J Krämer, 'Automated verification of function block-based industrial control systems' (2002) 42 *Science of Computer Programming* 101; Daniel Halperin et al, 'Pacemakers and implantable cardiac defibrillators: Software radio attacks and zero-power defences' (2008) *IEEE Symposium on Security and Privacy*, 129; Karl Koscher et al, 'Experimental security analysis of a modern automobile' (2010) *IEEE Symposium on Security and Privacy* 447; Stephen Checkoway et al, 'Comprehensive experimental analyses of automotive attack surfaces' (2011) *20th USENIX Security Symposium* 77) algorithms explanations to make them interpretable (See Cynthia Rudin, 'Algorithms for interpretable machine learning' (2014) *Proceedings of the 20th ACM SIGKDD International Conference on Knowledge discovery and data mining* 333) Cryptographic commitments, zero-knowledge proofs, fair random choices (on these techniques see again Kroll et al, ibid).

However, we can still assert with confidence that the basis of the debate surrounding liability regimes for the tackled new technologies have changed and are partially determined by the technologies they aim at ruling. Time is ripe to discuss how to unfold a multilayered accountability-based liability system using both:

a) existing and forthcoming experience/technology for accountability and
b) the existing/emerging regulatory framework at the EU level (e.g. GDPR is a clear example[38]).

Here we can only state that AI requires a gradual layered approach to liability grounded on accountability principles (already embedded in the EU legal system). In addition, we cannot illustrate here fully that AI requires the use of technology itself to unfold a multilayered accountable liability system and solve the 'splitting the bill problem'.

To conclude, let's have a closer look into this last issue.

Even when duly adapted, traditional tort liability rules are ineffective in sorting the allocation of liability and costs related to AI (recourse, contribution, joint and several liability, etc.); distributing the costs among the mentioned players, the public and with the insurance market. To the contrary, whatever liability basis is chosen (fault, strict liability, vicarious liability, no-fault, funds, etc.) predictable legal and computational accountability mechanisms effectively help splitting the bill in 'automated' and 'verifiable' ways at virtual no costs. A number of the causal connections and the correspondence to the 'required standard of conduct' can rely on legal computational accountability.

Note also that if the issue of apportioning the financial costs of liability is left to insurance companies by way of redress actions, the need to have objective criteria to redistribute the costs remains and can effectively rely on the accountability notion we are briefly introducing.

The link between the accountability principles and any liability regime remains essential.

38 'Accountability is an important area and an explicit requirement under the GDPR.' (WP29 'Guidelines on Automated individual decision-making and Profiling for the purposes of Regulation 2016/679', adopted on 3 October 2017, as last Revised and Adopted on 6 February 2018, at 29).

New Approaches: Form of Liability

Liability for Autonomous Systems: Tackling Specific Risks of Modern IT

Herbert Zech[*]

Recent developments in the area of Artificial Intelligence (AI) have been leading to increasingly autonomous systems, showing the capability of self-learning. In addition, self-learning made significant progress by the realization of multi-layered artificial neural networks with an ever-increasing complexity. These new technologies cause the emergence of new specific risks. Liability law may specifically address these risks.

I. Current AI – the phenomenon

Artificial Intelligence is a technology known since the 1950s when the term was coined in a research grant application for the famous 1956 Dartmouth Conference.[1] Broadly speaking, AI may be defined as the attempt to simulate human reasoning.[2] The development of AI encompassed expert systems, learning systems and finally cognitive systems.[3] However, until around 2010, although the theoretical background for neural networks already existed, AI relied on symbolic logic. The main goal was to describe logic processes as detailed as possible and with ever increasing

* Professor of Life Sciences Law and Intellectual Property Law, University of Basel.

1 Research proposal 'A Proposal for the Dartmouth Summer Research Project on Artificial Intelligenced' by J McCarthy/ML Minsky/N Rochester/CE Shannon, 1955 (available at <http://www-formal.stanford.edu/jmc/history/dartmouth/dartmouth.html> accessed 8 August 2018): 'We propose that a […] study of artificial intelligence be carried out […]. The study is to proceed on the basis of the conjecture that every aspect of learning or any other feature of intelligence can in principle be so precisely described that a machine can be made to simulate it.'.

2 A Lauber-Rönsberg, 'Im Gespräch: Künstliche Intelligenz und Immaterialgüterrecht' GRUR Newsletter 2/2017, 17.

3 M Šīrava, 'Euphorie Künstliche Intelligenz – Eine Bestandsaufnahme der technischen Entwicklung, Möglichkeiten und Grenzen aus Sicht der Praxis' GRUR Newsletter 2/2017, 7f.

complexity, and in doing so achieve results more and more similar to 'natural' thinking. Although results were impressive, like chess playing and even playing 'Jeopardy' such classical AI or GOFAI (good old-fashioned AI) was inherently limited. After 2010, with the advent of sufficient computer power to simulate larger neural networks, the picture changed completely. The already existing concept of multi-layered neural networks could be put into practice thereby simulating 'natural' brains. By now, the complexity of such networks equals, in number of simulated neurons and simulated synapses, brains of small mammals like mice.[4] This allows unprecedented flexibility and learning capabilities which are already used in everyday products like translation and language recognition.

The main difference between classical AI and deep learning is that only classical AI follows a precise step of logical rules (algorithms) whereas the behaviour of neural networks may only be described statistically (stochastical behaviour). The ability to describe such a trained behaviour and even reverse engineer it (i.e. explain which input caused the trained behaviour) is an area of intense research. Although the trained behaviour cannot be described as a fully (i.e. 100 %) reliable algorithm (but may, of course, be approximated), the status of a trained neural network, the so-called weights of every node in the network, can be described with perfect precision. Trained neural networks, therefore, can be replicated but their behaviour cannot be described with 100 % accuracy.

Another important characteristic is that neural networks can be used in a way where they never stop learning, just like natural brains. This is a huge advantage for creating self-adapting systems who can respond to changing environments. On the other hand, it creates huge problems in terms of foreseeability and reliability. Humans tend to perceive artificial systems as deterministic which will no longer hold true in the future.[5] It has to be noted that self-learning systems already had and have been real-

4 Around 10^8 (simulated) neurons or 10^{11} parameters (comparable to synapses). cf Jeremy Hsu, 'Biggest Neural Network Ever Pushes AI Deep Learning' (8 July 2015) <https://spectrum.ieee.org/tech-talk/computing/software/biggest-neural-network-ever-pushes-ai-deep-learning> accessed 8 August 2018 (record of $1,6 \times 10^{11}$ parameters). cf Suzana Herculano Houzel et al, 'Cellular scaling rules for rodent brains' PNAS 103 (2006), 12138, 12139 (<http://www.pnas.org/content/103/32/12138> accessed 8 August 2018): mouse $7 \pm 1 \times 10^7$ neurons, rat $20 \pm 1 \times 10^7$ neurons (with approximately 1000 synapses per neuron).

5 DC Dennett, 'The Singularity – an Urban Legend?' in J Brockman (ed), *What to Think About Machines That Think* (Harper Perennial 2015) 85ff.

ized with classical AI. Such systems also may change their behaviour due to input but always contain a core logic which remains unchanged. Neural networks, in contrast, develop their logical structure by learning. Moreover, they no longer behave deterministically in response to certain input. The most amazing development is the ability to set two networks as 'sparring partners', thereby creating a system which can learn and change its behaviour without any further input.[6]

Self-learning capability may be used in software systems (like language recognition) or in hardware systems (AI controlled machines) like robots and self-driving cars. Up until now, 'learning risks' in hardware systems were mitigated by releasing upgrades checked by humans instead of allowing constant changes without human intervention. This may not be sufficient for complex future applications like self-driving cars.

II. What distinguishes current AI from 'classical' IT?

When discussing current AI, two phenomena can be addressed which distinguish current AI from other 'classical' IT-systems: first, the capability of self-learning in general which may be called autonomy (coming in various degrees), and second, the new system structure of multi-layered neural networks which is also called deep learning.

1. Self-learning (autonomy)

Self-learning means, by definition, a loss of control since self-learning systems may be influenced by external stimuli – wanted or unwanted. This loss of control may be mitigated in several ways. It depends on how controlled the environment a system operates in is, the amount of permanent human control (by the operator or the manufacturer) and, reciprocally, the amount of influence learning can have on the behaviour of the system. As a general rule, the more a machine can learn, the less control the manufacturer has (which is important for product liability).[7] The capability of self-learning may be described as autonomy. According to *Russel/Norvig*, an

6 Example: Google's DeepMind playing chess <http://www.bbc.com/news/technology-42251535> accessed 8 August 2018.

7 See below at V.3.

autonomous agent can be defined as follows: 'To the extent that an agent relies on the prior knowledge of its designer rather than on its own percepts, we say that the agent lacks autonomy.'[8] An autonomous system can change its behaviour without human intervention, i.e. it can change the rules governing its behaviour independently.

2. *Multi-layered neural networks (deep learning)*

With the advent of neural networks and deep learning an additional degree of uncertainty has been introduced.[9] This is due to possible unexpected effects of new stimuli and to the inherent probabilistic nature of the behaviour of neural networks.[10] Trained behaviour of neural networks cannot be described as a deterministic algorithm and the contribution of individual inputs to changes of the behaviour cannot be described as a simple causal connection. Therefore, in advance, the behaviour of such systems can be predicted less accurately, and, in hindsight, it can be understood less precisely ('black box' problem[11]). However, the accuracy of predic-

---

8 SJ Russel/P Norvig, *Artificial Intelligence: A Modern Approach* (3rd edn, Pearson 2009) 40; E Hilgendorf, 'Interview JProf. Dr. Maximilian Becker & Sandra von Lingen mit Prof. Dr. Dr. Eric Hilgendorf' GRUR Newsletter 2/2017, 9: 'Wir verstehen autonome Systeme als solche technischen Systeme, die ohne menschliche Steuerung über einen längeren Zeitpunkt hinweg erfolgreich Aufgaben bewältigen können. Selbstlernende Systeme können ihre Algorithmen infolge von Erfahrungen weiterbilden, wobei das Lernen frei oder kontrolliert erfolgen kann.' In the area of robotics there is a definition of autonomy in ISO 8373:2012(en) 2.2: ability to perform intended tasks based on current state and sensing, without human intervention. The term is criticised as misleading by I Wildhaber/MF Lohmann, 'Roboterrecht – eine Einführung' AJP 2017, 135, 136. See H Zech, 'Zivilrechtliche Haftung für den Einsatz von Robotern – Zuweisung von Automatisierungs- und Autonomierisiken' in S Gless/K Seelmann (eds), *Intelligente Agenten und das Recht* (Nomos 2016) 163, 170f with further references.

9 Described in terms of autonomy, deep learning has realized higher degrees of autonomy.

10 G Lewis-Kraus, 'The Great A.I. Awakening' <https://www.nytimes.com/2016/12/14/magazine/the-great-ai-awakening.html> accessed 8 August 2018: 'It is important to note, however, that the fact that neural networks are probabilistic in nature means that they're not suitable for all tasks.'.

11 D Castelvecchi, 'Can we open the black box of AI?' Nature 538 (2016), 21ff; P Voosen, 'How AI detectives are cracking open the black box of deep learning' <http://www.sciencemag.org/news/2017/07/how-ai-detectives-are-cracking-open-

tion may be raised by specific measures like controlled learning (which is in conflict with the capability of self-adapting), minimum training, statistical analysis of the trained behaviour etc. The understanding of trained AI, i.e. the transparency of the 'black box', may also be raised by ongoing research.

III. Defining technology-specific risks of current AI

A technology-related or technology-specific risk is understood as a situation where a damage may occur caused by the use of a specific technology.[12] Some risks of AI are well known from other technological applications.[13] Complexity and the associated risk of unexpected system behaviour is typical for software in general. Another area of technology is robotics where AI is directly linked to hardware actuators causing risks of physical damage. However, self-learning systems in general and neural networks in specific raise problems which may, especially for legal purposes, be translated into technology-specific risks. Three such risks in connection with current AI can be discerned which could be called the autonomy risk (self-learning risk), the probability risk and the intransparency risk, respectively.

1. Autonomy risk (self-learning risk)

Firstly, all self-learning systems pose a specific risk associated with the ability to learn and accordingly to change their behaviour. This may call for specific counter-measures or technical restrictions according to the area of use, the environment and the skill of the operator. With increasing

---

black-box-deep-learning> accessed 8 August 2018; W Knight, 'The Dark Secret at the Heart of AI' <https://www.technologyreview.com/s/604087/the-dark-secret-at-the-heart-of-ai/> accessed 8 August 2018.

12 H Zech 'Haftungsregeln als Instrument zur Steuerung von "emerging risks"' in S Fuhrer (ed), *Jahrbuch SGHVR 2016* (Schulthess 2016) 17, 19. For a precise definition of technology see H Zech, 'Technizität im Patentrecht – Eine intra- und interdisziplinäre Analyse des Technikbegriffs' in A Metzger (ed), *Methodenfragen des Patentrechts. Theo Bodewig zum 70. Geburtstag* (Mohr Siebeck 2018) 150ff.

13 For a detailed description of the risks associated with IT due to complexity, connectivity, hardware connection and autonomy see Zech (n 8) 172ff.

learning abilities, the associated risk increases proportionally, i.e. the risk cannot be judged as merely existing or not but rather as increasing gradually according to the systems' architecture and capabilities.

If autonomous systems are implemented in hardware with actuators (autonomous robots) the autonomy risk may directly be realized in physical damages. Therefore, autonomous robots are especially problematic and, arguably, not allowable under existing law.[14]

2. *Probability risk of deep learning*

Secondly, neural networks in particular pose a further risk. The inherent probabilistic behaviour of a neural network decreases predictability independently from self-learning capabilities. Even if a neural network is trained under perfectly controlled circumstances and afterwards blocked from further learning its behaviour may only be predicted with a statistical margin of error. However, errors also occur in the ordinary machine world and a sufficiently low margin of error may suffice for declaring a neural network safe. From a legal point of view, this could be regulated by technical standards. Self-learning systems with neural networks being operated in open environments combine the autonomy and the probability risk.

In addition, probabilistic behaviour may make avoiding damages by third parties more difficult. From a legal point of view, this may be of relevance for the question of whether strict liability for AI is necessary or not.

3. *Intransparency problem (creating legal risks)*

The 'black box' problem also translates into difficulties to explain in hindsight why an AI system reacted in a certain way. Causal connections between training input and later system behaviour therefore may be difficult to elucidate. This, firstly, is due to a possible huge number of inputs from different sources (which also applies for classical self-learning) and, secondly, is inherent to the 'black box' nature of neural networks where the effect of known inputs may not be attributed precisely to changes in behaviour.

14 Zech (n 8) 192. G Wagner, 'Produkthaftung für autonome Systeme', AcP 217 (2017) 707, 728f.

In legal terms, this translates into problems with the proof of causality. Although such problems are known from other technological risks (like long term risks and multi-causal effects) the probabilistic nature raises new problems with the proof of causality hitherto only known for damages caused by animals or human intermediaries.

Generally speaking, the inherent intransparency of neural networks means that using a trained network does not necessarily entail understanding the underlying causality (leading to problems with the common understanding of technology as making use of known causality effects). This is comparable to the fact that big data analyses only generate insights into correlation and not into causality.

IV. New and old risks

Speaking about new technology-related risks necessitates comparing these risks with the ones caused by technologies already in use. Risks can by definition be quantified as the amount of damages multiplied by the likelihood of occurrence.[15] The estimate of a newly emerging risk entails a certain confidence interval. Similarly, the risk assessment concerning a specific AI system comes with a confidence interval which is inherently broader for deep learning systems but may be narrowed down by a better understanding of neural networks in general and by sufficient training and other safeguards for the individual system.

For public policy considerations, accepted risks of technologies already in use may be compared to the risk of replacing them with AI technology. An important example being currently discussed is the introduction of self-driving cars which necessarily have to be highly automated and may also have to rely on self-learning (although it is still unclear whether and to which extent the use of self-learning capability is necessary or whether even neural networks should be implemented in cars which seems extremely risky).

The alleged increased safety of automated cars over old cars bears significance for the admissibility of such cars. The underlying legal implication is that accepted risks represent a benchmark for the assessment of

15 Zech, 'Haftungsregeln als Instrument zur Steuerung von "emerging risks"' (n 12) 19f.

new risks. If the autonomy risk and the probability risk are lower than the accepted risk for the old technology which is to be substituted by AI, they are permissible. If 'autonomous' cars are actually safer than cars being driven by humans, they should, for instance, not be defective in the sense of product liability law.[16]

V. Specific risks as a legal tool

Identifying specific risks may benefit the legal analysis of liability law cases. The concept of technology specific risks, therefore, is an important instrument in technology-related jurisprudence. Moreover, technology-specific risks may even be used as elements in potential new legal rules (similar to the existing liability for genetic engineering according to § 32 GenTG[17]).

Generally speaking, the identification of technology specific risks may clarify legal liability rules as such, as well as their underlying economic function. It allows for a precise definition of sources of risks, potentially hazardous objects or hazardous activities. As an example, recent problems with regulating gene technology caused by genome editing could be resolved by a risk-based approach trying to distinguish between the specific risks of 'classic' gene technology and genome editing.[18] This would allow to answer the question whether organisms obtained by genome editing but indistinguishable from naturally occurring organisms should be covered by gene technology regulation.

---

16 cf Wagner (n 14) 733ff; Zech (n 8) 188f.

17 German Law on Genetic Engineering. § 32 (1) GenTG reads: 'If, as a result of the properties of an organism that is based on genetic engineering, someone is killed, their body or health is injured or a thing is damaged, the operator is obliged to compensate for the resulting damage.' Genetic engineering is precisely defined in § 3 (2) GenTG.

18 cf the pending request for a preliminary ruling of the CJEU on the notion of 'genetically modified organism', Case C–528/16 – Confédération paysanne and others.

1. Regulatory law

Harnessing technology related risks by means of direct intervention is the domain of regulatory law. The concept of technology specific risks makes it possible to design technology specific regulations. Technology specific risks may also be addressed by technical standards, allowing for greater flexibility and more details. Whether it is advisable to create a new law regulating AI in general or some of the abovementioned forms of AI is still an open question.[19]

2. Fault-based liability (tort law, contract law)

The concept of specific technology related risks may also be used for determining fault-based liability. By defining the duty of care in handling such risks it may be decided whether the use of a certain technology (a certain AI) is negligent or not. Based on specific risks also categories of cases (case groups) concerning the use of AI may be established. For example, different standards should apply for mere software systems and for hardware systems (direct AI-machine coupling). For defining the necessary measures and precautions, again, technical standards may be taken into account (but are not binding for the judge). Finally, standards and case groups for determining self-negligence may be based on specific technologies, too.

In the case of AI-related products, this means that duties of care for producers, distributors, commercial users, consumers and third parties have to be defined with regard to the specific technology and its optimal use for public welfare.[20] This, for instance, is especially important for consumers

---

19 A model for such a legislation could be the German law concerning critical IT infrastructure enacted in 2015 (*Gesetz zur Erhöhung der Sicherheit informationstechnischer Systeme* [*IT-Sicherheitsgesetz*] of 17. July 2015) which amended the law on the Federal Office for Information Security (BSIG). The European Parliament only called for civil law rules ('a directive on civil law rules on robotics') combined with a code of conduct ('code of ethical conduct for robotics engineers'), European Parliament resolution of 16 February 2017 with recommendations to the Commission on Civil Law Rules on Robotics (2015/2103(INL)), paras 51, 65 and annex.

20 For an overview of the potential liable parties see G Borges, 'Rechtliche Rahmenbedingungen für autonome Systeme' NJW 2018, 977, 980; Zech (n 8) 177ff.

as technology users. Without a clear limitation of the consumers' duties, new AI products are potentially not attractive enough to be broadly accepted.

3. *Product liability (defective products)*

Liability for AI is currently being discussed mainly as a product liability problem.[21] At least hardware implementing AI is a product in the sense of Art 2 Directive 85/374/EEC[22] ('movable' or physical thing).[23] According to Art 6 (1) Directive 85/374/EEC a product is defective when it does not provide the safety which a person is entitled to expect. Risks associated with AI may affect the safety of products. However, it has to be noted that product liability does not address the specific risks of these technologies. Instead, product liability seeks to mitigate or redistribute the 'risks inherent in modern technological production' (recitals of Directive 85/374/EEC).

Autonomy risk and probability risk can make products defective. Learning-risks may lead to products becoming defective by learning after sale (training defect[24]). However, it may also be argued that the mere learning ability in itself represents a product defect at the time when the product was put into circulation.[25] Due to the learning ability the manufacturer cannot control entirely whether the product may cause damages during its lifetime.[26] However, product safety and security does not require

---

21 See Wagner (n 14) 707ff; Communication from the Commission to the European Parliament, the European Council, the Council, the European Economic and Social Committee and the Committee of the Regions on Artificial Intelligence for Europe, Brussels, 25.4.2018, COM(2018) 237 final, at 3.3.

22 Council Directive 85/374/EEC of 25 July 1985 on the approximation of the laws, regulations and administrative provisions of the Member States concerning liability for defective products (OJ L 210, 7.8.1985, 29–33).

23 See Wagner (n 14) 714ff with further remarks on the applicability to software *per se*.

24 'Anlernfehler' (A Auer-Reinsdorff, public lecture, 28.10.2015, Munich); cf Article 7 (b) Council Directive 85/372/EEC of 25 July 1985.

25 Zech (n 8) 192.

26 Mady Delvaux-Stehres, 'Interview: MEP Mady Delvaux-Stehres (S&D) on Civil Law Rules on Robotics. European Parliament resolution of 16 February 2017 (2015/2103(INL))', GRUR Newsletter 2/2017, 16: '[…] personally, I cannot imagine that you put things into the market if you cannot foresee what they will do.'.

absolute control by the manufacturer or the absence of any risk. Rather, the product has to fulfil the reasonable safety and security expectations by potential customers (which should be determined on an economic welfare rationale).[27] Therefore, a product should be judged to be non-defective if its use generates benefits outweighing the unavoidably occurring damages.[28] As shown at IV., a comparison with existing products and accepted risks can be a proof for such a positive statistical overall balance. Moreover, regulatory law and technical standards can also serve as important signposts for the legally required level of safety (although they are not binding for product liability law, just like for tort law).

4. *Strict liability*

The identification of certain specific risks can also be used for the introduction of strict liability rules. The introduction of a strict liability for the use of a specific technology is – like regulatory law – a classical way of dealing with technology associated risks. The oldest example is the strict liability for steam trains.[29] From the perspective of economics, strict liability rules internalise negative effects of new technologies and therefore create an incentive to use these technologies only if they are safe enough and to develop existing systems further in order to make them safer.[30]

The existing German law knows no general clause for strict liability. However, it may be discussed whether the autonomy risk and the probability risk could be addressed by an analogy to the strict liability of animal keepers according to § 833 BGB[31] (German Civil Code, according to the

27 Wagner (n 14) 728ff.

28 Wagner (n 14) 733.

29 M Vec, 'Kurze Geschichte des Technikrechts' in M Schulte/R Schröder (eds), *Handbuch des Technikrechts* (2nd edn, Springer 2011) 3, 28.

30 See Zech, 'Haftungsregeln als Instrument zur Steuerung von "emerging risks"' (n 12) 3ff, 13ff with further references.

31 § 833 BGB: 'If a human being is killed by an animal or if the body or the health of a human being is injured by an animal or a thing is damaged by an animal, then the person who keeps the animal is liable to compensate the injured person for the damage arising from this. Liability in damages does not apply if the damage is caused by a domestic animal intended to serve the occupation, economic activity or subsistence of the keeper of the animal and either the keeper of the animal in supervising the animal has exercised reasonable care or the damage would also have occurred even if this care had been exercised.'.

second sentence of § 833 BGB strict liability does not apply 'if the damage is caused by a domestic animal intended to serve the occupation, economic activity or subsistence of the keeper of the animal').[32] This seems especially convincing for artificial neural networks with a size comparable to those of small animals.

The introduction of a strict liability rule for certain types of AI like self-learning systems, neural networks or products containing such systems would address their specific risks. Proof of causality problems could also be addressed: If certain risks pose specific problems of clarifying or proving causation, risk-specific rules for reversing the burden of proof may be introduced (e.g. in the German law on genetic engineering, § 34 GenTG[33]). The European Parliament called for a 'legislative instrument on legal questions related to the development and use of robotics and AI foreseeable in the next 10 to 15 years'.[34] It considered strict liability as a potential solution: '(T)he future legislative instrument should be based on an in-depth evaluation by the Commission determining whether the strict liability or the risk management approach should be applied'.[35] The Commission, however, decided to rely on product liability and announced to 'issue a guidance document on the interpretation of the Product Liability Directive in light of technological developments'.[36]

VI. Summary and outlook

Recent developments in the area of information technology, frequently addressed as Artificial Intelligence (AI), comprise the capability of self-learning (autonomy) and, as a special system architecture, multi-layered

32 See Borges (n 20) 981; Zech (n 8) 195f.

33 § 34 (1) GenTG: 'If the damage has been caused by genetically modified organisms, it is presumed that it was caused by the properties of these organisms, which are based on genetic engineering.'.

34 European Parliament resolution of 16 February 2017 with recommendations to the Commission on Civil Law Rules on Robotics (2015/2103(INL)), para 51.

35 European Parliament resolution of 16 February 2017 with recommendations to the Commission on Civil Law Rules on Robotics (2015/2103(INL)), para 53.

36 Communication from the Commission to the European Parliament, the European Council, the Council, the European Economic and Social Committee and the Committee of the Regions on Artificial Intelligence for Europe, Brussels, 25.4.2018, COM(2018) 237 final.

neural networks (deep learning). The use of self-learning systems and the use of multi-layered neural networks causes specific risks which may be seen as an example of technology risks. These risks may be called the autonomy risk (self-learning risk), the probability risk of deep learning, and, as a legal risk, the intransparency problem.

Addressing these specific new risks allows for a comparison with the risks of older technologies used for the same purpose. Moreover, such technology specific risks caused by the development or use of a technology (which may be the production, distribution or use of related products or the offering of related services) can be used as a legal tool. They may facilitate the analysis of liability cases under existing law or be used as elements in new legal rules. The concept of specific risks also helps to clarify the duties of care associated with the test for negligence. They can be used for establishing categories of cases by jurisdiction (case groups).

Technology related risks show the importance of interdisciplinary cooperation. The factual understanding of new technologies like self-learning systems or multi-layered neural networks has to be combined with the legal understanding of the concepts underlying liability law, regulatory law or other areas of law. This ensures that cases are correctly analysed according to existing law and that appropriate proposals can be made for changing the law.

As an outlook, it has to be mentioned that the current developments may turn AI into a transformative technology.[37] It is 'capable of significantly changing practice and reorganising concepts'.[38] Such a technology causes not only risks whose quantity (potential damage times likelihood) is uncertain but whose normative evaluation is also ambiguous (uncertainty whether effects are good or bad) and, even more, it may potentially

37 The term 'transformative technology' is explicitly mentioned for AI by the European Commission, Communication from the Commission to the European Parliament, the European Council, the Council, the European Economic and Social Committee and the Committee of the Regions on Artificial Intelligence for Europe, Brussels, 25.4.2018, COM(2018) 237 final, para 1. It was coined by the Nuffield Council on Bioethics, 'Genome editing: an ethical review' (2016) 12, 26 <http://nuffieldbioethics.org/wp-content/uploads/Genome-editing-an-ethical-review.pdf> accessed 8 August 2018, for characterizing genome editing; cf B Fateh-Moghadam, 'Genome Editing als strafrechtliches Grundlagenproblem', medstra 2017, 146, 148.

38 cf Nuffield Council on Bioethics (n 37) 12.

change social values (transformative potential).[39] Therefore, in the future, the law may be confronted with a task much more complex than simple risk management.

39 Nuffield Council on Bioethics (n 37) 26: '[…] genome editing is a potentially transformative technology, not merely in an economic sense but also in a moral sense, in that it has the capacity both to produce new differences in the world and to provoke new ways of thinking about differences in the world.'.

Causation and Scope of Liability in the Internet of Things (IoT)

Miquel Martín-Casals[*]

I. Introduction

1. IoT multiple layers and players

The Internet of Things (IoT) is a series of networked 'smart devices' that are equipped with microchips, sensors, and wireless communications capabilities. It involves several layers which encompass tangible elements (hardware-defined products), embedded and non-embedded software (software-defined products), supply of digital infrastructures (network fabric) and external processing and exploitation of data (external systems).[1]

Most of the IoT projects identified by IoT Analytics in its 2018 report are in Smart City (367 projects), followed by various other industrial settings (265) and Connected Building IoT projects (193).[2] The major categories of IoT technologies include 'smart' consumer technologies, wearables, 'smart' manufacturing and infrastructure technologies, and unmanned transportation[3]. The best known of these technologies are proba-

---

* Professor of Civil Law, Director of the Institute of European and Comparative Private Law, University of Girona. The author wishes to express his indebtedness to the Spanish Ministry of Economy and Competitiveness for the award of the [DER2016-77229-R] R&D grant which has made this research paper possible.

1 Rajkumar Buyya and Amir Vahid Dastjerdi (eds), *Internet of Things. Principles and Paradigms* (Elsevier 2016) 3ff.

2 The Americas make up most of these projects (45%), followed by Europe (35%), and Asia (16%) and there are large differences when looking at individual IoT segments and regions. In comparison to its 2016 ranking, Smart City (driven by government and municipality-led initiatives) has surpassed Connected Industry as the number one IoT segment of identified projects, while Connected Building (driven by widespread uptake of building automation solutions that increase operational efficiency and reduce costs) has climbed four places to become the third biggest IoT segment. See <https://iot-analytics.com/top-10-iot-segments-2018-real-iot-projects/> accessed 20 April 2018.

3 Andrea Castillo and Adam D Thierer (2015), 'Projecting the Growth and Economic Impact of the Internet of Things', available at SSRN: <https://ssrn.com/abstract=26

bly 'autonomous vehicles' or 'driverless cars', which permit cars to operate without human assistance and are expected to dramatically reduce the number of deaths and injuries in traffic accidents, and 'drones', which employ similar networked concepts to automate aerial operations. Other technologies such as wearables (watches, jewellery, clothes), that integrate networked devices and collect data, track activities, and customise experiences to users' needs, also promise to become widespread in the coming years, particularly in the areas of personal safety and security, health, wellness, fitness, personal organisation, and communication. In some cases, these new technological devices are not just worn, but implanted – such as pacemakers – or simply swallowed – such as 'smart pills'[4] – and will be able to sense the parameters of diseases, send data to monitoring centres or release medicines automatically.

The multiplicity and interdependency of layers involved in IoT technologies, and the wide variety of market players who contribute to their production, may make it difficult for IoT users to identify which layers or market players have caused harm. It is thus very likely that on many occasions users of IoT technologies may face legal uncertainty as regards who is responsible for the harm they suffer, all the more if, for instance, IoT hardware is supplied by producers of the IoT devices but software, data platforms or digital infrastructures are supplied independently by third-party contractors. Among many other legal questions, in the case of causation two basic questions arise: will our current legal rules and doctrines on causation, as they stand now, be able to solve the causal legal problems caused by IoT technologies? And if not, will they be able to evolve and to adapt to them or will new ones become necessary?

It is well known that IoT technologies may affect a wide variety of protected interests and thus that they can give rise, not only to personal injury and property damage, but also to pure economic loss and, most notably, to invasions of privacy. Taking into account that the main harmonising in-

---

18794> or <http://dx.doi.org/10.2139/ssrn.2618794> both accessed 8 February 2018.

4 Such as the smart-pill recently approved by the FDA for use in the United States (Abilify MyCite), which contains a drug and an ingestible sensor that is activated when it comes into contact with stomach fluid to detect when the pill has been taken and transmits data that can be accessed by the patient's doctors or caregivers. See <https://newatlas.com/smart-digital-pill-fda-approval/52187/> accessed 21 February 2018.

strument currently existing in the area of tort law, the Council Directive 85/374/EEC of 25 of July 1985 on the approximation of the laws, regulations and administrative provisions of the Member States concerning liability for defective products (hereafter, the Product Liability Directive or PLD), refers to personal injury and property damage only, this paper will focus on these protected interests and will not consider causation related problems that may arise when other protected interests have been violated.

After referring briefly to some general ideas about how legal evolution may react to meet the challenges of technological development, the first part of this paper deals with the lack of harmonisation of the rules on causation and with the different approaches to causation rules and doctrines in European legal practice. Additionally, it tries to provide an overview or a sort of roadmap to the problems related to causation by looking for a common language and framework in comparative legal literature and in some soft-law projects. The second part deals, firstly, with possible answers to problems posed by uncertain causation, which is not only the main problem in the area of factual causation, but also the most likely to arise in the context of IoT technologies and, finally, it also refers to foreseeability and to the doctrine of intervening causation as some of the main problems that may arise in the scope of liability area.

2. *Technological change and legal response*

At the beginning of the so-called 'Fourth Industrial Revolution'[5] a sensation of vertigo before the unknown invades not only politicians and business leaders but also lawyers and legal scholars. Although this seems a much more far-reaching revolution than the three previous ones, we can probably take some advantage from the lessons learnt from the past. In this regard, I would like to make three points only.

The first, probably not a very reassuring one, is that the types of new legal disputes that will arise from new technologies are often unforeseeable. We may say that there are a few things that we know that we know, and a few more that we know that we do not know. However, the most

---

5 Klaus Schwab, *The Fourth Industrial Revolution* (World Economic Forum 2016), 7 considers that it began at the turn of the century and is characterised by a much more ubiquitous and mobile internet, by smaller and more powerful sensors that have become very cheap and by artificial intelligence and machine learning.

worrying situation is that regarding that number of things that we do not know that we do not know.

The second point alludes to the 'adaptability hypothesis'[6], i.e. that the law and, in our case, the rules and doctrines on causation in tort law, will successfully adapt to solve reasonably legal disputes regarding damage caused by new technologies. This hypothesis may no longer be true if we refer it to the existing legal categories. However, as has been pointed out, the key to analysing whether existing legal categories make legal and social sense under a new technological regime is not about the legal category as such, but the rationale behind any given legal categorisation[7]. Accordingly, what must be evaluated is whether this rationale may be applied or not to a new dispute. In this sense, we may draw many lessons from challenges posed by technological and scientific developments in the past, such as the introduction of the telegraph or the steam engine, or more recently by products such as vaccines or by asbestos-related products[8].

The third and final point is a general one when dealing with tort law and although it is very well known it is often forgotten. For this reason, it deserves to be repeated: the principles and rules of tort law are not the only instrument available when disputes arise about who finally has to bear the consequences of a harm somebody has suffered.

In our case, probably more than in others, technological devices may make legal devices unnecessary or less needed. Thus 'black boxes', sensor systems, and other technological devices may produce proof of causation more easily than legal rules[9] or, at least, facilitate it. Additionally, the development of technology related to IoT may already take into account

---

6 John Bell and David Ibbetson (eds), *European legal development: the case of tort* (Cambridge University Press 2012) 138.

7 Gregory N Mandel, 'Legal Evolution in Response to Technological Change', in Roger Brownsword, Eloise Scotford and Karen Yeung (eds), *The Oxford Handbook of Law, Regulation and Technology* (Oxford University Press 2017) 225–245, 244–245.

8 Mandel (n 7) 244–245 and Jonathan Morgan, 'Torts and Technology', in Brownsword, Scotford and Yeung (n 7) 522–545. See also Miquel Martin-Casals (ed), *The Development of Liability in Relation to Technological Change* (Cambridge University Press 2010) 1–39.

9 Thus, for instance, Ujjayini Bose, 'The Black Box Solution to Autonomous Liability', 92 Washington University Law Review 1325 (2015), 1339ff considers that autopilot systems on airplanes provide the closest analogy to autonomous vehicles and

these and other legal needs ('regulation by design')[10]. Finally, social instruments, such as 'reputational damage', arising out of the scrutiny and attention of the media, can have a great impact on products of mass and lay consumption or that may cause harm to a broad group of users (such as in medical devices) and this may lead to the industry having an increased interest in the development of mechanisms that diminish the possible degree of doubt about who caused damage to whom.

As regards legal devices, tort law is by no means the only legal tool when trying to solve the challenges posed by IoT. There are also other legal devices, such as regulation, compensation funds or insurance, that may either replace or, most probably, complement tort law in this task[11].

II. Causation in its labyrinth: Rules and practice

1. Causation in the Products Liability Directive and its shortcomings

The Product Liability Directive leaves most issues referring to causation to national law.

Art 1 PLD indicates that 'the producer shall be liable for damage caused by the defect in his product', and Art 4 PLD adds that 'the injured person shall be required to prove the damage, the defect and the causal relationship between defect and damage'. These articles clearly point out that causation is a necessary condition for the producer's liability and that the burden of proof lies on the claimant[12]. However, since they do not lay down what causation actually means, what the standard of proof to be

that a solution for assessing tort liability to the manufacturer or the driver should be to require autonomous vehicles to carry an 'Event Data Recorder (EDR)', similar to the Flight Data Recorder (FDR) that airplanes carry onboard.

10 Lachlan Urquhart and Tom Rodden, 'A Legal Turn in Human Computer Interaction? Towards 'Regulation by Design' for the Internet of Things' (March 11, 2016), available at SSRN: <https://ssrn.com/abstract=2746467> accessed 8 August 2018. However, as regards the problems related to programming machines to make them act as much as possible in conformity to existing law see Mark A Chinen, 'The Co-Evolution of Autonomous Machines and Legal Responsibility' 20 Virginia Journal of Law and Technology 338 (2016) 378ff.

11 Morgan (n 8) 539–540, in the context of autonomous cars.

12 Piotr Machnikowski et al, 'Product Liability Directive', in Piotr Machnikowski (ed), *European Product Liability: An Analysis of the State of the Art in the Era of New Technologies* (Intersentia 2016) 85ff.

used to establish causation is or, in general, how causation must be proven, it leaves these issues to national law. Thus, it is for national law to establish whether causation is just a factual issue or whether it also requires that policy considerations, such as directness of the casual link, foreseeability of the damage, risk increase or others be taken into account, so as to keep its scope within acceptable boundaries. As regards how causation must be proven, both the standard of proof and what could be called 'alleviating devices' such as admissibility of prima facie reasoning or judicial presumptions, are also left to national law. Additionally, the Directive does not regulate either whether general causation can play any role in this issue or which solution must be adopted when uncertainty prevents the causal link being established according to the corresponding general rules.

Another relevant provision regarding causation is Art 5 PLD, which establishes that when two or more persons are liable for the same damage, they are jointly and severally (solidary) liable[13], but remits to the provisions of national law for the existing rights of contribution or recourse. The provision is also silent on how causation problems involving uncertain alternative tortfeasors are to be solved. Further provisions that to a greater or less extent may affect causation are Art 7 f) PLD, referring to cases where multiple manufacturers may be a cause of harm and one of them is a manufacturer of a component part. Pursuant to this provision, the manufacturer of a component part may escape liability when the defect is attributable to the design of the product in which the component part has been fitted or, even when the component part itself is defective, when the defect is attributable to the instructions given by the manufacturer of the product[14].

Finally, Art 8.1 PLD prevents the liability of the producer being reduced when the damage is caused both by the defect in the product and by the act or omission of a third party,[15] but also refers to the provisions of national law as regards the rights of contribution or recourse. In a similar way, Art 8.2 PLD allows reduction when damage is caused both by the defect in the product and by the fault of the injured person or any person for

13 Gert Straetmans and Dimitri Verhowven et al, 'Product Liability Directive' in Machnikowski (n 12) 72ff.

14 Machnikowski et al (n 12) 79.

15 Machnikowski et al (n 12) 87.

whom the injured person is responsible[16], but does not make any reference to the rules applicable to contributory negligence.

2. *Different legal approaches to causation in Europe*

The approaches to causation vary significantly from country to country. In an attempt to organise the results of comparative research Infantino and Zervogianni[17] have recently pointed out that, as regards causation, most European legal systems can be fitted into three different models. Although reasonable caution leads the authors to stress that they do not intend to establish a general taxonomy and that, when going deep into details, doubts about whether one legal system is properly classified in one or another model may arise, I think that for a broad general picture these models can be illustrative of the diversity of approaches to causation in Europe.

In a first model ('overarching causation'), which would include countries such as France, Italy, Spain, Poland and Bulgaria, for lack of preliminary filters (as, for instance, wrongfulness and protected interests) causation plays a central role as instrument to weigh up, not only the interests of the parties, but also policy interests. In this model, however, this weighing up of interests is not carried out openly but covertly, and causation is conceived as an objective element, barely analysed in any depth, which is mainly based on facts left to the decision of lower courts. Additionally, causation is generally submitted to high standards of proof, with alleviating devices, however, that may make results unpredictable. In cases of causal uncertainty this model tends to stick to an 'all-or-nothing' rule, but may accept loss of chance, mainly as a specific type of damage[18].

---

16 Machnikowski et al ibidem.

17 Marta Infantino and Eleni Zervogianni, 'The European Ways to Causation' in Marta Infantino and Eleni Zervogianni (eds), *Causation in European Tort Law* (Cambridge University Press 2017) 84–128.

18 Infantino and Zervogianni (n 17) 89–101. See also Bénedict Winiger, Helmut Koziol, Bernhard A. Koch and Reinhard Zimmermann (eds), *Digest of European Tort Law. Volume 1: Essential Cases on Natural Causation* (Springer 2007) (hereafter, *Digest I*); Cees van Dam (2013), *European Tort Law* (2nd. edn, Oxford University Press 2013), 307ff and Jaap Spier and Olav A Hazen, 'Comparative Conclusions on Causation', in Jaap Spier (ed), *Unification of Tort Law: Causation* (Kluwer Law International 2000) 127ff.

In a second model ('bounded causation approach'), which would include countries such as Germany, the Czech Republic, Greece, Portugal, Denmark and Sweden, causation is just one of the main conditions for the establishment of liability. It presupposes that all the previous filters (wrongfulness, legally protected interest) have been passed. In this model causation is rigid in its application, even dogmatic, and generally provides an open distinction between two stages (causation / scope of liability) with different functions. Generally it requires high standards of proof, but may allow the use of different standards of proof in certain situations and of alleviating devices that are more controllable than in the previous model. In cases of causal uncertainty it tends to stick to the 'all-or-nothing' rule and normally does not accept loss of chance[19].

Finally, in a third model ('pragmatic causation approach'), which includes countries such as Austria, The Netherlands, Lithuania, England and Wales and Ireland, courts are openly sensitive to the specific implications of their decisions and tend to propose flexible and case-tailored solutions. These solutions are not driven by the dictates of wide or limited tort law rules or by the dogmatic adherence to causation principles, but rather by a concrete and overt policy-making effort. Case law is open to approaches that are innovative and, in the case of causal uncertainty, departing from the 'all-or-nothing' rule, some countries may even allow proportional liability under specific circumstances[20].

Taking into account this diversity, it has been contended that causation is such a fundamental concept in the national law regimes that any possible interference by the European legislature would negatively impact their internal cohesion.[21] However, in my opinion, it is difficult to see why this should be so. Firstly, in spite of the fact that European legal systems have general tort rules on causation that differ from each other, an interchange of ideas fostered by comparative legal research and by soft-law projects such as the PETL[22] or the DCFR[23], and also by international legal writing

19 Infantino and Zervogianni (n 17) 101–116.

20 Infantino and Zervogianni (n 17) 117–128.

21 Machnikowski et al (n 12) 86.

22 European Group on Tort Law, *Principles of European Tort Law. Text and Commentary* (Springer 2005), Chapter 3. *Causation.*

23 Christian von Bar and Eric Clive (eds), *Principles, Definitions and Model Rules of European Private Law. Draft Common Frame of Reference (DCFR), Full Edition*, vol 4 (Sellier 2009), Chapter 4. *Causation.*

and other non-European soft-law references, such as the American *Restatements*,[24] contribute to a wider approach which may lead to convergence if national legislatures finally pass the bill-drafts now circulating in different European countries[25]. Secondly, if diversity prevails, this does not seem to preclude the possibility of introducing, in a certain legal area, a specific set of rules dealing with the problems tackled by causation, all the more if these rules are required by technological development and by a transnational market. It is true that this may lead to a hybrid system which does not conform any longer to all the traditional aspects of tort law, but this is something that has already happened internally in some legal systems[26] where their legislatures have introduced similar hybrid systems to try to give a satisfactory answer to new needs[27].

Due to the existing diversity, it is not possible to give a general account of the challenges that IoT may pose to causation starting from a particular legal system. In the same vein, it is also problematic to use a terminology that is that currently accepted in all or most jurisdictions. For this reason

---

24 Mainly, although not exclusively, The American Law Institute, *Restatement (Third) of Law of Torts: Liability for Physical and Emotional Harm*, vol 1, §§ 1 to 36 (American Law Institute Publishers 2010), Chapter 5. *Factual Causation* and Chapter 6. *Scope of Liability (Proximate Cause).*

25 Thus, for instance, the recent Belgian *Avant-projet de loi portant insertion des dispositions relatives à la responsabilité extracontractuelle dans le nouveau Code civil* (<https://justitie.belgium.be/sites/default/files/aansprakelijkheidsrecht_voorontwerp_van_wet.pdf> accessed 10 April 2018), under the heading « lien de causalité », contains nine long articles which, among other aspects, adopt the NESS-test in the case of a plurality of actual sufficient causes (Art 5.163) and proportional liability in the cases of loss of chance (Art 5.168) and multiple uncertain tortfeasors (Art 5.169).

26 See for instance § 84 (2) *Gesetz über den Verkehr mit Arzneimitteln (Arzneimittelgesetz – AMG)*, which facilitates the proof of causation of the medicinal product by presuming that the product has caused the damage if it is capable of causing the harm *in the circumstances pertaining to the individual case* [emphasis added], or § 34 (1) *Gesetz zur Regelung der Gentechnik (Gentechnikgesetz – GenTG)* which presumes that when the damage has been caused by genetically modified organisms, it has been caused by the genetically modified properties of these organisms.

27 One example of this extension beyond the traditional tort law rules on causation can be found in France in the *Loi Badinter* for traffic accidents introduced in 1985, which creates a hybrid system where traditional notions such as 'cause' are substituted by the idea of the 'implication' of the vehicle. See Geneviève Viney, Patrice Jourdain and Suzanne Carval, *Les régimes spéciaux et l'assurance de responsabilité* (4th edn, LGDJ 2017) 142ff.

the following analysis takes the above mentioned soft-law models and comparative legal literature as a reference.

3. *A general overview of causation related problems*

a) General v Specific causation

Technological development may give rise to new risks which are characterised by a high degree of uncertainty when establishing whether there is a causal link between the actor's activity and the damage suffered by the victim. In this context, a preliminary distinction between general (or 'generic') causation and specific causation seems to be necessary. The term general causation refers to whether the risk that a certain conduct or activity entails is capable to cause a certain type of harm (e.g. Can Wi-Fi radiation cause cancer?). By contrast specific causation refers to whether and to what extent, the risk posed by specific conduct or activity has caused the harm that the particular victim suffers (e.g. Did exposure to X-rays cause P's cancer, or was it P's smoking?)[28].

The distinction is not well entrenched in some European legal systems and is ignored in others[29], but it is important because if an activity is not capable to cause a damage, general causation is excluded, and then specific causation should also be excluded. The converse rule, however, is not true: if general causation is affirmed, specific causation must not necessarily be affirmed as well. Among other situations, the distinction can be useful in cases of multiple potential tortfeasors, where lack of general causation may 'negate' specific causation: if the activity of one of the defendants was not capable of causing damage, this defendant can successfully

---

28 Ingeborg Puppe and Richard W Wright, 'Causation in the Law: Philosophy, Doctrine and Practice', in Infantino and Zervogianni (n 17) 54ff. For a detailed account on the differences between general and specific causation see 'Comment on Subsection (a), § 28 Restatement (Third) of Law of Torts: Liability for Physical and Emotional Harm' (n 24) 404ff.

29 For instance, most Spanish tort law course books do not mention it. Also complaining about the little success of this distinction in France, Jean-Sébastien Borghetti, 'Litigation on hepatitis B vaccination and demyelinating disease in France. Breaking through scientific uncertainty?', in Miquel Martín-Casals and Diego M Papayannis (eds), *Uncertain Causation in Tort Law* (Cambridge University Press 2016) 11–42, 41–42.

exclude herself from liability. By contrast, generally speaking, proof of general causation is not sufficient and the claimant must establish, not only that the defendant's agent is capable of causing damage, but also that it did in fact cause the claimant's damage.

b) Causation versus scope of liability

Most legal systems draw a distinction between two stages in the assessment of the existence of a causal link. The first step, sometimes called 'factual causation' or 'causation of fact', aims at identifying whether the conduct or activity (hereafter, activity) of the defendant gave rise to the damage suffered by the claimant. In most ordinary cases the answer to this first step will enable the harm to be attributed the claimant and will be sufficient to close the enquiry. The second step called sometimes 'legal causation', 'proximate cause' or 'scope of liability' comes into play when causation has been established according to the rules applicable to the first step and when it is considered that attributing all the damaging consequences resulting from her activity to the defendant would be excessive. For this reason, it aims at limiting the consequences according to a series of relevant factors which are more concerned with questions of value, fairness and legal policy than with the factual existence or absence of a causal link. On these grounds, many legal systems consider that this second step goes beyond the causation enquiry[30], as do some soft-law texts[31]. In order to try to foster clarity, I will use the term 'causation' to refer to the first step and 'scope of liability' to name the second.

To establish causation most legal systems apply the 'conditio sine qua non' or 'but-for' tests which involves a counterfactual approach and provides that the tortfeasor caused the damage if the damage would have not occurred in the absence of the tortfeasor's activity[32]. Establishing causa-

---

30 Instead of many see Spier and Hazen (n 18) 127ff.

31 This is clearly the case in the Restatement Third, Chapter 5 (*Factual Causation*) and Chapter 6 (*Scope of Liability [Proximate Cause]*) and, in spite of a compromising common Chapter heading (*Causation*), also in the PETL (cf Arts 3:101 to 3:106 PETL in Section 1 (*Condition sine qua non and qualifications*) and 3:201 in Section 2. (*Scope of Liability*). By contrast, the DCFR does not draw the distinction and mingles in the same provision matters that pertain to the two domains (cf Art VI.-4:101 DCFR).

32 Zimmermann, in *Digest I* (n 18), 99–101, Spier and Hazen (n 18) 127ff.

tion may give rise to three sorts of problems, two of them related to this counterfactual approach (over-determination and pre-emption) and a third one independent on it (uncertainty).

Over-determination (a problem also known as real duplicative causes, concurrent causes or multiple sufficient causes) occurs when there are multiple activities (X and Y) and each of them was sufficient by itself to cause the damage. In these cases, a counterfactual approach leads to the counterintuitive result that none of them caused it, since if X would have not occurred Y would have caused the damage all the same and, conversely, if Y would not have occurred then X would have caused it[33]. This approach gives rise to a similar problem in cases of pre-emption, i.e. when an activity X is sufficient to cause a damage but another activity Y would have caused the same damage later. In these cases the counterfactual approach embedded in the 'but-for' test denies causal status to activities that appear intuitively causal[34]. To attributing causation where the 'but-for' test leads only to paradox, the NESS test (necessary element of a sufficient set), which analyses the real or potential duplicative causes in two different sufficient sets of elements, is a more satisfactory and comprehensive account of causation than the traditional *sine qua non* account.[35]

Uncertainty is the other major problem as regards causation and may have more bearing on the case of IoT technologies. Defective operation in any of the layers that make up an IoT ecosystem, mainly if the players in the market are different in each of them, may often raise questions such as who among them caused the damage or who caused the damage to which victim or what part of it. For this reason, uncertainty deserves more detailed treatment.

Finally, when dealing with the scope of liability, the complex IoT ecosystem may also pose some challenges as regards the foreseeability

---

33 Koch (2007), *Digest I* (n 18) 476–477. In these cases, instead of adopting an alternative test, some texts adopt a sort of modified test by merely prescribing that '… each act is regarded as a factual cause of the harm' (§ 27 *Restatement (Third) of Law of Torts: Liability for Physical and Emotional Harm*). In a similar vein, Art 3:102 PETL.

34 Koch (2007), *Digest I* (n 18) 501–504 and Spier and Hazen (n 18) 127–130.

35 See Richard W Wright, 'The Ness Account of Natural Causation: A Response to Criticisms', 285–322 and Chris Miller, 'NESS for Beginners', 323–337, both in Richard Goldberg (ed), *Perspectives on Causation* (Hart 2011). See, for instance the elegant way by which Art 5.163 of the Belgian *Avant-projet* solves the 'conditio sine qua non' paradox by using Wright's NESS-test.

analysis which, with restrictions and expansions, is the core of some of the factors used in some legal systems. Intervening causation may also play a role and, for this reason these two issues are analysed in more detail later on in this paper.

c) Burden of proof of causation and possible 'alleviating' devices

The burden of proof decides who has to prove one of more factual elements and the consequences that will ensue if the burden is not satisfied. A generally accepted rule is that both the claimant and the defendant are required to prove those facts on which they, respectively, base their claim or their defence. This rule is followed by Art 4 of the Directive when it places the burden of proof of causation on the claimant.

However, the burden of proof has two different aspects, which normally go together, but which can also be distributed between claimant and defendant. The first aspect, sometimes called 'burden of production' or 'evidentiary burden', refers to the burden of presenting evidence. The party that bears the burden is obliged to present it and runs the risk of not being able to present evidence on certain facts. By contrast, the 'burden of persuasion', sometimes also called 'legal burden', provides a mechanism to overcome a situation in which the facts that needed to be proven have not been (a so-called *non liquet* situation). The party who bears this burden runs the risk of losing if, in spite of all the evidence forwarded, uncertainty remains and the judge cannot decide according to the relevant standard of proof[36].

In this context, another important notion is the 'standard of proof', which refers to the degree of conviction that the evidence forwarded by the parties generates in the mind of the judge. If the required standard of proof is reached, the judge is convinced of the 'truth' of the relevant factual proposition and the case is decided accordingly. If the standard is not met, the case will be decided against the party who bears the burden of persuasion. The standard of proof applicable varies, not only among the different legal systems, but sometimes it also depends on specific situa-

---

36 Ivo Giesen, 'The Burden of Proof and the other Procedural Devices in Tort Law', 3–67 and Ernst Karner 'The Function of the Burden of Proof in Tort Law', 68–78, both in Helmut Koziol and Barbara C Steininger (eds), *European Tort Law 2008* (Springer 2009).

tions. In common law countries the applicable standard is the 'balance of probabilities' and is met if the judge is convinced that the relevant facts are more probable than not. By contrast, most continental European legal systems adhere to a higher standard that is sometimes expressed as a 'probability bordering certainty', which means that the judge must be convinced beyond reasonable doubt.[37]

It is submitted that when Art 4 PLD provides that the claimant bears the burden of proof of causation it refers to the burden of persuasion, but that this provision is not contrary to courts reversing the burden of production. This may be necessary – mainly in the cases of imbalance of information – to promote the effective protection that substantive law aims at offering to victims, since such protection would become illusionary if the claimant could not regularly provide the evidence needed.

Among other possible devices alleviating the proof of causation, a first one is to lower the standard of proof, since this also lowers the degree of evidence needed and leads to the consequence that fewer cases are decided on the burden of proof. Lowering the standard of proof is already used in some countries to alleviate the rigours of proof as regards the scope of liability[38] or the estimated amount of damages.[39]Another device is the presumptions of fact, which allows the judge to base the existence of a certain factual element on the presence of another fact that has been proven (reasoning by inference). They are also applied in many countries to alleviate the evidentiary risks and to prevent the burden of persuasion becoming the routine solution in some situations. Accepting such a presumption does not reverse the burden of persuasion, but shifts the burden of production to the other party who must then forward evidence to rebut the provisional decision of the judge.[40] Sometimes courts may even apply factors of association such as the strength of association (i.e. the stronger the association is, the more likely it is that it has a causal component), consistency (i.e. repeated observation of a relationship), temporality (i.e. the relevant factor precedes the outcome) and others.[41]

---

37 Giesen (n 36) 53ff and Karner (n 36) 71–72.

38 In Germany, § 287 ZPO.

39 In the Netherlands, Art 6:97 BW.

40 Giesen (n 36) 56ff.

41 See, for instance the use of the so-called 'Bradford Hill criteria' in the epidemiological context and their legal use, in spite of the fact that Hill himself said that none of his nine viewpoints could bring indisputable evidence for or against the

It is obvious that a consistent use of these and other alleviating devices could be useful to help solve the problems of proof of causation that may arise as a result of damage caused by the IoT technologies, without requiring the introduction of a general legal reversal of the burden of persuasion in order to protect the interests of the victims. A recent Report of the European Commission has recognised that 'the single most difficult stepping stone to receiving compensation for damages is the burden of proof on the injured person to demonstrate a causal link between the product defect and the damage' and it has pointed out that the ECJ 'has made doing this considerably easier by accepting national rules that help the injured person establish this proof, provided that this does not undermine the Directive's placing of the burden of proof on the injured person'[42] The Commission, among other commendable examples, mentions here the recent *Sanofi Pasteur* decision.[43] However, as this decision regarding the proof of causation in the case of damage caused by vaccines shows, the different approaches to causation and the thorny question of proof of causation may lead to very disparate results not only in different jurisdictions, but also in different courts of the same country[44]. In some countries, as has been the case in France with the *Sanofi Pasteur* decision, courts may be willing to

---

cause-and-effect hypothesis. See Austin Bradford Hill, 'The Environment and Disease: Association or Causation' (1965) Proceedings of the Royal Society of Medicine 58, 295–300 and Susan Haack, 'Correlation and causation. The "Bradford Hill criteria" in epidemiological, legal and epistemological perspective', in Martín-Casals and Papayannis (n 29) 176–202.

42 Report from the Commission to the European Parliament, the Council and the European Economic and Social Committee on the Application of the Council Directive on the approximation of the laws, regulations, and administrative provisions of the Member States concerning liability for defective products (85/374/EEC), COM (2018) 246 final, 5.

43 ECJ of 21 June 2017, Case C–621-15 *N.W, L.W & C.W v. Sanofi Pasteur MSD SNC, Caisse primaire d'assurance maladie des Hauts-de-Seine & Carpimko*, ECLI:EU:C:2017:484, where the Court of Justice ruled that the criteria used by lower French courts to establish causation do not run contrary to Article 4 of the Product Liability Directive 85/374/EEC, since this provision only sets the burden on proof, and not the means through which proof can be established. See Thomas Verheyen, 'Full Harmonization, Consumer Protection and Products Liability: A Fresh Reading of the Case Law of the ECJ', European Review of Private Law 1/2018, 119–140.

44 Eleonora Rajneri, Jean-Sébastien Borghetti, Duncan Fairgrieve and Peter Rott, 'Remedies for Damage Caused by Vaccines: A Comparative Study of Four European Legal Systems', European Review of Private Law 1/2018, 57–96.

bypass general causation and by considering associations such as 'temporal proximity between administering the vaccine and the occurrence of the disease', 'lack of personal and family history' and 'a significant number of reported cases' hold that causation has been established[45]. In cases like this, however, lower courts not subject to the unifying control of their corresponding Supreme Courts, may decide with thin evidence in such divergent and unpredictable ways to undermine the effectiveness of the rules regarding causation. The lesson should be learned and, in my opinion, the rules on causation for damage caused by IoT technologies should pay more attention to issues regarding proof of causation and avoid similar unsatisfactory results.

III. Uncertain causation in IoT and possible answers

1. 'All-or-Nothing' v. 'proportional liability'

Whenever defendants (Ds) are unable to establish proof of causation with the required standard of proof, courts must determine that causation has not been established and, accordingly, that Ds are not liable and that claimants (Cs) are not to be compensated for the damage they have suffered. The application of this 'all-or-nothing' rule in cases of causal uncertainty leads to the outcome that Ds are absolved from liability, although it is established that Ds acted tortiously and that Ds tortious conduct or activity (hereafter, activity) may have been a cause of Cs damage.

When uncertainty is recurrent or systemic, no-liability may be considered undesirable and then legislatures or courts may adopt one of these two solutions: (a) Preserve the all-or-nothing rule and hold all Ds solidary liable, allowing those Ds who can prove that they did not cause the damage to escape liability, or (b) adopt a rule of 'proportional liability' and hold each D severally liable, according to the established probability that the damage was caused by D's tortious conduct[46].

In the case of multiple indeterminate tortfeasors the practical results of solidary liability and of proportional liability are very close if all Ds are traceable and solvent. However if all Ds are not traceable or insolvent an important difference arises.

---

45 Borghetti (n 44) 78–86 and Verheyen (n 44) 131ff.

46 Koziol (2007), *Digest I* (n 18) 387–389, Spier and Hazen (n 18) 151ff.

Opting for solidary liability makes that the solvent and traceable Ds bear the risk of the insolvent or non-traceable ones. C, however, does not bear the risk of uncertainty since for her the result is the same as if uncertainty did not exist. As in the case of multiple determinate tortfeasors, C may claim the damage in full from any of them, and here even to those who may not have caused it. In extreme cases, this may even lead to a situation where the only D left and who, for this reason, cannot claim contribution from the others and, because of the existing uncertainty, may not have caused the damage, becomes eventually the only liable D and for the whole damage.

Opting for proportional liability, by contrast, distributes the existing risks between Ds and Cs. Thus, while Ds bear the risk of uncertainty and may be required to compensate for a damage they may have not caused, they will have to compensate according to the probability in which they contributed to causing the damage only. In their turn, Cs bear the risk of insolvency and non-traceability of the Ds.

It is contended that proportional liability seems to provide a better apportionment of the risks between Ds and Cs than solidary liability and for this reason legal writing[47] soft-law[48] and even legislatures[49] and courts[50] have sometimes proposed it as a more balanced solution for cases of causal uncertainty. However, the situations in which uncertainty may arise as regards causation are very different.

It may arise, for example, as regards uncertain causes in the past, when there is a plurality of tortfeasors (D1, D2, etc.) and it is unknown which of

47 Israel Gilead, Michael D Green and Bernhard A Koch (eds), *Proportional Liability: Analytical and Comparative Perspectives* (de Gruyter 2013).

48 Art 3:103, 3:105, 3:106 PETL and, to some extent, Art 3:1034 PETL.

49 § 1294 of the 2005 Austrian Draft. For a brief introduction with an English translation of the texts of this Draft see Helmut Koziol and Barbara Steininger, *European Tort Law 2005* and *European Tort Law 2007* (Springer 2006 and 2008), and more in detail Bernhard A Koch, 'Proportional liability for causal uncertainty. How it works on the basis of a 200-year-old code', in Martín-Casals/Papayannis (n 29) 67–86. See also Art 5.168 of the Belgian *Avant-projet* for proportional liability in the cases of loss of chance, and Art 5.169 in cases of multiple uncertain tortfeasors.

50 See, for instance, in Austria in the case of alternative causes if one lies within the victim's own sphere (Koch, 'Austria' 137) or in The Netherlands in the 2006 *Nefalit/Karamus* case of a smoker exposed to asbestos who contracted lung cancer (Keirse, 'The Netherlands' 333ff) or in Switzerland (Winiger, 'Switzerland' 470), all in Machnikowski (n 12).

them caused the damage (*alternative liability* or *indeterminate tortfeasors*); or when there is a plurality of tortfeasors (D1, D2, etc.) and a plurality of victims (C1, C2, etc.), but it is unknown which D caused damage to which C (*causally unrelated tortfeasors and victims* [e.g. *market-share liability cases*])[51].

Further uncertain causes in the past occur in situations where D's activity caused damage, but it is unknown which of the Cs is a victim and which suffer damage due to backgrounds risks or to other non-tortious factors which are independent of D's activity (*indeterminate victims* [*pollution cases*]). Also, where it is uncertain whether a single D, who acted tortiously and therefore increased the risk of harm, caused damage to a single C, it may well be, in these cases, that C is not a victim of a tort and D is not a tortfeasor (*risk increase*). A similar situation arises when uncertainty is not conceived in causal terms of increased risk, but rather as a reduction of C's chances not to suffer the harm and this reduction constitutes a standalone harm of 'lost chances' (*loss of chance*)[52].

Finally, uncertainty may also refer to which part of C's harm was caused by D (*indeterminate parts of harm*), to whether D's tortious conduct will inflict harm on C in the future (*unrealized risks with potential for future harms*), or involve a combination of the different categories[53].

However, no single legal system proposes proportional liability as the solution for all cases of uncertain causation. The shift to proportional liability may depend on several factors, such as the basis of liability (negligence/gross negligence, strict liability, vicarious liability), the relevant recoverable heads of loss, the magnitude of the damage, the number of tortfeasors, the number of victims, etc.[54]. It has also been contended that ranking the different categories of cases in which problems of casual uncertainty can arise may reflect the strength or weakness of the arguments in favour of imposing at least some liability, even when uncertainty as regards causation prevents the ordinary standard of proof from being satisfied.[55] However, to date no legal system has established detailed rules on

---

51 Gilead, Green and Koch (eds) (n 47) 12–13, 22–30.

52 Gilead, Green and Koch (eds) (n 47) 13–15, 31–44.

53 Gilead, Green and Koch (eds) (n 47) 15–17, 44–58.

54 Jaap Spier, Introductory Commentary to Arts 3:103ff PETL, in European Group on Tort Law (n 22) 46–47.

55 Ken Oliphant, 'Causation in Cases of Evidential Uncertainty: Juridical Techniques and Fundamental Issues' 91 Chicago-Kent Law Review 585 (2016) 591ff.

how to assess these or other factors in order to decide whether there should be proportional liability in a given context.

For these reasons, and depending on the policy grounds to be followed in a particular situation, it would not be too risky to affirm that proportional liability may offer an important alternative to an all-or-nothing approach when problems of uncertainty as regards damage caused by IoT arise.

2. *Hybrid systems and channelling*

A further alternative to explore in the case of multiple tortfeasors are the hybrid forms of solidary and several liability included in the *Restatement Third, Apportionment of Liability*.[56] Although not related to uncertainty, the Restatement provides for five different tracks in the case of liability of multiple tortfeasors for indivisible harm.[57] Leaving aside Track A (joint and several liability) and Track B (several liability), the other three are quite innovative and could be useful when solidary liability is not satisfactory because it imposes the complete burden of insolvency and non-traceability on one or few defendants, or when proportional liability is not satisfactory either because it imposes the same burden on the claimant.

Thus Track C (*Joint and Several Liability with Reallocation*), which is basically a system of liability that permits liability for uncollectible shares to be reapportioned among the plaintiff and any other defendants on the basis of the parties' relative responsibility, could be an alternative in order to mitigate the rigours of any of the two other 'all-or-nothing' or 'proportional liability' models.

In a case of multiple tortfeasors, reallocation between Ds and Cs could also take place above or under a certain threshold, in a similar way to that with Track D (*Hybrid Liability Based on Threshold Percentage of Comparative Responsibility*), which is a model that has the purpose of retaining solidary liability of the more significant defendants, but rejecting it in the case of minimally responsible ones.

Finally, it could be established that, in certain cases, property damage could follow a proportional liability rule, whereas personal injury could

56 The American Law Institute, *Restatement (Third) of the Law of Torts – Apportionment of Liability*, §§ 1-End (American Law Institute Publishers 2000).

57 Restatement (Third) of the Law of Torts – Apportionment of Liability (n 56) 160ff.

stick to solidary liability. This would be a distinction based on a higher protection for personal injury, and a remote variety of Track E (*Hybrid Liability Based on Type of Damages*), which draws a similar distinction but between pecuniary and non-pecuniary loss.

Although one must be aware that these hybrid system show pros and cons[58], they may offer additional flexibility.

Another legal device to be explored is the so-called 'channelling' of liability, which is a deviation from the principle that only the tortfeasor who caused the damage should be held fully liable for the loss and which is used in some liability statutes implementing international conventions[59]. Channelling attaches liability to a tortfeasor who becomes fully liable for the damage caused, regardless of whether it can be attributed to him or to others. Normally, statutes that provide for channelling also establish that it is exclusive, i.e. that the victim can bring a claim against the 'channelled' tortfeasor only. However, this does not mean that liability is finally allocated to this particular tortfeasor, since he has still the possibility of a right of recourse against the others[60].

It can be contended that in the case of multiple tortfeasors channelling is much more protective for victims since, it relieves victims of the burden of investigating who precisely the tortfeasor who caused the harm was. However, an important disadvantage for the victim is that, in the most usual cases where channelling is exclusive, she can no longer claim damages from other tortfeasors who may have also contributed to the loss she suffers. Thus, from the victims' perspective, solidary liability seems preferable since it allows them to bring their claim for full compensation against any of all the other possible tortfeasors[61]. Channelling also has disadvantages for the liability insurer of the channelled tortfeasor, since he may have to cover accidents in cases where the loss was not caused by his in-

58 Dan D Dobbs, Paul T Hayden and Ellen M Bublick, *Hornbook on Torts* (2nd edn, West Academic Publishing 2016) 901ff.

59 See Albert Verheij, 'Shifts in Governance: Oil Pollution', 133, Hui Wang, 'Shifts in Governance in the International Regime of Marine Oil Pollution Compensation: A Legal History Perspective', 197ff and Tom Vanden Borre (2007), 'Shifts in Governance in Compensation for Nuclear Damage. 20 Years after Chernobyl', 261ff, all of them in Michael Faure and Albert Verheij (eds), *Shifts in Compensation for Environmental Damage* (Springer 2007).

60 Michael Faure, 'Attribution of Liability: An Economic Analysis of Various Cases', 91 Chicago-Kent Law Review 603 (2016) 621ff.

61 Faure (n 60) 625ff.

sured tortfeasor, and when, eventual subrogation in the rights of the insured to get contribution from the other tortfeasors may become futile, since they may not be properly insured[62].

IV. Scope of liability and IoT

1. Foreseeability as a problem in the IoT

Since the application of the 'but-for' test yields the result that the defendant would be liable for everything which flows from his tortious activity, it is clear that policy factors are needed to limit the scope of the defendant's liability. Probably the most important and applied factor to establish the scope of liability in many European legal systems is, in one form or another, foreseeability, which is based on the idea that the defendant should be held liable only for the damage that a reasonable person of ordinary prudence put in his or her position would have foreseen as a likely result of his or her conduct. [63]Foreseeability is also reflected in soft-law projects.[64]

Foreseeability, however, raises doubts as to what must be foreseen (the damage in general terms, the specific damage, the risk), who must foresee it (an 'optimal observer', an 'experienced observer') and when foreseeability must be analysed (before/after the event). Thus, for instance, in Art 3:201 a) PETL, foreseeability seems to be treated as the most important factor, since it appears first on an open list of several factors, and the question of 'what' must be foreseeable refers to the 'damage', by 'whom' to a 'reasonable person' and 'when' to 'the time of the activity'. Other elements that qualify foreseeability are 'the closeness in time and space between the damaging activity and its consequences' and 'the magnitude of the damage in relation to the normal consequences of such an activity'. In

62 In this sense, Faure (n 60) 629 points out that if channelling has any effect on the insurability, it is more likely to decrease insurability rather than make liability insurable, since it does not provide adequate incentives to other tortfeasors who contributed to the damage.

63 Infantino and Zervogianni (n 17) 604–605 and Spier and Hazen (n 18) 131ff.

64 cf Art 3:201 a) PETL. By contrast, according to its commentary, p. 3571, Art VI.-4:101 DCFR, does 'neither confirm nor challenge' the various doctrinal approaches on this factor. However, foreseeability is an important factor in contract law, cf Art 9:503 PECL and III.- 3:703 DCFR.

the PETL, as in most legal systems that in one form or another start from the idea of foreseeability, this factor is not absolute and other factors may expand or restrict the scope of liability. Thus, sometimes tortfeasors may be held liable for damage that was not foreseeable due, for instance, to a specific vulnerability of the victim unknown to the defendant (the so-called *egg-shell skull* cases)[65] or, conversely, they may not be held liable even if damage was foreseeable, but the defendant did nothing to increase the ordinary risks of life to which the victim was subject to[66]. Another factor, the protective purpose of the rule[67] – which sometimes is presented as a better substitute for the foreseeability test altogether[68] – may sometimes expand the scope of liability and lead to holding defendants liable for damage that, in spite of not being foreseeable, falls within the protective purpose of the rule that has been violated or, on other occasions, may restrict the scope of liability when foreseeable damage does not fall within the protective scope of the rule. Additionally, other factors such as the basis of liability or the nature or value of the protected interest, may point in the direction of a wider scope of liability, as in the case of damage caused with gross negligence or intent, or in the case of personal injury, or in the opposite direction of a narrower scope, as in the case of strict liability or pure economic loss[69]. Moreover, in a given situation, some factors may point towards expanding liability, whereas others may point in the opposite direction.

IoT may give rise to specific legal challenges to the concept of foreseeability used to assess the scope of liability, not only for the lack of previous experience with regard to new technologies, but also for the use of artificial intelligence (AI). This is because one of the fundamental differences between the decision-making process of a human being and the decision-making process that takes place with AI is that artificial intelligence systems may generate solutions that even an objective reasonable human

65 Not specifically mentioned in Art 3:201 PETL, but see Spier in his Commentary to this article in European Group on Tort Law (n 22) 62.

66 Art 3:201 d) PETL.

67 Art 3:201 e) PETL.

68 Thus for instance in Germany, regarding the criticism to foreseeability in the so-called *Adäquanzkriterium* version and in favour of the protective purpose of the rule (*Schutzzweck der Norm*) as the most relevant factor, see Hermann Lange and Gottfried Schiemann, *Schadensersatz* (3rd edn, Mohr 2003) 90ff and Hein Kötz and Gerhard Wagner, *Deliktsrecht* (13th edn, Franz Vahlen 2016) 84ff, 92ff.

69 Art 3:201 b) and c) PETL.

being, no matter how 'optimal' or experienced 'observer' she is, would not expect. It has been contended that human beings, affected by the cognitive limitations of the human brain, cannot analyse all or most of the information at their disposal when confronted with time constraints and, for this reason, they often settle for satisfactory rather than optimal solutions.[70] By contrast, the ever increasing computational power of modern computers allows AI programmes to search through many more possibilities than a human being in a given period of time, allowing AI systems to analyse potential solutions that humans may not have even considered[71]. Moreover, even if to date the unexpectedness of AI actions may be rather limited in scope, the development of AI systems will raise the frequency of situations and unexpected behaviour will increase. If legal systems choose to view the experiences of some learning AI systems as so unforeseeable that it would be unfair to hold the systems' designers liable for harm that these systems cause, victims might be left with no way of obtaining compensation for their losses. In the context of scope of liability it thus seems that foreseeability presents a vexing challenge to any legal system wishing to solve the problem of affording redress to victims of AI-caused harm.

A better approach to dealing with the scope of liability question for damage caused by IoT technologies would be to rely upon theories based on the scope of the risk created by the defendant's activity. The American Restatement builds the scope of liability factors around a risk test and considers that 'an actor's liability is limited to those harms that result from the risks that made the actor's conduct tortious'[72]. This 'Harm within the Risk' (HWR) theory is not utterly alien to European practice, since it can

---

70 Matthew U Schere, 'Regulating Artificial Intelligence Systems: Risks, Challenges, Competencies, and Strategies', 29 Harvard Journal of Law & Technology 353 (2016) 363ff.

71 Schere (n 70) 363–364, points out that a particularly intriguing example comes from a cancer pathology machine learning program (C-Path). While pathologists suspected that studying components of the supportive tissue (stroma) surrounding cancerous cells might, in combination with studying the actual tumour cells, aid in cancer prognosis, C-Path found in a large study that the characteristics of the stroma were actually a better prognostic indicator for breast cancer than the characteristics of the cancerous cells themselves – a conclusion that stood at odds with both common sense and prevailing medical thought.

72 § 29 *Restatement (Third) of Law of Torts: Liability for Physical and Emotional Harm.*

already be found in the bases of some tests already applied in Europe[73] and, more specifically, in the 'protective purpose of the rule' factor when taken as an alternative test[74].

AI is a source of risk that exceeds the more familiar risks that have their only source in human behaviour. For this reason, it has been pointed out that even in the case of harm caused by unforeseeable behaviour resulting for AI alterations carried out by the system itself, its programmers should also be held liable. In this case the harm occurs as a realisation of a risk which is inherent to AI in accordance with the dictate of the initial programming which enables the AI system to alter its behaviour according to subsequent experiences[75].

A general rule establishing the HWR-test, however, is not sufficient to solve all problems and other factors are also required. In fact, most of the additional factors mentioned in the *Restatement (Third)* sound very similar to those already mentioned in the context of the foreseeability-test, but the tune is now played in the key of risk. This is the case, for instance, of the 'pre-existing physical or mental condition or other characteristics of the person' (the *egg-shell skull*, again), which are taken into account to expand the HWR-test when a harm is of a 'greater magnitude or different type than might reasonably be expected'[76]. Factors that also expand the scope of liability are those related to the activity of rescuers or of persons giving medical or other aid to the victim[77] or to acting recklessly or with

---

73 Thus Infantino and Zervogianni (n 17) 606 point out that the idea often substantiates some other tests, such as the adequacy test (Austria, Bulgaria, Poland and Portugal) and the foreseeability test (England).

74 Infantino and Zervogianni (n 17) 606 and Kötz and Wagner (n 68) 94 who consider that the protective purpose of the rule, understood as referring to those damages that are the continuing effect of the risk that made the tortfeasor liable, together with the 'general risks of life', which are attributable to the victim, enable a better solution without requiring the speculation involved in the foreseeability test.

75 Schere (n 70) 366–369.

76 § 31. *Preexisting Conditions and Unforeseeable Harm.* 'When an actor's tortious conduct causes harm to a person that, because of a preexisting physical or mental condition or other characteristics of the person, is of a greater magnitude or different type than might reasonably be expected, the actor is nevertheless subject to liability for all such harm to the person'.

77 cf § 32. *Rescuers* and § 35. *Enhanced Harm Due to Efforts to Render Medical or Other Aid.*

intent[78]. By contrast, factors that limit liability are for instance, when the tortious conduct has not increased the risk of harm[79] and the so-called 'Intervening Acts and Superseding Causes'[80], which can be rather relevant in the context of the IoT technologies.

2. *The relevance of intervening causation in the IoT technologies*

Intervening causation would encapsulate the idea that when an act or an event has intervened between the defendant's activity and the claimant's injury, the defendant should no longer be liable because this act or event has 'broken the chain of causation' and his or her activity no longer operates as the effective cause of the claimant's damage[81].

In the internet of things ('IoT'), where devices may be hacked and used to carry out devastating and costly attacks, cyber-attacks are typical intervening causes for damage caused by defective software, since they are not only tortious acts by a third party, but also criminal acts. Cyber-attacks may cause not only pure economic loss, but also important property damage, and although they are difficult to avert, they are highly foreseeable, given the widely acknowledged insecurity of IoT devices. Therefore, it has been contended that given the tremendous costs incurred by the victims of denial-of-service (DoS) and other network attacks, the central role that connected devices play in these attacks, and the large number of potential victims, it is likely that cyberattacks will increase IoT-related litiga-

---

78 § 33 *Scope of Liability for Intentional and Reckless Tortfeasors*. '(a) An actor who intentionally causes harm is subject to liability for that harm even if it was unlikely to occur. (b) An actor who intentionally or recklessly causes harm is subject to liability for a broader range of harms than the harms for which that actor would be liable if only acting negligently. In general, the important factors in determining the scope of liability are the moral culpability of the actor, as reflected in the reasons for and intent in committing the tortious acts, the seriousness of harm intended and threatened by those acts, and the degree to which the actor's conduct deviated from appropriate care'.

79 § 30. *Risk of Harm Not Generally Increased by Tortious Conduct.* 'An actor is not liable for harm when the tortious aspect of the actor's conduct was of a type that does not generally increase the risk of that harm'.

80 § 34. *Intervening Acts and Superseding Causes.*

81 Douglas J. Hodgson, *The Law of Intervening Causation* (Ashgate 2008). For the current weight of this factor in European tort law, Infantino and Zervogianni (n 17) 607–609.

tion and that the rules of intervening causation may be used as a legal device to limit or exclude liability of IoT market players.[82]

However, both the PETL and the DCFR consider that the intervening causation factor is neither autonomous nor useful when establishing the scope of liability, since the problems it tries to solve are ultimately solved by a distribution of risks between the subjects involved and according to other factors, such as foreseeability or the protective purpose of the rule already mentioned[83]. It is also contended that the advent of more refined tools for the apportionment of liability, such as comparative responsibility, comparative contribution, and substantial modification of joint and several liability, has also undermined the reasons that were behind this factor.[84] Following the HWR-test, the *Restatement (Third)* provides when the harm that occurs arises from a risk other than one of those that was among those that made the actor's conduct tortious, the actor is not liable, and the presence of an intervening act that is also a cause of the harm does not affect this conclusion[85].

It has been affirmed that cyber-attacks are within the scope of liability of IoT players, since they should be considered reasonably foreseeable given the widespread recognition of the risks they pose[86]. In any case, foreseeable or not, they are risks inherent to IoT technologies and apportionment of liability will be better served with the rules of concurrent liability or contributory negligence of the victim and whenever an IoT market player fails to adopt the adequate precautions against the risks of improper conduct, even criminal conduct, of others, he may be held liable if such an intervening cause materialises.

---

82 Alan Butler, 'Products Liability and the Internet of (Insecure) Things: Should Manufacturers Be Liable for Damage Caused by Hacked Devices?' 50 University of Michigan Journal of Law Reform (2017) 913–930, 915.

83 Spier (n 65) Commentary of Art 3:201 PETL, para. 11–12, 100, and Commentary of Art VI.-4:101 DCFR in von Bar and Eric Clive (n 23) 357.

84 See Comment a. § 34 *Restatement (Third) of Law of Torts: Liability for Physical and Emotional Harm* and Michael S Moore, *Causation and Responsibility. An Essay in Law, Morals, and Metaphysics* (Oxford University Press 2009) 254ff.

85 *Restatement (Third) of Law of Torts: Liability for Physical and Emotional Harm*, § 34 *Intervening Acts and Superseding Causes*, which provides that 'When a force of nature or an independent act is also a factual cause of harm, an actor's liability is limited to those harms that result from the risks that made the actor's conduct tortious'.

86 Butler (n 82) 924–925.

V. Conclusion

The multiplicity of layers and market players involved in IoT technologies may make it difficult for users to identify who caused the harm they suffer. Causation problems are not new, but they have not been tackled in depth by European law so far. The Product Liability Directive (PLD) has dealt with the most basic aspects of causation only (such as burden of proof or joint and several liability), but has left most issues to national law. Since the approaches to causation vary very significantly from country to country, if the same pattern is followed with IoT technologies, the result would be that the rules and doctrines applicable to important problems that may arise in the context of IoT technologies, such as uncertain causation or scope of liability, could give rise to very different results across Europe. The disparity of results would be increased by the acceptance of differing national procedural devices alleviating the burden of proof of causation. Although these devices may be necessary to effectively protect the rights of the victims, they may undermine a harmonised regulation on the basic elements of causation and foster an uneven application of causation for damage resulting from IoT technologies across Europe.

Since it is almost impossible to talk about causation related problems considering the particularities of all European legal systems, the paper has resorted to comparative European and international legal literature and to soft-law projects, such as the PETL, the DCFR and the American *Restatements*, to establish a basic conceptual framework (such as general v. special causation, or causation v. scope of liability) in order to analyse the basic tools that may be available to solve causation problems that damage caused by IoT technologies may pose.

As regards causation strictly speaking, uncertain causation seems to be the most pressing problem. It is submitted that the most widespread 'all-or-nothing' solution may be considered undesirable when uncertainty is recurrent or systemic, and then other devices such as proportional liability, hybrid forms of solidary and several liability and channelling, may provide alternative legal instruments. To switch to these alternative instruments is not a neutral move and it is not valid for all situations. It should be carried out piecemeal and will depend on policy grounds and on which legal interests are to prevail in a certain situation. It is submitted, however, that they may offer enough flexibility to give satisfactory answers to the causation problems posed by damage caused by IoT technologies.

In the case of scope of liability, it is submitted that a test that is built around the basic idea of foreseeability, with complementary rules that tend either to expand or restrict the scope of liability in particular situations, is probably not the most adequate for an area where a lack of previous experience with regard to IoT-technologies may make the test futile and where the characteristics of an ever increasing use of AI-technologies may make foreseeability based on human experience inappropriate. For this reason, a 'Harm within the Risk'-test, built around the idea that the liability of a tortfeasor is limited to those harms that result from the risks that made his conduct or activity tortious, with the corresponding complementary rules, and which is similar to the approach adopted by the *Restatement (Third)*, may be more appropriate. The HWR-test may also be applied to cases of the so-called 'intervening causation', and together with other legal devices, such as apportionment in cases of concurrent liability or contributory negligence, may satisfactorily establish the scope of liability of all the persons involved.

Discussion Panel

Consequences of Digitalization from the National Legislator's Point of View – Report on a Working Group

Eva Lux

It was a great honor to participate in the 4th Münster Colloquia on EU Law and the Digital Economy. The truly insightful conference offered a rare opportunity to get together with a number of experts working on issues concerning robotics and liability.

As a result of advancing digitalization and connectivity, the technical, economical, but also societal relevance of data, data services and technical devices is steadily increasing in all aspects of life. As a matter of fact, the changes induced by digitalization also raise questions from the legislator's point of view.

Therefore the Spring Conference of the Federal State's Ministers of Justice has decided in June 2015 to initiate a working group headed by the federal state of North Rhine-Westphalia. The working group's aim is to examine the impact of digitalization on civil law and to identify a potential necessity for additional regulation. At the Conference of the Federal State's Ministers of Justice on June 21st/22nd 2017, this working group called 'Digitaler Neustart' ('Digital Reset') has submitted its report which it had developed in cooperation with a large number of federal states as well as with the Federal Ministry of Justice and Consumer Protection (available at http://www.digitaler-neustart.de).

In its report, the working group analysed if there is cause for legislative action, and if so, what the action should look like. The working group's goal was to ensure that there exists a reliable legal framework which enables digital change while maintaining freedom, equality, democracy and justice for private citizens as well as for companies.

The subjects covered in the working group's report are data ownership, digital contracts, digital personality rights and digital legacy.

Under the umbrella term of 'data ownership', the working group analysed the issue of whether the legal quality of digital data needs to be defined by statutory law, possibly by establishing a new exclusive right. The working group furthermore discussed different forms of 'digital contracts' and focused on the question of to which extent new types of contracts should be incorporated into the German Civil Code (BGB) or if prevailing contract types must be supplemented with digital forms of contracts. The most important aspect of the third topic 'digital personality rights' focused on the question as to whether the statutory framework has to recognize and protect the digital personality. Finally, a separate chapter of the report has been dedicated to all topics revolving around 'digital legacy'.

The conclusions of the working group are generally based on the principle that there is no need for legislative action, insofar and as long as the current ('analogue') law provides viable rules for the consequences of digitalization and the courts can be entrusted with providing appropriate solutions by applying the existing legal framework to new circumstances.

Based on this principle there is cause for legislative action in some areas. But, all in all, the working group considers German civil law to be well equipped to handle and cope with many challenges of the digital world.

But, for example in regard to autonomous systems, the working group concluded nonetheless that there may be a gap of liability. Not only for this very important issue but also regarding some other crucial topics the Spring Conference of the Federal State's Ministers of Justice decided in June 2017 to continue the work of the group which focuses on two main topics at the moment:

First, big data and algorithms and, secondly, Robotic law. Additionally the group takes a look at questions in connection with the blockchain-technology.

Regarding liability for autonomous systems, the group focuses on two issues: autonomous driving and autonomous systems in a medical setting. Initially, experts illustrate the current state of the art to the group, since it does not want to work with science fiction, but with scenarios, which will soon be reality.

The group's aim is to find a balance between consumers' and companies' interests. It is important not to obstruct innovation, but to protect consumers in an adequate way at the same time. On the one side, consumers have to be certain, that a damage caused by an autonomous system will be compensated in the end. On the other side producers need certainty regarding the pressing questions.

However, it has to been worked out precisely, if and where there currently are gaps of liability. Is our liability system with for example risk-based liability in traffic or product liability efficient enough for new technologies? The more autonomously a system acts and the more it is able to learn on its own, the more we have to rethink our current rules of liability and check if they still lead to adequate results.

An open question is, if it is reasonable to draft a liability framework for autonomous robots, which is uniform and overarching categories. Possibly, it would be more expedient to create categories of robotics and to decide in each case, if there is a cause for legislative action and, if necessary, discuss the specific form of liability rules.

Here, characteristics of robotics, which are relevant for the determination of liability, have to be taken into account. For example, this includes the ability to learn und to decide, or also the structure of each area of application.

All in all, there are many questions to be answered. Measured against the speed in which the digitalization currently progresses the legislator is demanded to find these answers as soon as possible.

Contributors

Cristina Amato
Professor of Comparative Law, University of Brescia

Georg Borges
Professor of Law, Chair for Private Law, Legal Informatics, German and International Business Law, Legal Theory, Saarland University

Jean-Sébastien Borghetti
Professor of Private Law, University Paris II Panthéon-Assas

Giovanni Comandé
Professor of Private Comparative Law, Scuola Superiore Sant'Anna Pisa, and Director of Lider-Lab

Ernst Karner
Professor of Civil Law, University of Vienna, and Director of the Institute for European Tort Law and the European Centre of Tort and Insurance Law

Bernhard A Koch
Professor of Civil and Comparative Law, University of Innsbruck

Sebastian Lohsse
Professor of Roman Law, Comparative Legal History, Civil Law and European Private Law, University of Münster

Eva Lux
Ministry of Justice, North Rhine-Westphalia

Miquel Martín-Casals
Professor of Civil Law and Director of the Institute of European and Comparative Private Law, University of Girona

Reiner Schulze
Professor of German and European Civil Law, University of Münster

Gerald Spindler
Professor of Civil Law, Commercial and Economic Law, Comparative Law, Multimedia- and Telecommunication Law, University of Göttingen

Dirk Staudenmayer
Head of Unit 'Contract Law', DG Justice and Consumers, European Commission. Honorary Professor at the University of Münster

Gerhard Wagner
Professor of Civil Law, Commerical Law and Economic Analysis of Law, Humboldt-University of Berlin

Herbert Zech
Professor of Life Sciences Law and Intellectual Property Law, University of Basel

FSC
www.fsc.org
MIX
Papier | Fördert
gute Waldnutzung
FSC® C083411

Kolibri 360 GmbH
Ferdinand-Jühlke-Straße 7
99095 Erfurt, Deutschland
produktsicherheit@kolibri360.de